School organisation and pupil involvement

International Library of Sociology

Founded by Karl Mannheim

Editor: John Rex, University of Warwick

Arbor Scientiae
Arbor Vitae

A catalogue of the books available in the **International Library of Sociology** and other series of Social Science books published by Routledge and Kegan Paul will be found at the end of this volume.

School organisation and pupil involvement

A study of secondary schools

Ronald King
Institute of Education, University of Exeter

Routledge & Kegan Paul

London and Boston

First published 1973
by Routledge & Kegan Paul Ltd
Broadway House, 68–74 Carter Lane,
London EC4V 5EL and
9 Park Street,
Boston, Mass. 02108, U.S.A.

Printed in Great Britain by
Western Printing Services Ltd, Bristol

ISBN 0 7100 7610 X

Library of Congress Catalog Card No. 73–75942

To Rita

Contents

Acknowledgments

This book is based upon research supported by the Schools Council at the University of Exeter Institute of Education from 1967 to 1970. The idea of asking the Schools Council to support a research project concerned with the sociology of the school existed in the University before I took up my lectureship there in 1966. Professor Robin Pedley (now of the University of Southampton) asked me to help in the framing of the proposal, and later invited me to direct the research. I am grateful to him for having asked me to do so, and also for his interest and encouragement throughout its many stages.

At an early stage the project was proposed as a joint one with the University of Bristol Institute of Education. This idea was not fully developed, but I am grateful to Professor William Taylor for his efforts in getting the project started, and to Nicholas Gillett for his valuable help during the survey period.

It would be difficult for me to acknowledge adequately the important contribution made by my two research assistants. Mrs Joan Fry was part of the team for the whole three-year period of the project. I am particularly grateful to her for her administrative skill and her unshakeable commonsense. Gary Easthope (now at the New University, Ulster) joined us for the second two years. His methodological expertise and undogmatic sociology were very valuable. Between them they took on the main load of the very exhausting fieldwork, the tedious but essential coding processes, and the hours of often unfruitful calculations. I hope there were enough moments of satisfaction to have it made worth while.

I should like to thank the chief education officers who gave us permission to ask the schools to help us, the headteachers who gave us access to their schools and some of their valuable time, the teachers who helped in many different ways, and the pupils who completed the questionnaires. These thanks are extended to the headteachers, teachers and pupils of the Exeter schools who were so helpful during the pilot stage.

Finally I should like to thank my colleague Dr Paul Kline for his statistical advice and my wife for her support and her typing of the original research report, which forms the basis of this book, under less than ideal conditions.

Introduction

This study was an attempt to answer three basic questions about the nature of the educational process. The purpose of this Introduction is to present those questions, under headings reflecting the title of the book, and to discuss why they were worth asking.

School organisation

How do secondary schools organise the behaviour and learning activities of their pupils? What are the differences in organisation between types of school, and how may they be explained?

Until quite recently it was fashionable to point to a conspicuous gap in the British literature of the sociology of education. The social survey tradition of research had led to a considerable knowledge of success and failure in the British educational system. This large-scale approach, with an emphasis on educational output, was complemented by studies concerned essentially with the human input, and concentrating upon the family as an agency of socialisation. The concept that linked these two approaches was social class.

Educational success, in terms of passing the eleven-plus, gaining certificates, staying on in the sixth form, and entering university, was shown to be more commonly associated with middle-class rather than working-class pupils. The family studies were based essentially upon the idea of social class sub-cultural differences in patterns of child rearing or primary socialisation. That the middle-class child tends to internalise norms, values and beliefs, and acquire knowledge and modes of thought, which are similar to those encountered in the learning situation of the school. Conversely, that the working-class child, especially those from what are known as 'rough' or 'deprived' homes with fathers in unskilled manual occupations, tends to be in cultural discontinuity with school.

This brief summary fails to give a proper account of the many developments associated with these two approaches, but to do so would involve a summary of most of what is regarded as being the sociology of education. However, the outline serves to indicate the conspicuous gap in the research—the school. Something was known about educational inputs and outputs, but little about through-put.

From the late sixties onward a number of British studies began to be published which began to bring the school into research focus. These consisted mainly of case studies of single schools, and include that of David Hargreaves (1967) of a modern school, Colin Lacey's (1970) and my own (1969a) of grammar schools, Mays and his associates (1968) of a comprehensive school, and Julienne Ford's (1970) of a comprehensive, a grammar and a modern school.

Surveys of larger samples of schools began to appear including those by Weinberg (1967) of boys' public schools, Wober (1971) of girls' public schools, and Royston Lambert and his associates (1968) of a range of boarding schools. In addition, the interest in the re-organisation of secondary education was associated with two large-scale surveys of comprehensive schools, by Monks (1968) and by Benn and Simon (1970). Although these comprehensive-school studies used social survey techniques they were basically atheoretical in that they did not attempt to explain what they reported from any distinct theoretical perspective.

Case studies can be very valuable in opening up new areas of inquiry, in generating new theoretical ideas, or in testing new methodologies. However, strictly speaking, the knowledge gained only applies to that one school. To reach conclusions about many or all schools on the basis of a case study is to use reductionism, which may be fallacious. Only an extension of the research to an acceptable sample of schools could test the truth or falsity of such conclusions. It is part of the English conception of the school that each has, or should have, its individual, perhaps unique, characteristics. A case study cannot reveal which elements of a school are particular and which universal.

The research situation was, therefore, one where a number of small-scale studies had described and explained aspects of the sociology of the school, and a number of large-scale studies had described aspects of one kind of school, the comprehensive, without explaining sociologically what was described.[1] The gap in the sociology of education was partly filled, but there was still a space

[1] Royston Lambert's work on boarding education which both describes and explains a large sample of schools, is not yet completely reported.

for research which described and explained the organisation of a range of secondary schools.

Our attempt to do this was focused on the organisation of pupil learning and behaviour, and to a large extent excluded teacher/teacher relationships and what is generally called the administration of the school.

Pupil involvement

To what extent and in what ways are pupils involved in the school? What differences exist in the levels and types of involvement of pupils of different ages, sex, ability and social background, and how may they be explained?

There is quite an extensive literature of studies of pupils' attitudes and dispositions towards school. A few are sociological, notably the longitudinal study of Hilde Himmelweit (1954, 1963), but most are psychological or atheoretical.

Most of these studies sampled pupils from a number of schools and report the pupils' responses to questions about school for the whole sample or for contrasted categories of pupils, for example, boys against girls. This method of analysis ignores the possibility of there being variations in the pupils' experiences from one school to another. Our ideas about the individuality of schools suggests that such variations are a possibility. This research tested the possibility by analysing the data on pupils' school involvement for individual schools. This method of analysis is not without its problems, some of which are discussed in Appendix B.

School organisation and pupil involvement

To what extent and in what ways is the pupils' involvement in the school related to the internal organisation of the school?

The asking of this question arose principally from the sociological studies of academic streaming in schools. Case studies of grammar schools (King, 1969a; Lacey, 1970), a modern school (Hargreaves, 1967), and a comprehensive school (Holly, 1965) had shown associations between stream status and pupil involvement in school. The mean levels of involvement of pupils in top streams, measured in terms of favourable attitudes to school and voluntary participation in school activities, were higher than those of pupils in lower streams.

No study has established causality between streaming and involvement, but the evidence suggested the possibility of some relationship between this particular organisational structure and pupil disposition,

3

which might be paralleled in other aspects of the school. A particular example is the organisation of the school uniform. Are variations in the extent of the prescription of the uniform related to the degree of the pupils' acceptance of the uniform?

It should be stressed that the possibility of this positivistic re-lationship between structure and involvement was put to the empirical test. The simple proposition that structure (in the form of streaming) determines involvement had already been shown not to be completely acceptable, in that the experience of streaming was found to vary with the social characteristics of the pupils. In my own case study the experience of both the top and bottom streams was different for the first and second generation grammar-school boys, indicating that in part the pupils' definition of the situation was derived from meanings they brought into it from their home backgrounds.

Answering the questions

The answers to these three basic questions are based upon data obtained from two surveys; one of schools, the other of pupils.[1] An outline of the survey methods is given in Chapter 1, and more details in Appendix A. Chapter 1 also introduces the theoretical approach used in treating the data from the surveys.

The chapters that follow suggest answers to the questions about organisation and involvement for different aspects of the schools. The final chapter collates these and provides an overview to the whole study.

[1] A third survey, of pupils' friendship choice, is reported in King and Easthope (1973).

1 The approach

The Introduction discussed the three basic questions which the chapters that follow this one attempt to answer. This chapter outlines how the information was obtained and treated in order to provide those answers, and does so under headings representing the three questions. In each case the methods used to obtain the data are described in outline and then, in more detail, the conceptual scheme used in the treatment of the data.

A more detailed account of some aspects of the sampling and methodology is given in Appendix A, and details of the statistical analysis in Appendix B.

The organisation of the school

The schools' survey

The purpose of the schools' survey was to obtain data concerning the organisation of pupil learning and behaviour.

The sample consisted of seventy-two schools which were reasonably representative of the national (England and Wales) distribution of schools by size, sex composition and status (Table 1). The schools were drawn from seven local authority areas in the south-west of England. Between them they serve a city with half a million population, one of a quarter of a million, two towns of 100,000, many smaller towns, and a large rural area.

Four important methods were used in the survey:

1. A self-completion questionnaire for the headteacher or his delegate.
2. The content analysis of documents provided by the school.
3. Direct, non-participant observations in the school.
4. Interview(s) with the headteacher and other staff.

These four methods were used to collect mainly two kinds of information concerned respectively with the how and the why of the situation. First, data concerning the organisation of all aspects of the school directly affecting the pupils, including learning groups, curriculum, games, out-of-school activities, assessments, uniform,

TABLE 1 *Schools' survey sample—actual and ideal numbers*

Status	Small	Medium	Large	Very large	All
Modern					
boys'	4	3	0	0	7 (6·8)
girls'	2	4	0	0	6 (7·0)
mixed	10	9	3	2	24 (27·5)
all	16 (18·5)	16 (15·5)	3 (7·0)	2 (0·3)	37 (41·3)
Comprehensive					
boys'	0	0	1	0	1 (1.3)
girls'	1	0	1	0	2 (1·3)
mixed	0	2	5	7	14 (10·8)
all	1 (1·7)	2 (3·2)	7 (4·8)	7 (3·7)	17 (13·4)
Grammar					
boys'	1	4	1	0	6 (5·8)
girls'	0	3	3	0	6 (5·5)
mixed	1	1	4	0	6 (5·7)
all	2 (3·0)	8 (7·0)	8 (6·8)	0 (0·2)	18 (17·0)
All schools					
boys'	5	7	2	0	14 (13·9)
girls'	3	7	4	0	14 (14·0)
mixed	11	12	12	9	44 (44·0)
all	19 (23·2)	26 (25·7)	18 (18·6)	9 (4·2)	72

Notes. Small, < 400; medium, 401–600; large, 601–1,000; very large, > 1,000.

The grammar sample actually consisted of sixteen grammar schools, one boys' technical school, and one girls' selective secondary school not designated a grammar school, both *de facto* grammar schools. Figures not in brackets show actual numbers of schools; those in brackets the ideal numbers by the 1969 statistics (see Appendix A). Fifteen of the comprehensives were of the 11–18 type; one was for 11–15 and the other for 14–18.

House, prefectorial and pastoral care systems. Second, headteachers were asked to explain their purpose in choosing to organise the school in the way they did. In addition, information about the social characteristics of the pupils was obtained.

The scheme of analysis

The survey provided over one thousand items of data about the organisation of each of the seventy-two schools. Each item was classified using a scheme of analysis which views the organisation of the school as complex and multivariate. It is a truism that the organisation of schools is widely variable. The scheme is an attempt to analyse this phenomenon by posing three important sets of ways in which school organisation may vary. These *organisational variables* are:

(a) Activity variables
(b) Structural variables
(c) Contextual variables

(a) *Activity variables* The two principal activities of a school are considered to be the transmission of educational knowledge and the transmission of modes of approved behaviour. The term *instrumental* is used to describe those processes used in the transmission of knowledge, and the term *expressive* for those used in the transmission of approved modes of behaviour. Schools may vary in the knowledge and modes of approved behaviour they transmit, and in the activities used in their transmission.

A further distinction is made between the process or activity of transmission, and the judgments, including the use of rewards and punishments, of the performance of the pupils in the assimilation of what is transmitted. Thus there are four basic types of activity:

1. Instrumental activities, e.g. doing homework.
2. Instrumental performance, e.g. marks collected for homework.
3. Expressive activities, e.g. entering school when the bell rings.
4. Expressive performance, e.g. detention for lateness.

The other officially recognised activities of the school are classified according to their association with the prefectorial, House, pastoral care and games systems, and with out-of-school activities, although it is recognised that often these may also be classified as either instrumental or expressive, as when, for example, the House system is used as a basis for academic competition.

(b) *Structural variables* Schools vary in the way they structure, or in the ordinary sense, organise, these different kinds of activities. Four such structural variables are used in this approach; standardisation, formalisation, specialisation and ritualisation.

7

Standardisation, in the form of rules, routines and set procedures is a basic aspect of all organisations. It establishes where the organisation ends and the rest of the world begins. Homework extends school into the home and into the night. A ban on eating on the way home brings school into the street and out of 'school hours'.

Many of the activities that occur in schools are not officially standardised, and therefore are not strictly speaking organisational. Much of what goes on in playgrounds and staffrooms is neither planned nor deliberately structured. More importantly, much of what goes on in the classroom is also extra-organisational, because teachers in British schools are generally allowed a great deal of autonomy in the teaching situation. This is an aspect of the professional nature of the teacher's role which is achieved through specific training and qualifications rather than by being employed in a particular school. Although some processes may be standardised throughout the school, much of the learning is planned and structured by individual teachers with a degree of independence from the school context. The school may standardise pupil behaviour, but individual teachers have their own standards and their own personalised techniques of control.

Formalisation refers to the organisational use of paper in such forms as lists, written rules, records and memoranda. The timetable is an excellent example of formalisation in the school.

The *specialisation* of activities among pupils is usually made on the basis of three salient pupil characteristics; age, sex and imputed ability. Pupils of different ages, sexes and imputed abilities may be taught different things, expected to behave in different ways, may be controlled, punished and rewarded in different ways.

The House and prefectorial systems may also be considered to be the basis of other principles of specialisation.

Ritualisation refers to the use of symbols. A symbol is simply defined as a thing representing or typifying something else. Symbols in schools have two forms; ceremonials, as in the school assembly, and emblems, tangible symbols such as plaques and badges.

(c) *Contextual variables* The activities of schools and the organisational structures associated with them occur in situations or contexts which may vary from one school to another, and may affect the activities and their organisation. These contextual variables may be broadly classified as being either internal or external, without implying that a definite boundary exists between the school and other social systems.

Internal contextual variables are of two kinds; those concerned with resources, and those that condition the nature of those resources.

The most important resources of a school are its pupils. Variations in their social characteristics give rise to the following variables:

1. Age composition
2. Sex composition
3. Ability composition
4. Social composition

The size of the school in terms of the number of pupils, is another important resource variable, as are the physical plant and material provision of the school. (Teachers, too, are resources that vary in number and in their social characteristics.)

The important conditioning variables include:

1. The administrative status of the school, which may vary in terms of financial control (maintained, voluntary-aided, etc.), religious affiliation, sex composition, and selectivity (modern, grammar, comprehensive, etc.)
2. The charter and articles of government
3. The school's recent social history
4. The school's ideology

External contextual variables are more difficult to define. Strictly speaking the external context of the school consists of the total social system, and it is therefore difficult to know which of the enormous number of things which may vary outside the school may be related to what happens inside the school. (For a review, see Eggleston (1967).) The following may be important:

1. The social characteristics of the local area, including its social class composition and density of population.
2. The local occupational structure.
3. The local educational structure, including provision of further education and relationships between schools in terms of co-operation and competition.
4. The national educational structure, including the provision of higher education.[1]

Some of these external contextual variables are part of the broad distinction made between urban and rural areas. Others are related, directly or indirectly to internal variables. For example, the social composition of a non-selective school operating alone will be a reasonable representation of the local social composition.

Table 2 provides a summary of the organisational variables that make up the scheme of analysis.

[1] Not all of these variables were included in this study.

TABLE 2 *Organisational variables*

Activity variables		*Structural variables*	*Contextual variables*
Transmitted Educational knowledge	*Transmission* Instrumental activities Instrumental performance	Standardisation Formalisation Specialisation	*Internal* Resource: plant, size, age, ability,
Modes of approved behaviour	Expressive activities Expressive performance	(by age, sex and ability) Ritualisation	sex and social compositions. Conditioning: status, history, ideology.
House, games, prefectorial, pastoral care, out-of-school activities			*External*

The measurement of school organisation

The data relating to the organisation of each school were classified and grouped under headings representing the various organisational variables described in the previous section.

Eighty-five contextual variables were derived in this way, for example, the percentage of pupils whose fathers had manual occupations.

One hundred and thirty structural variables were obtained. Some of these were numbers, for example, the number of games played against other schools. Others were percentages, for example, the percentage of out-of-school activities for girls. However, the largest category were specially constructed scales of a fairly sophisticated kind.

The attempt was to produce scales that were as near 'perfect' as possible. A perfect or ratio scale has a fixed zero, equal scoring intervals, and a particular score indicates a particular characteristic of what is being measured. It is often referred to as being unidimensional. When such scales are constructed for studies of attitudes the Guttman technique of scalogram analysis is often used (See Selltiz *et al.*, 1965). However, Levy and Pugh (1969) have proposed and used another technique for organisational analysis which uses Brogden's biserial correlation as a form of item analysis. This has advantages over the Guttman technique in that it takes into account the degree to which a given item is out of sequence with the pattern of a perfect scale and makes no assumptions of a normal distribution.

An example of such a scale is that for the measurement of the age-specialisation of expressive activities, that is, how the school regulates the behaviour of pupils of different ages (Table 3). A school's score is obtained by the addition of the number of items which are present or exist in the school.

TABLE 3 *Age-specialisation of expressive activities scale*

Items. Age differences in	Frequency	Item analysis value
Cycle parking	7	0·767
Playground entrances	11	0·854
Use of corridors or stairs	15	0·749
School entrances	27	0·732
Playground areas	28	0·836
Cloakroom areas	37	0·828
Registration groups	63	0·886

Mean item analysis value 0·807; mean score on scale (2·61 N = 72; S.D. = 1·70).

11

Levy and Pugh (1969) have pointed out that the adopting of a particular analysis for organisational data has implications for a theory of organisational behaviour. The choice of measuring organisational structures using unidimensional scales implies that a sequence of decisions is taken when activities become organised, or that one decision usually leads to another particular decision.

The scale for the measurement of age-specialisation of expressive activities implies that a decision to have different entrances for pupils of different ages will be closely linked to that to have special areas of the playground for the different ages. Another implication is that the next decision is more likely to be the creation of age-specialisation of corridors or stairs rather than playground entrances or cycle parking. This theory of teacher decision-making behaviour was not tested in this research. The major interest was not in the detailed aetiology of the structural variables but in their identification and measurement, their relation to one another and to the contextual variables, and more importantly, to the involvement variables.

The approach to the school as an organisation

The survey methods and the scheme of analysis were constructed and validated in pilot schools during the first year of the research.

The scheme was derived from a number of sources, the three principal ones being the theoretical papers on the sociology of the school by Basil Bernstein (1966a, b), the work of Derek Pugh and his associates of the Industrial Administration Research Unit of the University of Aston in Birmingham (see Hinings *et al.* (1967); Pugh *et al.* (1963, 1968)), and my previous research in a single school (King, 1969a). It was formulated in an attempt to meet the three important features that a conceptual approach to the school as an organisation should ideally possess. (It is not claimed that the ideal has been met.)

(a) The approach should be congruent with approaches that have been used in the analysis of other types of organisation.

(b) The approach should be particular enough to account for the special characteristics of schools as organisations, enable distinctions to be made between schools, and also account for the unique features of individual schools.

(c) The approach should enable connections to be made between the macro-sociology of education in terms of its societal aspects, and its micro-sociological aspects, including pedagogy and learning.

Condition (a) is necessary because it is recognised that schools are organisations and must therefore be susceptible to either partial

analysis using approaches generated in the field of industrial so
logy, or to low-level analysis using approaches formulated for
comparison of organisations.

Whilst it is recognised that schools are like factories and offices in
some respects (and churches and prisons too), a common-sense view
is that these similarities are less important than the things that lead
us to regard schools as being different to other organisations. As
Caplow (1964) has pointed out, schemes for the comparative analysis
of organisations are usually based upon variations in a single
important feature. In Blau and Scott's (1963) scheme, for example,
this is the prime beneficiary principle. Its application leads to schools
being classified with universities, churches and hospitals as client
beneficiary organisations.

The principal sociological approaches to organisational structure
have utilised the concept of bureaucracy. The extent of its use is
reflected in Etzioni's (1964) suggestion that the terms 'organisation'
and 'bureaucracy' are virtually synonymous.

A number of studies, mainly American and mainly centred on
teachers, have treated the school as a bureaucracy. (See the study
of Anderson (1968) and the review of studies by Brown and House
(1967).) Weber's (1948) ideal-type bureaucracy forms the starting-
point of these and other applications of the concept. Everyday
experience of schools confirms their conformity with many of the
items forming the original ideal-type. Tasks are distributed as official
duties, carried out by technically qualified, specialist staff (teachers).
There is a hierarchical authority of offices with the headteacher at the
top. Formally established rules and regulations (including syllabuses
curricula) and govern actions and decisions. Reservations might be
made, however, about the application of Weber's suggestion that the
officials (teachers) have an impersonal orientation towards their
clients (pupils). This suggestion and other elements of the ideal-type
have been criticised in their wider application. It is not, however,
intended to rehearse these criticisms or to review the revisions and
variations that have been made of the original concept of bureaucracy. (See for example Albrow (1970) and Pugh et al. (1968).)

Of the many developments of the concept of bureaucracy that of
Pugh and his associates seemed most appropriate for an approach
to the organisation of the school. Following the work of Hall (1963),
they analyse the concept into six structural variables; standardisation, formalisation, specialisation, centralisation, configuration and
flexibility. Standardisation, formalisation and specialisation are
integral to the approach used in this study. Configuration and
centralisation are briefly referred to. In addition a non-bureaucratic
variable, ritualisation, was added for reasons argued in Chapter 4.

The approach of Pugh and his associates develops only the

structural aspects of bureaucracy, leaving the orientation of the participants as problematic and open to investigation. In this study the orientation of the headteachers was investigated through the schools' survey, and that of the pupils through the investigation of involvement to be described later.

The main strength of this multivariate approach is that it enables comparisons to be made of the organisation of different kinds of school and of individual schools, so meeting one aspect of condition (b).

Condition (b) also leads to the question, what are the special features of schools as organisations? The common-sense answer is that schools are places where pupils are taught and learn things. This suggests that the distinctive feature of the school is not necessarily its bureaucratic structure, as Bidwell (1965) has suggested, but the nature of its activities.

In this study the main activities of the school are classified as being instrumental or expressive. This dichotomous classification of educational activities has several antecedents and parallels in the analysis of the whole process of education. Weber (1948), in his discussion of the education of the Chinese *literatae*, made the distinction between specialised or expert education, and charismatic education. Durkheim (1961) contrasted moral education with intellectual education. More recently Basil Bernstein has made an analysis of the culture transmitted by the school into two components; the instrumental and the expressive: (1966a)

> I propose to call that complex of behaviour and activities in the school which are to do with conduct, character and manner, the *expressive culture* of the school, and the complex of behaviour and the activities which generate it, which have to do with the acquisition of specific skills, the *instrumental culture.*

It is Bernstein's analysis which forms the basis of the classification used in this study. Its particular strength is the way in which it enables connections to be made between schools as social systems with the general social system of society. Bernstein suggests that each cultural order is associated with different sources of external legitimacy, has different functions in relation to society, and different social effects within the school. The instrumental order is principally legitimised by the work order since, ultimately, its major societal function is occupational placement, often mediated through the examination system. The interpersonal competition it generates under conditions of objective, universalistic assessment is potentially divisive within the school. The more diffuse expressive order is legitimised by the dominant social group in society, in modern Britain the loosely defined middle class. Its principal societal function is the preparation of pupils for the more general non-occupational positions in adult society, usually consonant with their social status. Unlike the instrumental order, the expressive, Bernstein suggests, is potentially consensual within the school. Performance in the common morality is assessed more subjectively and there may be particular-istic elements in the assessment of performance, in terms of the age, sex and other characteristics of the pupils.

Bernstein's analysis has a definite coherence, in that relationships are established between function, control and legitimacy, and between the school and its social context. Its particular treatment of the instrumental-expressive distinction suggests ways in which the sociology of the school may be linked to both the macro- and micro-sociological aspects of education, so possibly meeting condition (c).

In many ways Bernstein's analysis is similar to two discussions of the educational process by Talcott Parsons. The first is his essay, 'The School Class as a Social System' (1959b) which is based upon an analysis of capacities:

> Capacities can also be broken down into two components, the first being competence or the skill to perform tasks involved in the individual's roles, and the second being 'role-responsibility' or the capacity to live up to other people's expectations of the interpersonal behaviour appropriate to these roles.

The second is his essay on general theory in sociology in Merton *et al.* (1959) in which he applies his theoretical perspectives to the American educational system. Here, in a variation of the familiar functional problems paradigm, he uses the terms instrumental and consumatory to represent a means/ends distinction. In a footnote he suggests that consumatory might be substituted by expressive, so bringing his discussion into line with his use of the instrumental/expressive distinction in connection with other social systems, in-cluding the nuclear family (in Parsons and Bales, 1956).

However, Bernstein's use of the distinction is not exactly the same as Parsons's. Parsons links it to the external and internal functions of the system. Bernstein's analysis indicates that both the instru-mental and expressive have internal and external functions in relation to the school.

The use of the distinction in this study is not, however, being justified on the basis of its utilisation in either formal or substantive theories of a functionalist kind. Instead, it is contended that the elements of an instrumental/expressive distinction are held in the general consciousness.

Clyde Kluckhohn (1964) in a discussion of forms of cultural learn-ing suggests there are two kinds, technical and regulatory, which correspond very closely to the instrumental and expressive activities used here. He perceptively points out that common speech makes a similar distinction in the two connotations of the word 'good', either in the sense of being morally and socially amenable, or in the sense of being skilful and accomplished. Colin Lacey (1970) has also shown how teachers use 'good' in connection with both a pupil's school work and his behaviour.

This idea of the duality of the educational process exists in the official reports:

> The task of education in the technological age is thus a double one. On the one hand, there is the duty to set young people on the road to acquiring the bewildering variety of qualifications they will need to earn their living. On the other hand, running through and across these vocational objectives there is a duty to remember those other objectives of any education . . . concerned with the development of human personality and with teaching the individual to see himself in due proportion to the world in which he has been set. (Central Advisory Council for Education (1959), p. 53.)

This is echoed in a secondary-modern headteacher's account of his school which formed part of the sample:

> Our aim as a school is to help children grow up to learn to understand themselves and something of the world into which they will be going. Although we are conscious that it is not possible to make a division we tend to think of them in terms of social and academic development.

Many of the arguments about the nature and purpose of education seem to spring from the different degrees of importance placed upon the instrumental and the expressive by those in disagreement.[1]

This study does not use the instrumental/expressive distinction in exactly the same way as Bernstein. A further distinction is made between what is transmitted and the transmission process. Thus instrumental activities are concerned with the transmission and acquisition of educational knowledge; together they form the instrumental order. Expressive activities are concerned with the transmission and inculcation of approved modes of behaviour; together they form the expressive order.

A further difference is the place of ideas, beliefs and values in relation to the instrumental/expressive distinction. In Bernstein's

---

[1] One final piece of evidence:
Author to son (then aged seven): Why do you think children have to go to school?
Son (without a pause): To learn about things and to learn how to behave themselves.

usage values are transmitted through the expressive component. 'The expressive culture of the school can be considered to be the source of its shared values . . .' (1966b). However, the acquisition of knowledge, through instrumental activities, is assumed to have behavioural consequences, and the possibility of value-change. In addition it is recognised that the transmission of values takes place not only by the internalisation of the content transmitted, but also by the experience of the transmission process. Thus the transmission of values cannot be easily separated from the transmission of knowledge. Similar considerations may be true of the transmission of ideas and beliefs.

A third difference also concerns the place of the ideas, beliefs and values, those held by the superordinates of the system; collectively their ideology. Bernstein appears to give primacy to the expressive order when he writes, 'We are talking about the expressive culture when we make pronouncements about the aims of education' (1966b). A more satisfactory paradigm (illustrated in Figure 1) would be to propose that the values, ideas and beliefs held by the superordinates of the system, the teachers, headteachers and administrators, are concerned with both the selection of knowledge to be transmitted, the approved modes of conduct to be transmitted, and the methods used for their transmission.

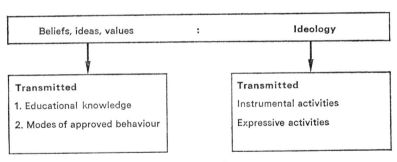

FIGURE 1

* These relationships are further discussed and elaborated in the last chapter of the book.

Pupil involvement

The pupils' survey

The purpose of the survey was to measure the degree and kind of involvement pupils had in relation to different aspects of school.

The sample consisted of 7,457 pupils drawn from a sub-sample of thirty schools included in the schools' sample (see Table 4). The pupils were from the second-, fourth-, fifth-, and where appropriate, seventh-year groups.

TABLE 4   *Pupils' survey—school sample*

| | | | Size | | Very large | All |
		Small	Medium	Large		
Modern	Boys	2	2	0	0	4
	Girls	2	2	0	0	4
	Mixed	2	2	2	0	6
	All	6	6	2	0	14
Comprehensive	Boys	0	0	0	0	0
	Girls	1	0	0	0	1
	Mixed	0	2	3	2	7
	All	1	2	3	2	8
Grammar	Boys	1	1	1	0	3
	Girls	0	1	1	0	2
	Mixed	1	1	1	0	3
	All	2	3	3	0	8
All schools	Boys	3	3	1	0	7
	Girls	3	3	1	0	7
	Mixed	3	5	6	2	16
	All	9	11	8	2	30

Two methods were used in gathering data relating to pupils' involvement in school:

(a) The sampled schools provided information about each pupil's father's occupation and score in the verbal reasoning or other test used in secondary selection.

(b) Each pupil completed a questionnaire. They were asked to make estimates of the age they would leave school, their expectations of the post-school education and occupation. They were also asked to write down the school clubs they attended and the positions of responsibility they held in the school. The major part of the questionnaire consisted of fifty-five statements about school, each of which the pupils were asked to tick if they agreed, or cross if they disagreed.

The measurement of involvement

In this study the term involvement was defined as affective-evaluative orientation. Specifically it refers to the pupil's emotional disposition towards, and judgments of, the school situation.

Two basic methods were used to measure the involvement of pupils in school:

(a) Pupils' self-reported behaviour in terms of joining clubs, holding of positions of responsibility and their expectations of post-school education were used as behavioural indices of involvement.

(b) The fifty-five statements about school which the pupils were asked to agree or disagree with formed items of seven scales constructed to measure involvement in ways similar to the measurement of attitudes. A twenty-six item Thurstone-type scale measured general involvement in the school. Six shorter scales measured involvement in the following particular aspects of the school: expressive activities, instrumental activities, school assembly, House system, school uniform and pastoral care.

Table 5 shows the scale used to measure expressive involvement. Each pupil's score was obtained by the summation of the number of agreements with items forming the scale.

TABLE 5   *Expressive involvement scale*

	Judges' score (range 0–9)	Per cent agreement	r Item/ total score
Most school rules are necessary	6·6	82	0·73
The punishments are fair in this school	7·1	72	0·80
School helps you get on with people	7·2	86	0·50
The school helps you see what is right and wrong	7·6	77	0·60
You can't run a school unless the pupils behave themselves	7·2	76	0·69
The school expects you to behave in a reasonable way	6·6	98	0·63

Range of scores 0–7; mean score 4·9 (N = 7,457; S.D. 1·15).
N.B. The numbers are explained in Appendix A.

The concept of involvement

The concept of involvement occurs quite widely in the literature of organisations. It is often left undefined or else authors implicitly or explicitly accept the definition proposed by Etzioni (1961): 'Involvement refers to the cathetic-evaluative orientation of an actor to an object, characterised in terms of intensity and direction.' There are a number of reservations that should be made about this definition. The term cathexis, which has its origin in the theories of Talcott Parsons, is not easily defined. Parsons variously refers to it as 'a line of action' or 'the attachment to objects which are gratifying and rejection of those which are noxious' (1951). A suggested clarification and improvement used here is to substitute cathexis with affective, so that involvement refers to affective-evaluative orientation.

Etzioni proposes that involvement may vary in intensity from high to low and in direction, which may be positive or negative. Reservations must be made about a direction dimension of involvement. Basically the problem is one of operationalisation. The measurement of both positive and negative involvement would require a ratio scale with a fixed zero. Such scales are difficult to construct and, furthermore, as the discussion of scales for structural variables made clear, their use implies that the variable being measured is unidimensional. But in Etzioni's definition involvement has at least two aspects, cathexis and evaluation, each of which may be analysed into a number of dimensions. It is clear that any division between positive and negative involvement would be an arbitrary one.

The choice of a Thurstone-type scale to measure general involvement was made because it produced a fit between the method of measurement and the nature of that which was being measured. Involvement contains effective and evaluative elements; the school is a complex social object which may evoke a number of different evaluative and affective responses. A ratio scale would be inappropriate to measure what is clearly a cluster or syndrome of dispositions. A Thurstone-type scale is an appropriate one for measurements of this kind in that a particular score on the scale may represent agreement with a different combination of statements forming the scale. The implied theory of organisational behaviour is that there are many ways in which a pupil may manifest high or low involvement in the school.

The six short scales used to measure particular aspects of involvement are also interval scales, but although they have fixed zeros (no questions agreed with) they may not be regarded as ratio scales, and like the Thurstone-type scale a given score may represent different patterns of agreement with the questions.

School organisation and pupil involvement

In his *Comparative Analysis of Complex Organisations* (1961) Etzioni makes a secondary analysis of a wide range of existing studies to illustrate his propositions about organisations. One of these, and perhaps the most important, is that there is a relationship between the kind of power used by the superordinates of the organisation and the involvement of the subordinates. The principal form of power used in schools, he suggests, is normative, and the congruent form of involvement this tends to be associated with in the pupils is moral involvement, characterised by its high intensity and positive direction.

It is not intended to make an extended critique of Etzioni's approach to organisations; some reservations have already been made about his definition of involvement. The point of this short discussion is to stress that in this study the forms of power used in schools were not presupposed, and more importantly, the relationship between organisational structure and the degree and type of involvement of pupils was not assumed but investigated. In each school relationships were sought between the measurement of the structural variables and the measurements of the pupils' involvement in the activities concerned.

Thus the results of the two surveys and some of the answers to the first two basic questions, were brought together to answer the third question. The answers to all three questions are given in the chapters that follow.

2 General involvement in school

This chapter is concerned with the pupils' general involvement in school, the way it relates to their social characteristics and to the type of school they attend.

The first section presents the general involvement scale and describes the ways in which the scores on the scale are related to the pupils' social class, sex, age and ability.

The second section deals with the relationships between the pupils' scores on the scale and the type of school they attend. The schools are typified according to variations in certain key contextual variables including size and status, sex, age, social and ability compositions.

The general involvement scale

The items forming the general involvement scale are given in Table 6. A pupil's score is the mean score for the number of items agreed with. Further information on the construction and use of the scale is given in Appendix A.

Pupils' social characteristics and involvement

Three important social characteristics of pupils are considered in relation to general involvement. They are, sex, age and social class.

Each of these pupil variables represents a social characteristic that exists within the culture in terms of shared meanings, for example the shared meaning of being a boy or a girl, or of being twelve or fifteen. The inclusion of social class rests upon the evidence suggesting a consciousness of social class stratification in young people, and its almost axiomatic inclusion as an independent variable in

TABLE 6 *The general involvement scale*

Item	Scale score	Agreement %
This is the best school around here	8·3	53
I enjoy learning new things	8·2	97
I will be sorry to leave school	7·8	48
School assembly is a good start to the day	7·6	43
School helps you to see what is right and wrong	7·6	77
I respect most of the teachers in the school	7·1	89
I like most teachers in this school	6·8	87
I like doing games	6·5	76
School work is usually interesting	6·3	79
I usually enjoy school	5·9	81
It is not difficult to be well behaved in school	5·9	75
The main reasons for working hard is to get a good job	5·3	94
Teachers should set us a good example	4·4	95
The school's job is to get us through the exams	4·4	60
It is impossible to obey all the rules	4·0	60
We should have more freedom in school	3·9	68
I dislike taking exams	3·4	55
There are too many rules in this school	2·6	41
There is no one to take your problems to in this school	2·3	33
School assembly is a waste of time	2·1	47
Doing games is a waste of time	2·1	15
I do not get on well with most teachers	1·8	20
I will be glad to leave school	1·1	42
I have no respect for the teachers in this school	1·0	14
This is the worst school around here	1·0	11
School is a waste of time	1·0	6

Mean score 5·7 (N = 7,457; S.D. = 0·63); split half coefficient of reliability 0·73.

N.B. The scores did not appear in the questionnaire and the items were randomly arranged with the questions forming parts of other scales.

studies in the sociology of education. (See Himmelweit *et al.* (1954); Ford (1970).)

Unlike sex or age, social class is not easily operationalised as a categoric statistic. In this study the dichotomous classification of middle class/working class is used, largely because the small numbers of pupils in the groups to be analysed prevents the use of a multiple classification. The classes were operationalised by fathers' occupation; non-manual middle class, manual working class. The use of the class terminology is preferred to that of the occupation because the occupation is being used as the best single clue to a whole complex of characteristics which constitute the social class sub-cultures. (See Sugarman (1967).)

Social class and involvement

The over-achievement of middle-class children compared with working-class is well established and forms the core of much of the sociological discussion of education. (See King (1971).) It is therefore interesting to find that it is by no means always the case that middle-class pupils are on average more involved in school than working-class pupils of the same age and sex in the same school (Table A, Appendix C). Its occurrence was highest in the second year, lowest in the fifth year. The incidence of this 'over-involvement' of the younger middle-class pupils was more marked in mixed comprehensive schools than in any other types of school.

Social class differences in educational attainment have been explained using a number of different theories. (For a review see King (1971).) In sociological studies of education the most common explanation or theory has been what may be called the culture gap or cultural discontinuity theory. (For a critique of the theory see Witkin (1971).)

Briefly, the theory proposes that the culture transmitted by the educational system, in terms of knowledge, norms, values and beliefs, is related to that of the dominant group in society, which in modern Britain is identified as the loosely defined middle class.

Thus there is a 'gap' or discontinuity between the culture of the working-class child and that of the educational system which is manifest in lower levels of attainment compared with those of middle-class children. The theory has been posed, implicitly in several different forms, and a documentation of its application becomes virtually a bibliography of the sociology of education.

Do these results showing that middle-class pupils are not always more involved in their schools than working-class pupils mean the relegation of the cultural discontinuity theory? Two reservations must be made about these results. First, the results of other more specific measurements of involvement do show significant and widespread class differences with middle-class pupils showing the higher levels of involvement. These measures are particularly the behavioural indices of involvement, including the taking up of positions of responsibility, joining school clubs and expectation of post-school education (see Chapters 3, 6 and 7 respectively).

24

This is linked with a second reservation. A favourable disposition and evaluation of school, as indicated by a high general involvement score, does not necessarily imply good behaviour, hard work or academic success. As Blake and Davis (1964) point out, values are not causally related to behaviour. R. H. Turner (1964) calls this gap between values and behaviour, value-relevance. Thus some pupils may hold values which relate to high involvement but are not relevant for their behaviour. This may be more typical of the working-class pupil. The values implied in high involvement in school may have more relevance for middle-class pupils so that high involvement may be more often related to educationally successful behaviour.

Sex differences in involvement

There is a tendency for the second-year girls of all types of mixed school to show higher levels of involvement than boys in the same school (Table B, Appendix C).[1] This sex difference is least common in the comprehensive schools. It persists into the fourth year in modern schools, but disappears in other schools at this age, and is almost completely absent in the fifth year of all types of school.

Several studies of children in primary schools have shown that girls tend to show a better adaptation to school than boys, and this effect is confirmed to continue into the early years of the mixed secondary school. (For example Kellmer-Pringle et al. (1966); Mitchell and Shepherd (1967).) A possible explanation is basically a psycho-cultural one; that girls have traits which lead to higher school involvement. One such trait that may be suggested is that girls show a more ready compliance with authority than boys. (See Wright (1971).) Among adults this may be shown in the tendency for women to vote Conservative more often than men, irrespective of social class.

A possible mechanism for this sex differentiation in early involvement is that the good-pupil role in mixed schools has a female sex-typing. That the orderliness, politeness, acquiescence, quietness and neatness of the female stereotype are congruent with the teachers' ideal-expectations of pupils. These expectations may also exist in single-sex schools but they cannot be given a visible sex connotation.

Age differences in involvement

Two common age differences in involvement are found: a fall in the mean involvement score from the second to fourth years; and a rise

[1] There is little difference between the social classes in this respect.

from the fourth to fifth years (see Table B, Appendix C). There were no differences between the social classes in these respects.

The second- to fourth-year fall in involvement is particularly associated with both boys and girls in mixed grammar schools, and is least common for both sexes in mixed modern schools. The pattern is not invariable; in three schools, one mixed modern and two mixed comprehensives, boys in the fourth were significantly more highly involved than those in the second year.

It is a commonplace observation that some of the eager and interested pupils of the early years of the secondary school become the troublesome pupils of the middle years. Weinberg (1967) has suggested a status deprivation explanation of the phenomenon; that the middle-year pupils know the ways of the school and its limits of tolerable behaviour, but they are deprived of the status given to the older pupils with its associated expectations of commitment to the school. This effect may be reinforced, especially in non-selective schools, as some pupils perceive that they will soon be leaving school.

The pattern of a higher mean involvement in the fifth year compared with the fourth year is particularly associated with pupils of both sexes in comprehensive schools and mixed modern schools.

Two possible mechanisms may account for this difference. First, a socialisation explanation; that the anticipation of the external examinations produces a rise in involvement. The second explanation is mainly applicable to non-selective schools; that the fourth-year leavers had low involvements and their leaving raised the mean level of involvement.

Whatever the usefulness of any of these explanations the problem remains of explaining the non-occurrence of the phenomena, and in a few cases their actual reversal.

Involvement and other pupil characteristics

It is generally accepted that the best single predictor of academic ability is the intelligence test, particularly verbal tests. Each pupil was placed in one of six ability cohorts (see Table 7) according to his or her test score in the verbal reasoning for secondary selection (or in some cases the supplementary tests described in the Appendix A). A limited number of cohorts were used rather than actual scores because of the variation in the tests used and the age of the data for most older pupils.

It might be expected that the more able pupils would be more involved in school than the less able, since they would find school work easier. No simple relationship was in fact found between ability and involvement.

Ability, as defined by intelligence test scores, has no social sig-

26

nificance for pupils who are kept unaware of these test results. Ability, so defined and measured, only has social significance when it is used for selection purposes, for allocation to different secondary schools or different streams. (See Horobin *et al.* (1967).) Even in these circumstances the precise measurement of ability itself does not enter the consciousness of the pupils, or influence their social identities and behaviour in the way that age, sex and possibly social class do.

There were no significant differences in the levels of involvement of pupils whose fathers had agricultural occupations compared with pupils of the same age and sex in the same school, whose fathers had non-agricultural occupations.

Involvement and type of school

The schools were typified according to variations in a number of their contextual variables.

Relationships between contextual variables

Of the eighty-five variables a number of key variables may be distinguished using two criteria. First, they have a well-defined cultural meaning; thus, the sex-composition of a school is a key variable but, it is argued, the proportion of pupils receiving school meals is not. Second, they correlate highly with many other variables.

The key variables that emerge are, first, the conditioning variables of status and sex composition, and second, the resource variables of the number of pupils, and the age, sex, ability and social compositions. Table 7 shows the relationship between some of these variables. It excludes sex composition because there was little significance within schools of a given status, but includes a number of minor variables of some interest. The table refers to the main sample of seventy-two schools. The data for the smaller sample was essentially similar.

Table 7 (together with Table 1) indicates that a reference to modern schools in general refers to mixed schools that are small or medium in size, with predominantly working-class pupils of average and below average ability, who are mainly in their first to fourth years of schooling, but virtually none in the sixth or later years.

The term comprehensive, used generally, refers to mixed schools in urban areas which are large or very large, with predominantly working-class pupils of a wide range of ability, who cover the whole range of ages but with most in the younger age range.

The term grammar school, used generally, refers to single-sex schools which are medium sized or large, with predominantly middle-class pupils of above average ability, covering the whole age range.

27

TABLE 7 *School contextual variables*

	Modern (n=37)	Status Compre- hensive (n=17)	Grammar (n=18)
Social composition (%)			
Manual workers' children	70·0	67·7	42·4
Agricultural workers' children	10·3	3·6	8·2
Father unemployed	2·7	2·5	0·3
Incomplete families	6·2	5·2	1·9
Receiving free meals	17·6	14·4	6·6
Ability composition (%)			
IQ 120 or over	0·3	7·3	46·2
110–119	6·9	16·2	44·7
100–109	28·6	25·6	8·9
90–99	32·9	27·6	0·2
80–89	20·0	15·9	0·0
79 or under	10·9	8·1	0·0
Age composition (%)			
1st year	23·4	20·3	16·1
2nd year	23·1	20·0	15·5
3rd year	22·8	19·9	15·0
4th year	22·5	20·6	16·4
5th year	7·9	12·0	15·8
6th year	0·4	5·0	10·9
7th year	0·0	2·2	9·5

Care must be taken to remember that these modal or average types of school by status conceal wide variations in the individual schools. The variations in size and sex composition are given in Table 1 and indicate an overlapping between schools by status. However, every grammar school had a lower percentage of manual-workers' children, a higher percentage of very able pupils, and a higher percentage of pupils in their seventh year, compared with all other schools. As other research has implied there are considerable overlaps in the ability and social compositions of modern and comprehensive schools. (See Monks (1968); Ford (1970).)

School status and involvement

When the mean scores on the involvement scale for pupils matched by age and sex were compared in schools of different status, no consistent or significant differences were found. Individual schools were characterised by both high and low average levels of involvement but these were not characteristically either grammar, modern or comprehensive schools.

Sex composition and involvement

Sex composition was found to be related to level of involvement in only one situation. Second-year girls in both girls' grammar schools had lower mean involvement scores than the second-year girls in each of the three mixed grammar schools (Table B, Appendix C).

School size and involvement

The enormous literature on the relationship between the size of an organisation and the orientation of the participants suggests that larger schools would be associated with lower levels of involvement. (For a review see Campbell (1965).) There was no simple relationship between school size and mean levels of involvement.

This result is perhaps surprising, but, as later sections will show, the large schools had introduced pastoral care and House structures which were partly intended to prevent the feelings of impersonality among pupils, which are assumed to be endemic in such schools.

Social class composition and involvement

A number of studies have indicated that the social composition of a school may have an effect upon pupils' educational ambition and performance. (See, for example, Eggleston (1967); Wilson (1959).) These results might suggest that working-class pupils in predominantly middle-class schools show a higher involvement than those in predominantly working-class schools, and that middle-class pupils in predominantly working-class schools may show a lower involvement than those in predominantly middle-class schools. No evidence was found for either of these effects.

School location and involvement

There were no simple relationships between involvement and a school's location in terms of being in a rural area, small town, housing estate or slum area.

Material provision and involvement

There was no simple relationship between material provision, such as age of building, and involvement. However, the free responses of pupils in the questionnaire indicated that they were concerned about material provision. It was not the case that pupils in new, well-equipped schools had no complaints, and that pupils in old, poorly-equipped schools had many. In each situation pupils expressed dissatisfaction about the absence of the facility that they might reasonably expect to be provided with next. Thus pupils in a new, well-equipped school complained that they did not have their own swimming pool. Pupils in old, poorly-equipped schools complained about the state of the lavatories and wished for proper changing-rooms.

Religious foundation and involvement

Six schools in the sample had religious foundations but as a group they had no special involvement characteristics.

General involvement in school

The results of this chapter indicate that although the internal and external contexts of schools are widely variable, these variables are not directly related to the level of the pupils' general involvement in the school.

The existence of differences in mean levels of involvement between schools supports the idea of each school having its own unique culture, since they indicate different degrees of the sharing among pupils of dispositions towards the school. These differences probably arise from the interaction of many factors including the social characteristics of the pupil, the context of the school, the activities and their organisation, as well as their non-organisational interaction within pupil peer-groups, and with teachers in the learning situation.

Within schools the differences in the degree of involvement are related to the social characteristics that the pupils bring into the situation.

This chapter has ignored the activities of the school and the way they are structured or organised. These are dealt with in the chapters that follow, as are the relationships between them and pupil involvement.

3 The expressive order

The expressive order of the school consists of the modes of approved behaviour it transmits and the activities used in their transmission. This chapters concerns the way in which expressive activities are organised, and the pupils' involvement in them.

The first section deals with the organisation of pupil behaviour, in terms of the way it is standardised, formalised and ritualised. The specialisation of expressive activities by age, sex and imputed ability, is dealt with in later chapters, as are the special aspects of the expressive order, school uniform and assembly.

The next section on pupil involvement first describes the methods used to measure involvement in expressive activities. The measurements are then related to the social characteristics of the pupils, the type of school they attend, and the organisation of expressive activities.

The organisation of expressive activities

Five structural variables or basic methods of organisation are described:

1. Standardisation of expressive activities
2. Standardisation of expressive performance
3. Formalisation of expressive activities
4. Formalisation of expressive performance
5. Ritualisation of expressive performance

The standardisation of expressive activities

The following description of the pupil's school-day illustrates the extent to which expressive activities were standardised in the sample of seventy-two schools. The percentage incidence is given in brackets.

No matter how you travel to school there are rules about it. At the bus stop adults must be allowed on first (29 per cent), and if you come by special bus or coach you have a definite seat (15 per cent), and are supervised (49 per cent) to make sure you abide by the special rules of behaviour (24 per cent). Using your bike requires permission (65 per cent), and when you get to school you must put it in a particular place (21 per cent). Motor bikes, scooters and cars may be prohibited (13 per cent, 13 per cent and 19 per cent respectively), and if you can use them remember the special rules about their use (53 per cent). However you come to school, remember not to eat things on the way (19 per cent).

When you arrive, come into the playground by the correct entrance (39 per cent) and stay in your own area (60 per cent), and remember not to play any of the banned games (51 per cent), and not to eat (11 per cent). Do not enter school until the special entry time (64 per cent). Wait for the whistle or bell (64 per cent), then stand still (8 per cent), and then line up (17 per cent) to enter by the correct door (78 per cent). When in school remember which corridors or stairs you must not use (54 per cent), and which part of the cloakroom you can use (85 per cent). Remember that you can only enter the cloakrooms at certain times (47 per cent), and to use your individual place in it (53 per cent).

The journey to the hall for assembly will be supervised (65 per cent), as will your entry into the hall (93 per cent). When you go to class queue outside the door (40 per cent) and do not enter unless the teacher gives permission (31 per cent).

The building will be cleared during breaktime (82 per cent). If you are allowed in your formroom at any time remember you must not do school work (13 per cent) or homework (17 per cent), talk (4 per cent), play games (13 per cent), or records (47 per cent) and you must not eat (56 per cent). Queue for your dinner (81 per cent) in silence (7 per cent) and then go to your special place (28 per cent) on your particular table (50 per cent) where you will be supervised (56 per cent). You may not leave the table when you wish (78 per cent), wait until you are instructed (60 per cent) and then either leave with the other members of your table (72 per cent) or leave when everyone in the dining room is finished (11 per cent). If you are not forbidden to bring sandwiches (42 per cent) then remember you must have permission to do so (11 per cent). You are not allowed to leave school during dinner hour (83 per cent) unless you first receive permission (79 per cent). You are not allowed in your formrooms during the dinner hour (82 per cent).

Remember that all the rules about coming to school also apply when you are going home.

The items classified under this heading were not susceptible to being scaled using the item-analysis technique mentioned in Chapter 1. This may be an indication of a decision-making process that was not very sequential, but rather piecemeal. An authentic example is the introduction of rules about playing with hard balls in the playground after a window had been broken. However, a simple summated scale was obtained by the addition of the incidence of 55 items which occurred in more than 10 per cent and less than 90 per cent of all the schools (see Table C, Appendix C). The average score for all schools was twenty-seven.

The extent of the standardisation of expressive behaviour was less in comprehensives than other schools, and tended to be lower in girls' schools (Table 8).

TABLE 8 *Standardisation of expressive activities, mean scores, summation scale*

	Boys SM	Girls SM	Mixed SM	All SM	All CS	Boys GS	Girls GS	Mixed GS	All GS
n	7	6	24	37	17	6	6	6	18
mean	28·0	25·3	28·0	27·4	23·1	29·1	26·9	29·1	28·5

Legend. SM secondary modern; *CS* comprehensive school; *GS* grammar school (see note to Table 1, Chapter 1).

Some individual items have a particularly high incidence in certain categories of school. The 'adults first in the bus queue' rule occurred in five of the six girls' modern schools but in none of the boys' modern schools. Lining up before entering school was more associated with boys' schools than girls' (29 per cent compared with 7 per cent; mixed schools occupied a median position of 16 per cent). Sandwich lunches were forbidden in 86 per cent of girls' schools compared with 50 per cent of boys'. Pupils queued outside rooms in about half the modern schools compared with a third of grammar schools and a quarter of comprehensives.

There is no evidence to indicate that large schools standardised more than smaller ones, except through rules about entrances and corridors, often associated with split sites. This apart, there is little evidence that the material provision of the school was directly associated with the extent or kind of standardisation. In one LEA area a number of schools had been built to the same plan, but each had a different degree and type of standardisation. What sometimes happened was that a material feature of the school was given as a reason for a particular standardisation. In one boys' modern school the pupils were marched (literally) in single file by their teachers from one class to another. The reason given was that the corridors and stairs were very narrow, but in the sample in general there is no evidence of marching or single filing associated with narrow corridors, so that the rule was probably more associated with the teachers expectations or experience of the pupils' behaviour when not controlled in this way.

The standardisation of expressive performance

Pupil behaviour is constantly assessed within schools. Some assessments become standardised. Latecomers were automatically punished in 44 per cent of schools and in 25 per cent of them a further punishment followed an excessive (variously defined) number of latenesses. In 14 per cent there were regular inspections of appearance.

Thirty-two per cent of schools used a system of marks or points to reward good behaviour. The award of points was in the gift of the teachers, and the criteria for the award of points appeared to be mainly personalised and subjective. In most cases bad behaviour could lead to a deduction of points, and the collecting of a certain number of points often lead to a further reward. In one girls' modern school a weekly reward of leaving school a quarter of an hour early on Friday was made to the class with the highest points average. For the winning form of the year there was a celebration party.

Seventy-four per cent of headteachers caned pupils for misbehaviour. Forty-nine per cent of deputy heads and 42 per cent of other senior staff also caned. In only four schools did all the teachers use the cane. The criteria for receiving the cane were, as in receiving points, particular to the pupil rather than the misdemeanour. Thirty-three per cent had automatic caning for a few offences, smoking in school being one of the most common. Of schools, 51 per cent held regular detentions.

Only three of these items were scalable, so that the scale for standardisation of expressive performance is a four-point one (Table 9).

TABLE 9   *Standardisation of expressive performance scale*

Items	f
Collecting a number of points leads to further reward	11
Other senior staff cane	30
Deputy head canes	35

Mean item analysis value = 0·966; mean score 1·06 (N = 72; S.D. = 1·04).

The standardisation of expressive performance showed a great deal of variation by school context. High mean scores on the scale (Table 10) were particularly associated with modern schools and boys' schools, so that the highest score was for boys' modern schools and the lowest for girls' and mixed grammar schools.[1]

TABLE 10   *Standardisation of expressive performance scale mean scores*

	Boys SM	Girls SM	Mixed SM	All SM	All CS	Boys GS	Girls GS	Mixed GS	All GS
n	7	6	24	37	17	6	6	6	18
mean	2·00	0·50	1·33	1·32	1·29	0·83	0·00	0·00	0·28
S.D.	1·07	0·50	0·99	1·04	1·02	0·69	0·00	0·00	1·04

These results are reflected in the correlations of the scale scores with the age, ability and social compositions of the schools (Table 11). It is clear that high levels of standardisation are associated with a high proportion of pupils who are young, less able and working-class. These together with the sex variable are an analysis of the high score for boys' modern schools.

TABLE 11   *Correlations of standardisation of expressive performance scores*

Ability composition (by IQ)	%	120+	110+	110+	90+	80+	79−	
	r	−0·43	−0·31	0·28	0·42	0·43	0·31	
Social composition (by occupational group)	%	1	2	3	4	5	6	
	r	−0·40	−0·49	−0·18	0·47	0·11	0·30	
Age composition (by year group)	%	1st	2nd	3rd	4th	5th	6th	7th
	r	0·50	0·37	0·29	0·35	0·10	−0·40	−0·45

Note. The sixfold occupational classification was similar to that used in the Young Leavers Report 1968. (The correlation against mean IQ was −0·43, and against the percentage of manual pupils 0·24.)

The use of a *behaviour point reward scheme* occurred in more than half the modern schools compared with one in five comprehensives and only one grammar school. Among modern schools it was higher in the single-sex schools than the mixed ones.

[1] The sex differences are to be expected as two-scale items refer to caning.

The incidence of the use of caning was strongly linked to sex composition. Only one boys' school did not cane, and only one girls' school did so. Nine out of ten mixed schools did cane. Only in the boys' modern school was it found that all the teachers were empowered to cane. In contrast not a single boys' modern school used regular detentions.

One external contextual variable of some significance was location. Schools in country districts had large proportions of their pupils brought in by special buses each day. These schools could not operate a fair system of punishing lateness because lateness was not usually the pupils' fault. They did not give after-school detentions because all the pupils had to be on the buses for home.

The formalisation of expressive activities

The two most common forms of the use of paper to control expressive activities were school rules, found in 81 per cent of schools and uniform lists, found in all but three schools. Three items form the scale for this structural variable (Table 12).

TABLE 12   *Formalisation of expressive activities scale*

Items	f
Cycle passes	19
Speech or open day programme	51
School rules	58

Mean item analysis value $= 0 \cdot 832$; mean score $1 \cdot 78$ (N $= 72$; S.D. $= 0 \cdot 71$).

The mean scores were highest in grammar schools (Table 13).

TABLE 13   *Formalisation of expressive activities scale mean scores*

	Boys SM	Girls SM	Mixed SM	All SM	All CS	Boys GS	Girls GS	Mixed GS	All GS
n	7	6	24	37	17	6	6	6	18
mean	1·57	1·83	1·58	1·62	1·88	2·00	1·83	2·17	2·00
S.D.	1·05	0·37	0·64	0·71	0·76	0·82	0·37	0·37	0·58

This was reflected in the incidence of school rules which occurred in all but one grammar school but in only three quarters of modern and comprehensive schools. The use of paper in social control requires a reliable standard of literacy on the part of pupils. The correlation between the schools' mean ability level and the scale score was 0·27 which is significant at the 5 per cent level. As may be expected the scale score was also positively correlated with the proportion of older pupils; 0·24 for the percentage of seventh year, −0·26 for the percentage of first.

The formalisation of expressive performance

The four commonest uses of paper in the assessment of pupil behaviour form parts of the scale (Table 14).

TABLE 14 *Formalisation of expressive performance scale*

Items	*f*
Detention list displayed	10
More than one punishment book	15
Detention book	28
Late list	43

Mean item analysis value = 0·823; mean score 1·33 (N = 72; S.D. = 1·07).

The formalisation of expressive performance was strongly associated with boys' grammar schools (Table 15). The low score for mixed schools is probably partly explained by their high incidence of bussing, which is associated with the low incidence of late procedures and detentions, which appear as scale items.

TABLE 15 *Formalisation of expressive performance scale mean scores*

	Boys SM	Girls SM	Mixed SM	All SM	All CS	Boys GS	Girls GS	Mixed GS	All GS
n	7	6	24	37	17	6	6	6	18
mean	0·86	1·33	0·96	1·00	1·76	2·67	1·67	0·50	1·61
S.D.	0·64	0·94	0·89	0·87	1·16	0·94	0·47	0·50	1·11

The ritualisation of expressive performance

The act of caning could be classified as a ritual, and I have made a speculative analysis of this elsewhere (King (1969b)). The two items forming the scale both refer to the use of a points-award system for behaviour (Table 16). In some schools the use of tokens such as

TABLE 16 *Ritualisation of expressive performance scale*

Item	*f*
Cup or prize for general behaviour competition	26
Cup or prize presented at speech or open day	12

Mean item analysis value = 1·00; mean score 0·53 (N = 72; S.D. = 0·76).

'merit certificates' may be regarded as further acts of ritualisation. The ritualisation of expressive performance was highest in modern schools especially the single-sex schools (Table 17).

TABLE 17   *Ritualisation of expressive performance scale mean scores*

	Boys SM	Girls SM	Mixed SM	All SM	All CS	Boys GS	Girls GS	Mixed GS	All GS
n	7	6	24	37	17	6	6	6	18
mean	1·14	1·17	0·50	0·73	0·29	0·33	0·67	0·00	0·33
S.D.	0·99	0·90	0·58	0·79	0·57	0·75	0·94	0·00	0·75

Correlations between structural variables

Only one significant zero-order correlation was found between the four item-analysis scales for expressive structural variables. The correlation between the formalisation and standardisation of expressive performance was 0·35 which is significant beyond the 1 per cent level. This suggests that when schools are concerned with how well the pupils are behaving they include the use of paper in conjunction with rules and punishments.

Transmitted modes of approved behaviour

The previous section of this chapter described and analysed the way expressive activities were organised or structured in schools. These activities were concerned with the transmission of approved modes of behaviour, which can be identified by two important methods. First, by the examination of statements made by headteachers about their expectations or ideals of pupil behaviour. The sources of the statements discussed here were obtained from the documents sent to us by the schools. These included introductory letters to new parents, statements of school philosophy, school rules and speech-day addresses. In every case it was assumed that the statements were either written by the headteacher or had his or her approval. They are all examples of the formalisation of approved modes of behaviour.

Unlike the public schools analysed by Weinberg (1967), or the medieval school documented by Sylvester (1970), there were few explicit or detailed descriptions of the model pupil.

This diffuseness is a reflection of that found in the general culture. In modern democratic pluralised societies like Britain there exists a range of acceptable life styles, so that precise prescriptions do not always exist for behaviour in all situations. What the statements often do is to endorse the observation made by Baron (1955) that the English conception of the school is that of a discrete community, and so the description of the pupil is as a member of that community, happy, loyal, with a feeling of belonging.[1]

'We aim to be a well-ordered, happy community. (Modern-school headteacher.)

This image of the pupil as a member of the community is linked with the socialisation purposes of education. It is also related to the wide scope of interest the teachers are expected to have in their pupils, as well as the welfare functions of the school in providing dinners, health and dental checkups.

A second method of identifying the modes of approved behaviour transmitted by the school is to make inferences from the expressive activities employed. In this study only those activities which became structured are considered and little account can be taken of the expressive activities that occur within the domain of the teachers' autonomy, which are personalised and non-organisational. Given this limitation an examination of the standardisation, formalisation and ritualisation of expressive activities indicates that the behaviour expected of the pupils in this connection is not especially that of a member of a community, although the notion of the school as a community is used to legitimate the behaviour, by appeals for loyalty to the school.

The prevailing image of the ideal pupil that emerges is that he or she is punctual, well-behaved, neat and tidy, with a respect for ownership and property. To be well-behaved includes not smoking, fighting, chewing gum, dropping litter, being rude to teachers or the public. According to the typology of social class behaviour suggested by Cohen (1955), and used by Hargreaves (1967) in his study of a secondary-modern school, many of these characteristics of the ideal pupil are characteristically middle-class. To this extent, at least, all of the schools could be regarded as being middle-class institutions.

It could be argued that much of the organisation is simply to allow the school to function efficiently. Royston Lambert's (1966) classification of school goals includes such a special category, organisational, in addition to instrumental and expressive goals. Here is perhaps a confusion between purpose and function. The purpose of having a controlled entry into school in the morning may be to make the entry more efficient; one of its undoubted outcomes is to modify pupil behaviour. At the level of justification many expressive activities have a dual purpose; to permit the education processes to continue effectively, and to socialise the pupils into approved modes of behaviour. Thus the lateness rules are not only an attempt to bring learning groups together efficiently but also to internalise the importance of punctuality.

[1] In a few cases schools used the term 'family' to indicate the degree of belonging expected of the pupil.

> In a large school like this there must be a sound routine to ensure reasonable working efficiency and safety for people and property. Definite standards of behaviour with such a sensible routine are sound policies to adopt towards the upbringing of all young people. (Headteacher, mixed modern school)

This is the collapsing of the means and ends of schools that Lambert (in Lambert *et al.*, 1968) has already described in the public schools. In a sense schools are transcendental organisations that attempt to create for present purposes situations to have future consequences. This is implied in the idea of the school as a society or a microcosm of society and points to Bernstein's (1966b) distinction of the internal (school) and external (societal) functions of the expressive order. More specifically it is also made explicit by some headteachers who claim the legitimacy of the work order for their rules for pupil behaviour.

> I insist on good standards of discipline . . . because it will create a greater respect for the school among the general public, including employers. (Letter to parents. Headmaster, mixed modern school)

It has already been shown that expressive activities were differently organised in schools of different kinds. In particular it varied with the age, sex, ability and social composition of the school. This may indicate two related things; that different models of behaviour exist for different types of pupil, or that the norms or standards of performance vary for the different types of pupil. This distinction is a difficult one to disentangle. There was a tendency for boys' schools, both modern and grammar, to refer to a gentlemanly model of behaviour. 'The School Rule. Every boy must behave as a gentleman on all occasions.' (Boys' grammar school.)

Similarly there was a tendency for girls' schools, especially grammar schools, to use a 'young lady' model. Such models were rarer in mixed schools, and it is of interest that no mixed school made explicit models of how pupils of different sexes should behave towards one another.

An examination of the organisation of expressive activities implies a lower standard of expectation of behaviour for boys, particularly when they are young, not so able and working-class; all of which may be claimed to concur with the general cultural expectation of behaviour. There is some evidence of an expectation of a higher, perhaps different, standard of behaviour for girls. The judgments of good behaviour seem to be based less on the breaking of rules and more on the girls' demeanour even when actually observing them. Thus the only girls' school to cane its pupils did so only for cases of deliberate disobedience or repeated rudeness or insolence. Our observations suggest that the look on a girl's face and the way she stands can be interpreted as insolence in some girls' schools.

Expressive involvement

Two methods were used to measure the pupils' involvement in expressive activities, one attitudinal the other behavioural.

The six items of the seven-point scale for expressive involvement were shown in Table 5, Chapter 1.

A number of behavioural indices are available to measure expressive involvement. Measurements of the incidence of being punished for misbehaviour, or teachers' ratings of behaviour, proved to have little discriminating power in our pilot trials. The behavioural index used was based upon the proposition that the model of the pupil transmitted by the school was that of a member of a community. Pupils were asked in the questionnaire to give what official positions they held in the school. The incidence of holding at least one such position was taken as being a positive index of expressive involvement. The holding of such a position, be it prefect, blackboard monitor or library help, indicates the holding of a communal role in addition to the basic and involuntary pupil role. The weakness of the measure is that the degree of self-selection and teacher-selection involved in filling the positions is not known. However, it is argued that in general teachers select for jobs of responsibility those pupils who appear to be both willing and able.

Social class and expressive involvement

Bernstein (1966a) has suggested that working-class pupils may be less involved in the expressive culture of the school than middle-class pupils. An examination of the differences in the mean scores on the expressive involvement scale for pupils matched for age and sex within individual schools does not support the suggestion. Examples are found of significantly higher involvement for middle class over working class, but what is more interesting is that in some types of school there was a tendency for higher working-class involvement. This occurred:

(a) In the fourth year of girls' modern schools
(b) For girls in the fourth year of mixed grammar schools
(c) For girls in the fifth year of mixed comprehensives
(d) In the fourth year of boys' grammar schools (see Table D, Appendix C).

However, the measurement of involvement by occupancy of positions followed the expected pattern more closely. In several situations middle-class pupils held more positions than working-class. This was particularly clear in:

(a) The second year of girls' modern schools
(b) The fifth year of girls' comprehensive schools
(c) The second and fourth years of boys' modern schools
(d) The second year of boys' grammar schools
(e) For boys in the fifth year of mixed grammar schools.

The only significant reversal was for fourth-year boys in mixed grammar schools (see Table E, Appendix C). It is interesting to note that the middle-class over-representation was most common in single-sex schools. It is possible that in mixed schools sexual identity has primacy over social class identity in some situations.

These results suggest that the pupil's disposition towards the expressive aspects of the school is not directly related to his social class of origin, but that the conversion of a favourable disposition into approved behaviour is more common among middle-class children. Thus working-class pupils do tend to legitimise the essentially middle-class model of behaviour transmitted by the school, even if they are not always willing to act upon it.

Sex and expressive involvement

Although at particular ages in individual mixed schools the differences in the mean scores on the involvement scale for boys and girls were sometimes significant, there were no consistent patterns associated with either sex, social class, age or type of school.

Consistent differences in the rate at which pupils of different sexes held school positions were only found in mixed grammar schools, where boys tended to occupy school positions more frequently than girls at every age-level (Table F, Appendix C).

Age and expressive involvement

The only clear age-pattern for the mean scores on the involvement scale was that of the fourth year being lower than that of the second year. However, this only occurred consistently in boys' grammar schools and for girls in mixed grammar schools (Table G, Appendix C). There were no consistent age differences related to class.

In contrast to this relative lack of age differences at the attitudinal level, the measurements of holding school positions showed a marked pattern of increasing incidence with age. This occurred in virtually every school, for both boys and girls.

There is little doubt that this pattern is due to the way opportunities for holding positions favour older pupils.

Expressive involvement and type of school

Possible associations between the type of school, in terms of the contextual variables of size, status and sex composition, and level of involvement, were investigated by comparing the mean scores of pupils matched by age and sex. Only one example was found. Girls in the second year of grammar schools were on average less involved in the girls' schools compared with those in the mixed schools.[1] (Table H, Appendix C.)

However, when the rates of occupying positions were compared, second-year girls in girls' grammar schools scored more highly than those in mixed schools (Table I, Appendix C).

Boys and girls in the fifth year of modern schools generally held more positions than those in comprehensive schools (Table I, Appendix C). This is a reflection of their higher age-status and their holding many of the official positions occupied by the sixth formers in the comprehensives.

Involvement and the organisation of expressive activities

The degree and type of organisation of expressive activities has been shown to be widely variable, but these variations were not significantly related to degree of expressive involvement. Thus the pupil's orientation to the control of his behaviour is not *directly* related to any of the rules, rewards or punishments used by the school. This does not mean that organisation does not affect involvement, but that it does not determine it.

A likely intervening variable is the teaching staff. It is they who operate the rules, rewards and punishments. Much of the expressive order is not organised but mediated by individual teachers generating personalised expectations of pupil behaviour and using personalised rewards and punishments.

Expressive involvement, consensus and conflict

The results of the measurements of involvement indicate that pupils of different ages, sex and social class tend to show similar levels of acceptance of the expressive order within most individual schools. This, and the generally high mean scores on the involvement scale, may be taken to indicate a general level of consensus between pupils and their teachers, as to how they should behave in school. This is

[1] This is similar to some of the results of Dale (1967).

not surprising, as it would be difficult for schools to continue in their present form without such a reasonable consensus.

This overall consensus of sentiments that exists in most schools is probably a resultant of the interaction of a number of variables. The model of pupil behaviour transmitted and the type of organisation vary with the kind of pupil a school recruits. In addition, it is likely that the criteria used by individual teachers in making assessments of pupil behaviour are similar to those used in the organisation; age, sex, social background and, perhaps, ability.

This proposition of a general consensus does not exclude the possibility of conflict, but this analysis suggests it would be between individual pupils and the school rather than groups of pupils with similar social characteristics. Sentiments such as 'I don't like the cane. I hate this rotten school' were not uncommon in the free comments on the questionnaire. However, it would be wrong to assume that a pupil who is punished is inevitably in conflict with the school; a punished pupil may consider the punishment to be quite legitimate. Every boy in a group of fourth-year low-stream pupils from a boys' modern school that were interviewed in the pilot stage, had been frequently caned. (All the teachers in the school had canes). When they were asked about caning one replied, 'If they didn't cane us we wouldn't behave ourselves would we?' The others were in agreement.

4 School rituals

The concept of ritual makes only rare and unimportant appearances in approaches used in the study of organisations. Etzioni (1961), for example, subsumes its use under the heading of normative power, together with the manipulation of mass media, the allocation of esteem, and other rather disparate items.

Most of the literature of ritual is anthropological, but there do exist two contributions specifically dealing with ritual in schools. The first is a chapter on Ceremonials in Waller's classic, *The Sociology of Teaching* (1932). Some of Waller's ideas are taken up, extended and combined with others from anthropological studies in the speculative analysis, 'Ritual in Education', by Basil Bernstein and his associates. Bernstein defines ritual as 'an expression in action as distinct from thought of man's active attitudes towards those non-empirical aspects of their reality, which are expressive of ultimate values'. This definition is concerned with the function of ritual and does not form a satisfactory basis for an operational definition concerned with the form or structure of ritual. In the anthropological context Turner (1964) defines ritual as 'prescribed formal behaviour for occasions not given over to technological routine, having reference to mystical being or powers'. Clearly the school assembly with its interpolation of religious worship falls within this definition. Turner goes on to describe the symbol as the smallest unit of ritual, hence a basic definition used in this study; ritual consists of the use of symbols. However, Turner's definition of symbols as 'objects, activities, relationships, even spatial units in a ritual situation', is not so useful in the context of the school, because symbols are used outside 'ritual situations'. The school uniform, for example, is usually worn all the time in school. Clearly Goody's (1961) suggestion that rituals can be used outside of magical-religious situations must be accepted, a point that is supported by Bocock (1970) who makes a distinction between civic and religious rituals. Hence a symbol may be simply

45

defined as a thing representing or typifying something else. Turner's definition gives examples of symbols; Bernstein's of what may be symbolised.

The investigator of ritual in the school faces two problems: how to recognise a symbol and how to establish what it symbolises. Symbols used in schools seem to be of two kinds: ceremonials and emblems. The symbol of the ceremony lies in its form, regularity and repetition. Emblems are tangible and include uniforms, badges, plaques, flags and cups. Such symbols may be detected using a number of methods. The most commonly used in this study was the use of the Weberian *Verstehen* analysis. All the investigators had shared in the cultural experience of education both as pupils and teachers, and so could claim to be reasonably sensitised for the detection of symbols. In addition, Leach (1964) has suggested that emblemic symbols have a non-rational relationship to what they symbolise. Thus school colours vary from school to school but (presumably) symbolise some of the same things in each school. Ceremonials may be recognised by the stability of their form, and possibly from the observed and stated orientation of the participants; do they look as if they were taking part in a sacred ceremony? Care must be taken in the use of the observation technique, in that civic ceremonies do not necessarily have a sacred reference, and in any case, as Mary Douglas (1966) has pointed out, the participants in religious rites do not necessarily appear to be behaving in a reverent or other special sort of way.

Several methods were used to infer what was symbolised by the rituals observed. Here again the observer's own experience was valuable, but in addition headteachers were asked in interview to comment on the value of both the school uniform and assembly, as well as other ritualised activities, and a content analysis was made of references to such rituals in the documents sent to us by schools. Questions on the purpose of the school uniform and assembly were also asked of pupils in the group interviews at the pilot stage.

This chapter presents the two major rituals of the expressive order of the school, the school uniform and school assembly, and a note on speech days. The ritualisation of the House system, prefectorial system, games, school work, age and sex differences are described and discussed in later chapters.

The school uniform

Definition and prescription

Every school had some kind of school uniform; 95 per cent had a uniform list; but it was only compulsory for all pupils in 78 per cent of schools. The extent to which different items of clothing were standardised and defined as being part of the uniform, and the extent to which each item was prescribed to be worn is given in Table 18.

TABLE 18 *Definition and prescription of items of uniform (percentages)*

	Boys		Girls	
Item	Defined	Prescribed	Defined	Prescribed
Shoes	52	48	76	69
Socks/stockings	41	34	76	67
Skirt/dress/ trousers	93	79	98	93
Shirt/blouse	79	68	95	91
Tie	95	86	91	78
Jumper/Cardigan	66	26	93	60
Blazer	95	78	88	21
Topcoat	52	24	76	43
Scarf	43	3	57	3
Cap/hat/beret	57	22	62	24

Note. Boys refers to boys' and mixed schools; *Girls* refers to girls' and mixed schools (N = 58 in each case).

Uniform and type of school

Four item-analysis scales were constructed for the measurement of the definition and prescription of uniform, and are reported in Tables Y and Z, Appendix C. Table 19 indicates the way these measurements relate to school status and sex composition.

Uniforms were most extensively defined for boys in mixed grammar schools and comprehensives, less so in boys' modern schools. The definition of the girls' uniform showed less variation, but was least extensive in mixed modern schools. The extent of the definition of the uniform correlates positively with the degree of prescription (boys r = 0·34; girls r = 0·31). Among boys closer prescription was associated with the grammar schools, and with the mixed schools in each status category. The pattern for girls is of higher prescription in the grammar schools, but there is little variation between the single-sex and mixed schools.

The item-analysis scales do not permit comparisons to be made of sex differences in uniform. Table 19 shows that for comparable items of uniform the definition and prescription was generally higher for girls than boys. Shoes, for example, were defined and prescribed for about half the cases of boys, but for nearly three-quarters of the girls. It may appear from this that somewhat higher standards of appearance are expected of girls, and that the closer definition and prescription of the uniform for boys in mixed schools stems from the higher standards realised or expected of the girls. However, it should be recognised that although particular items of clothing were prescribed for girls the definition of the items was often diffuse and capable of many variations. Summer dresses were often allowed in different colours, patterns and styles.

TABLE 19   *Mean scores definition and prescription of uniform scales—boys and girls*

	Boys SM	Mixed SM	All SM	All CS	Boys GS	Mixed GS	All GS
Boys							
Definition n	7	24	31	15	6	6	12
mean	1·71	3·08	2·77	4·07	2·83	4·83	3·83
S.D.	1·39	2·00	1·96	1·29	2·11	2·19	2·37
Prescription							
mean	2·43	4·17	3·77	5·20	4·17	6·33	5·25
S.D.	2·13	2·43	2·47	1·42	2·34	2·43	2·62

	Girls SM	Mixed SM	All SM	All CS	Girls GS	Mixed GS	All GS
Girls							
Definition n	6	24	30	16	6	6	12
mean	4·50	3·08	3·37	3·75	4·33	4·83	4·58
S.D.	0·50	1·63	1·58	1·15	0·47	0·37	0·49
Prescription							
mean	2·83	2·17	2·50	2·94	4·50	4·33	4·42
S.D.	1·57	1·55	1·69	1·56	0·76	1·11	0·95

A school's uniform policy is part of a general concern about pupil appearance. Sixty-five per cent of schools had rules about hair style or length. These were most common in boys' grammar schools and girls' modern schools.

It is difficult to know whether schools were applying different standards. The word 'sensible' was most commonly used by head-teachers in writing or talking about the matter. At the time of our fieldwork there was enormous variation in the acceptance of side-burns on boys (not below the ear in one school).

Only four out of the fifty-eight schools for boys allowed the wearing of jeans, five would allow boys to come without ties, nine without jackets. Three out of the fifty-eight schools for girls did not expressly forbid the use of make-up. Here perhaps the distinction can be made between what is intended to happen, what is allowed to happen, and what actually happens. Older girls in many of the schools were obviously wearing discreet make-up, even where its use had not been extended to them as 'privilege'. It is difficult to believe that this was not also visible to the teachers. Although the tie was a common masculine element in the uniform of girls only one school allowed girls to wear trousers.

Most schools checked pupils' appearance by a random inspection of individual pupils but in ten schools regular class inspections were used.

Uniform as symbol

In their comments on the importance of uniform headteachers did sometimes mention what may be described as its utilitarian or even rational purposes. These include being able to identify pupils on school trips, and the proposition that the school uniform was 'suitable clothing for school'. Comments were also made about the inculcation of neatness, good taste and pride in appearance, but both the rational and the overtly socialising purposes were clearly subordinate to the symbolic value of the uniform. Its recognition as a symbol was made clear by this kind of comment, 'The wearing of the school uniform demonstrates respect for the things the school stands for.'

What is symbolised by the wearing of the uniform may be inferred from the purposes it is supposed to serve. They include:

(a) Removes social differences
(b) Promotes pride in membership of the school, high morale and corporate spirit
(c) Prevents competition in dress (especially between girls).

The wearing of uniform is an expressive activity, it is a school-approved mode of behaviour. It was argued in the previous chapter that the model of approved pupil behaviour was that of a member of the school as a community. The stated purposes support this argument, some explicitly – 'Uniform promotes unity and community'. The school uniform has basic role-defining functions. (See Wood (1966).) When a child puts on his uniform it is a symbolic acceptance of his pupil-role – 'Distinguishes home from school', as one headteacher put it. It is common in schools for a negligent wearing of the uniform to be interpreted as indicating actual or potential rejection of the processes of the school.

By defining the pupil as a member of the school community the uniform makes latent the other identities that may either form a threat to the pupils' allegiance to the school (for example, the teenager role), or introduce social and economic inequalities which may

49

prevent the formation of consensus essential to the idea of a community. The making of all pupils equal in this way is part of the English sense of fairness, that all should be equal in the competition for achievement. In addition the elimination of conflict and competition which has its origins outside enables the school to create its own forms of competition and tension, in both its academic and sporting activities.[1]

Most, but not all, headteachers supported the idea of school uniform strongly. Some were opposed to its use but conceded that parents liked it and that it gave the school a good name. Another opposed it on the grounds of its imposition of uniformity, an argument that was reversed by another headteacher, who claimed that it made children more individual, in that they were responded to as people rather than as the identities suggested by their clothes. Among modern-school headteachers the uniform was seen as a 'status symbol' and the pursuit of a 100 per cent turnout vigorously sought. Our observations suggest that schools only make the uniform compulsory when virtually all the pupils are wearing it voluntarily.

The acceptance of uniform

The pupils' involvement in, or acceptance of, the school uniform was measured using a short two-item, three-point scale (Table 20).

TABLE 20   *Uniform involvement scale*

Item	Judges' score	Per cent agreement	r item/ total score
I am proud to wear the school uniform	8·4	50	0·817
Having a uniform gives the school a good name	6·8	66	0·792

Mean score 1·2 (N = 7,457; S.D. = 0·78).

We were unable to make measurements based upon pupil behaviour in relation to uniform. Although general observations were made, the resources required to check, for example, every pupil's appearance against the school's expectation, would have to be enormous.

Social class and acceptance of uniform

The acceptance of school uniform did not vary significantly by social class within schools.

[1] Nearly all schools forbade the wearing of badges of non-school organisations and jewellery.

Assuming that pupils respond to the uniform as a symbol, then it is clear that there is little difference in the acceptance of the membership of the school community among the social classes, which is a confirmation of the results from the measures of expressive involvement.

Two reservations should be made about this statement. First, children from different social backgrounds may have a different conception of the nature and purpose of membership of the school community, and of the school uniform. Second, a high acceptance of the uniform may not be directly related to the extent to which it is worn and the manner of its wearing.

Sex and acceptance of uniform

There is a clear tendency for girls to accept school uniform more than boys, a generalisation that holds for the different ages and in different types of mixed school (Table J, Appendix C).

This difference is probably a cultural one because with only two exceptions there were no significant differences of levels of involvement between pupils matched by age and sex, in single-sex and mixed schools matched by status. The exception was in fourth-year and seventh-year girls in grammar schools. The mean scores in all three mixed schools were higher than in the two girls' schools (Table J, Appendix C).

This general pattern is perhaps a little surprising in that conventional wisdom assumes that girls are more resentful of the school uniform than boys. Here, as with social class, it may be that the significance of uniform and its implied membership of the school, is different for boys and girls. Other possible partial explanation rests at a less deep level. Some girls, in interviews and in their free responses in the questionnaire, said that they liked the uniform because they could then avoid the problem of what to wear each day, and reserve their more fashionable clothes for the evenings and weekends. In addition it was fairly common for older girls to be consulted about the style and colour of summer uniform. Boys' uniforms showed little variation by season or style.

Age and acceptance of uniform

The most conspicuous age-pattern found for both sexes in schools of all situations and sex composition was that of a lower mean involvement in the fourth year compared with the second (Table J, Appendix C). In boys' grammar schools and for boys in most comprehensives the fifth-year mean score was lower than the fourth.

This lowered acceptance with age may be organisational, but it

51

most probably also reflects the teenagers' increased encounter with social groups outside the school such as youth clubs and courtship groups, and their exposure to the vestments of the teenager role, so vigorously disapproved in many schools.

Acceptance of uniform and uniform policy

There were no significant relationships between the extent to which the uniform was either defined or prescribed and the pupils' acceptance of the uniform.

The school assembly

Control and structure of the school assembly

The following description provides the incidence of certain structural features of the school assembly found in the sample schools.

Pupils enter the school hall supervised (93 per cent) by the prefects (12 per cent) or the teachers (82 per cent). They enter by age (60 per cent) and take up special positions for each age-group (88 per cent). Within age-groups they enter by their teaching-group (43 per cent) and take up positions special to that group (53 per cent). The older pupils sit whilst the younger ones stand (15 per cent). The prefects process in (3 per cent) and take up their special positions (44 per cent). In mixed schools boys and girls enter separately (39 per cent) and take up separate positions (61 per cent). The prefects enter separately by sex (52 per cent).

The teachers process in (7 per cent), or enter separately from the pupils (47 per cent), wearing gowns (15 per cent), and take up their places on the platform (29 per cent). They sit while the pupils stand (31 per cent). The headteacher enters separately from all others (83 per cent) wearing a gown (46 per cent), and carrying a Bible (7 per cent). The pupils stand specially for his entrance (21 per cent), as do the teachers (28 per cent), and he takes up a position on the platform (92 per cent) behind a lectern (65 per cent).[1] The headteacher is the only adult to speak during the assembly (17 per cent). Only prefects read the lesson (28 per cent).

When this assembly is over the headteacher leaves separately from all others (81 per cent), and the teachers process out (43 per

[1] In one comprehensive school formed by the amalgamation of three schools there were two ex-headteachers on the staff who took turns with the existing head 'for old times sake'.

cent). The pupils leave in the same groups that they entered in but in the reverse order.

This is a description of an assembly without content but this structure of processions and ceremonials is repeated in some schools five days a week for nine months of the year. The structure is a reflection of the status system and authority structure of the school. The pupils are differentiated by age, sex and ability. Pupils with power over other pupils, the prefects, exercise that power and present themselves as a separate group. The teachers, as power and status superordinates, are separated from the pupils and elevated on the platform. The most high, the most conspicuously separated and the most active participant, holds the most powerful position in the school – the headteacher in three-quarters of the schools, usually in consultation the school halls of England, but Edmund Leach (1964) in his study of the Kachin reached this similar conclusion; 'ritual serves to express the individual's status as a social person in the structure system in which he finds himself for the time being.'

The form and content of the assembly were controlled by the headteacher in three quarters of the schools, usually in consultation or in conjunction with other teachers. Older pupils and prefects were allowed into the process in 44 per cent and 31 per cent of schools respectively; younger pupils in 40 per cent of schools.

Separate assemblies for pupils of different ages occurred in 40 per cent of schools, although not everyday, and two mixed schools had separate assemblies for boys and girls, probably related to their being on a dual site. Separate House assemblies occurred in 30 per cent of schools and pupils stood in House groups in the school assembly in 22 per cent of schools.

The structure of assembly in different types of school

Six item-analysis scales were constructed for the measurement of the structure of the school assembly. Details of their construction appear in later chapters. The mean scores for schools varying by status and sex composition are given in Table 21.

The ritualisation of age-differences was particularly associated with single-sex modern schools and girls' grammar schools. Ability differences were most ritualised in modern schools, least in comprehensives and boys' grammar schools. Prefects were highly ritualised in boys' and mixed grammar schools. Teachers were also highly ritualised in these schools, as well as in girls' modern schools. The headteacher was most highly ritualised in boys' grammar schools (perhaps the closest to the public school archetype), but girls' grammar and modern schools also score highly.

TABLE 21 Ritualisation of assembly scales – mean scores

Scale:		Boys SM	Girls SM	Mixed SM	All SM	All CS	Boys GS	Girls GS	Mixed GS	All GS
	n	7	6	24	37	17	6	6	6	18
Ritualisation of:										
Age differences	mean	2·29	2·83	1·67	1·97	1·59	1·33	2·67	1·50	1·83
	S.D.	0·45	0·37	0·90	0·88	0·97	0·75	0·47	0·96	0·96
Ability differences	mean	2·00	2·00	1·92	1·95	0·71	0·83	1·83	1·17	1·28
	S.D.	1·31	1·41	1·32	1·33	1·27	1·21	1·34	1·34	1·37
Prefects	mean	0·57	0·50	0·58	0·57	0·53	1·17	0·33	1·17	0·89
	S.D.	0·49	0·50	0·64	0·59	0·61	0·93	0·47	0·69	0·81
Teachers	mean	0·86	1·33	0·83	0·92	0·82	1·83	1·00	1·50	1·44
	S.D.	0·83	0·75	1·25	1·12	0·98	1·07	0·58	0·76	0·90
Headteachers	mean	2·00	3·17	2·33	2·41	2·47	3·67	3·33	2·17	3·06
	S.D.	0·93	1·57	1·14	1·24	1·46	1·37	0·94	1·21	1·35
Sex differences	mean	—	—	1·79	—	1·14*	—	—	1·33	—
	S.D.			1·08		1·12			1·11	

*Mixed comprehensives n = 14.

Mixed schools tended not to ritualise age and ability relationships as much as single-sex schools, perhaps giving primacy to the ritualisation of sex differences.

Grammar schools, especially for boys, ritualised power positions in the school; prefects and more importantly, teachers and headteachers. This is reflected in the correlations between age, social class and ability compositions with the scale scores (Table 22). Ritualisation of power positions is associated with older, bright pupils from middle-class homes; of all the types of pupils in the sample, those most likely to occupy what are known as leadership positions in society.

TABLE 22   *Correlations of ritual and contextual variables* ($N = 72$)

| | Ritualisation | |
Context	Teachers	Headteachers
Social composition (per cent manual)	− 0·32†	− 0·18
Ability composition (mean IQ)	0·25*	0·28*
Age composition—per cent 1st year	− 0·32†	− 0.29*
per cent 7th year	0·22	0·13

* 5 per cent significant.   † 1 per cent significant.

A crude index of the overall degree of the ritualisation of the school assembly is obtained by the summation of the scores on the five scales that apply to all schools, i.e. excluding the ritualisation of sex differences. Table 23 indicates that girls' schools, especially modern schools, were the most highly ritualised type of school, although the lower scores of mixed schools partly reflect the exclusion of the sex-differentiating ritual.

The low score of comprehensive schools may be partly explained by their being mainly mixed schools (fourteen out of seventeen). It may also be due to the newness of such schools, as tradition is an importance source of legitimacy for rituals. It could also be related to an ideology which tends to view pupils of different ages, and particularly of different abilities, as being of equal value.

TABLE 23   *Degree of ritualisation of the school assembly*

	Boys SM	Girls SM	Mixed SM	All SM	All CS	Boys GS	Girls GS	Mixed GS	All GS
n	7	6	24	37	17	6	6	6	18
mean	7·72	9·54	7·33	7·82	6·12	7·83	9·16	7·51	8·50

Headteachers sometimes expressed the wish to keep the school hall more or less exclusively for school assembly and special, often ritualised, occasions, such as prize-givings. The sanctity of the hall was often polluted by the presence of PE fixtures and apparatus, floor workings and dining furniture. Sanctity was fostered by displays of cups, plaques of scholarship winners and other records of school-approved success.

An attempt was made to measure the sanctity of the school hall in terms of its being reserved for assembly and special occasions. The scale is given in Table 24.

TABLE 24   *Sanctity of school hall – scale*

Item	*f*
No PE fixtures or apparatus	50
No dining furniture	43
No floor markings	35
Plaques on the wall	10

Mean item analysis value 0·827; mean score 1·92 (N = 72; S.D = 1·09).

It is clear that the hall was most sanctified in grammar schools, especially those for boys (Table 25).

TABLE 25   *Sanctity of school hall – mean scores*

	Boys SM	*Girls SM*	*Mixed SM*	*All SM*	*All CS*	*Boys GS*	*Girls GS*	*Mixed GS*	*All GS*
n	7	6	24	37	17	6	6	6	18
mean	1·29	2·00	1·62	1·62	1·82	3·17	2·50	2·17	2·61
S.D.	1·03	1·41	0·95	1·07	0·78	0·90	1·26	0·69	1·06

Correlations between structural variables

The correlation between the degree of ritualisation of teachers and headteachers is 0·35, which is significant at the one per cent level, and indicates a strong association between these two forms of ritual. The correlation between age and ability ritualisation is more significant at 0·42, and probably indicates that a decision to differentiate between pupils by their ability statuses is concomitant with that to differentiate them by age.

The content of school assembly

This analysis of the school assembly has concerned only its ritual structure. We were unable to make satisfactory measurements of the content of the assembly. A great deal of variation in content was observed in the seventy-two assemblies studied. Attempts were made to record the number of hymns, prayers and readings, their sources and performers, but they were not altogether successful. The definitions of a hymn and a prayer are different when, as in some schools, one verse of the hymn is sung, then a prayer, then another verse and another prayer. In addition many schools varied the content of the assembly on a daily, weekly or seasonal basis, so that only the content analysis for a large sample of assemblies in each school would be satisfactory. Assemblies also included items by the choir, orchestra, soloists, and even dramatic performances. Our cross-checks on the structure of the assembly, observing one, asking the headteacher and ultimately the pupils and staff about it indicate that it shows little variation within schools.

Similar problems arose in the measurement of the length and frequency of assemblies, but there is one authentic case of a two-assembly per day school, which indicates the effect of a highly particular contextual feature. A small rural mixed modern school had a dismissal assembly at the end of the day. This was to facilitate the pupils getting on the school buses for home. The county authority had introduced larger buses which were unable to turn in the narrow approach road to the school. Pupils assembled in the hall in their bus groups and were dismissed a group at a time after a prayer, to walk down to the bottom of the road to the waiting buses.

The meaning of school assembly

Two sources are used in this discussion of the meaning of the school assembly: the statements made by headteachers about its importance and the observations and measurements made of the structure of assemblies. The headteachers suggested three important purposes for the assembly: religious, communal and communication.

The religious purpose of school assembly is perhaps its most manifest one and was stressed by 54 per cent of the headteachers. In a few cases the assembly was seen as an antidote to a secular society – 'Acts as a counterweight to the humanist ethic of society'; 'more important than ever because local churches are badly supported'. Four headteachers denied the religious value of school assembly, and four suggested they would probably not hold an assembly if the legal requirement were changed. These latter were not necessarily expressing anti-religious sentiments; one of these headteachers thought that compulsory religious observance was bad for the faith.

The communal purposes of assembly were stressed by 68 per cent of headteachers. The phrases used to express it included: 'Communal value', 'brings everyone together', 'development of corporate attitudes', 'pulls school together', 'together to start the day', 'sense of community', 'corporate identity'.

This was sometimes linked to the religious purpose, as in the use of the phrase, 'corporate worship', but in many cases the communal was mentioned without any reference to the religious.

It was suggested in the discussion of both the expressive order and the school uniform that the model of the pupil held by the school is one of a member of a community. The school assembly also propagates this model. It is a daily reminder of the resumption of the pupil role – 'a good start to the day'; 'gets pupils in the right frame of mind'. The school assembly not only marks off the school as a group of like-situated individuals, but also distinguishes it from other parts of the social system, including the pupils' homes and other schools. The announcement of games results in assemblies, which occurred in 89 per cent of schools, is an aspect of this.

The importance of this communal purpose among headteachers is indicated by the solutions created in large schools where it was difficult to get all the pupils into the school hall. One response was to leave out one age-group on each day of the week, and headteachers often reported with considerable regret that they had to hold assemblies split by age. Its general cultural importance is further indicated by the fact that large school halls continue to be built at great capital expense.

The value of the school assembly for communication purposes was stressed by 29 per cent of headteachers, and in a few cases headteachers thought this was its only value. However, others tried to eliminate or minimise this use of assembly. It was common for the deputy-head to make the announcements, so making a secular/sacred distinction between the communication and religious content. In one school, a Catholic mixed modern, the secular business was dealt with first and then the pupils turned round to face the other end of the hall for worship.

The inference already made of the meaning of the school assembly as a daily display of the authority relationships within the school is partly confirmed by some of the statements made by headteachers – 'the pupils get to know who the staff are'; 'the pupils get to know me.' The term authority has somewhat pejorative connotations in everyday use and heads may have been reluctant to use it, but this is what is being expressed when communications are made in assembly. If the headteacher makes an announcement to the whole school, the fact that *he* is making it to *everyone* is part of the message.

There is a fusion between the religious, communal and communication or authority presentation purpose of the assembly. The school community is the body of worshippers; worship sanctifies the community, and the idea of the school as a community is legitimised by these connections. The authority of the headteacher and the teachers is fused with the authority of religion. Disrespectful behaviour in assembly is an offence both to the school and to the faith, to the headteacher and to God.

Involvement in school assembly

Involvement in the school assembly was measured using a two-item, three-point scale (Table 26).

TABLE 26   *School assembly involvement scale*

Item	Judges' score	Per cent agreement	r item/ total score
I usually enjoy school assembly	6·6	33	0·919
School assembly is a good start to the day	7·6	43	0·911

Mean score = 0·8 (N = 7,457; S.D. = 0·89).

To infer the individual pupil's involvement from his behaviour in assembly would be an enormous task. We observed wide variations in behaviour from the apparently reverential to the casual, the uninterested and the disruptive.

Social class and the acceptance of school assembly

Although in individual schools at particular age-levels there were a few significant social class differences in levels of involvement, there was no consistent pattern. Acceptance of the school assembly appears to have little to do with class.

Sex and involvement in school assembly

Girls in mixed schools showed a higher level of involvement in the assembly than boys (Table K, Appendix C). This generalisation also holds true within the social classes.

It is difficult to decide to what extent this sex difference is a cultural one or organisational, i.e. one arising in mixed schools. There were no consistent differences in mean scores for pupils in single-sex schools, compared with pupils of the same sex and age in schools of the same status. This suggests that the sex difference in mixed schools is a cultural one, but the mean scores of girls in girls' schools were not consistently higher than those for boys of the same age in boys' schools of the same status.

Two related explanations may be made of these results. The higher involvement of girls may rest with their more ready acceptance of the religious content of the assembly. Religious observance is somewhat sex-typed in British society, women attend church more often than men, and so the boy/girl differences may be basically cultural. (See Robertson (1972).) It may also be the case that girls find the rigid hierarchical pattern of authority implied in the structure of the assembly more acceptable than boys. It has already been argued that women tend to be more conservative, more status-assenting and more compliant than men, and that to some extent these are cultural expectations. It is possibly that these explanations are linked; that the kind of religious authority implied in the worship, and the kind of school authority implied in the structure of assembly, are both hierarchical, immutable, omniscient, omnipresent and omnipotent.

Age and involvement in school assembly

In almost all schools fourth-year pupils had lower mean scores than the second year (Table K, Appendix C). This was found for both sexes, irrespective of social class, in all types of school. In most schools the mean involvement scores, keeping sex and social class constant, were highest for the second year.

This decline in involvement with age parallels the age-patterns observed for general, expressive and uniform involvement. Religious observance is known to decline during adolescence; perhaps older pupils are less ready to accept the kind of authority implied in the assembly. At a less deep level of analysis, perhaps the fifth former attending his thousandth assembly may be less inclined to agree that it is a good start to the day, than a second former at his two hundredth.

Involvement in assembly and its structure

There were no significant correlations between the degree and type of structuring of the assembly and the involvement of pupils of different ages, sexes and social classes.

Seventy-nine per cent of girls' schools allowed pupils of all ages to participate in the arranging and conducting of the assembly, compared with 39 per cent of mixed and 7 per cent of boys' schools. This kind of participation was not directly related to the level of involvement. Pupils in schools with participation did not score consistently higher than those in schools without participation.

Ritual, conflict and consensus

The measurements of pupils' involvement in the expressive order reported in the previous chapter were interpreted as indicating general levels of consensus among pupils and teachers within most schools. It is clear that the particular aspects of the expressive order examined in this chapter, uniform and school assembly, were not associated with such a consensus, and that conflict, in terms of differences in levels of acceptance, exist between pupils and teachers, as indicated by low mean scores on the scale. Conflict of this kind also exists between pupils of different ages and more especially of different sexes. This conflict is mainly felt rather than enacted in behaviour, and it is likely that the sacred connotations of the rituals keep it at that level. Attendance at the school assembly is not voluntary and for a pupil to challenge it in any way would require courage.

The school-imposed rituals of assembly and uniform are strongly suffused with emotion for both teachers and pupils, and form important sources of organisational tension. Among the militant pupils of the Schools Action Union the abolition of uniforms and the voluntary attendance of assembly are important points of policy. (See Times Educational Supplement, 7 November 1969.) My former colleague, Gary Easthope, observed a long and heated staff-meeting which was almost entirely devoted to a discussion of which button, or buttons, on the boys' blazers should be done up. They eventually resolved on a middle button rule.

Headteachers and many teachers regard the observance of the school uniform as a constant test of the individual pupil's allegiance to the school, and the school assembly as a daily test of that of the total population. The ideology of the school as a community both masks and legitimates the exercise of authority involved. In some schools the pupils filed quietly and obediently into the hall for assembly. In others they were pushed and shouted at, cajoled and threatened into waiting in silence for the headteacher's entry. Such occasions are remarkable feats of social control, where the reluctant pupils outnumber the teachers twenty to one.

Willard Waller (1932) called the school 'a gigantic agency of social control'. Teachers and headteachers in many secondary schools seem to view the control they exercise over their pupils as being tenuous. It is perhaps curious to think that a headteacher, the most powerful person in the school, and legally responsible for good discipline, may hold such a view, even if for obvious reasons, he may not explicitly express it. Perhaps they recognise, as Waller pointed out, that they ultimately only exercise control with the consent of the pupils.

The maintenance of discipline is a major concern of new teachers. (See, for example, McIntyre et al. (1966).) Most of them do eventually keep reasonable order, but the processes involved in doing so are still essentially mysterious. They cannot, for example, be made explicit to student teachers. The ability to control a class is regarded as a gift or something to be slowly acquired, often the hard way, on the job.

The school uniform is, however, tangible, and the manner in which it is worn susceptible to the most precise and reassuring kind of inspection and regulation. Thus the observance of school uniform becomes a quickly applied test of the individual pupil's allegiance or acceptance of the school's authority. Waller (1932) pointed out that teachers exercise general control by close attention to detail and minor deviations, such as the width of a margin. The school uniform can be used as a most refined form of control. In the school already mentioned it was focused on one button.

There is a certain paradox surrounding the use of ritual control in schools. Despite headteachers' apparent concern about the maintenance of order there is little evidence that any school had a serious social control problem. However, the two aspects of the school organisation that many pupils in most schools did not legitimate were the school assembly and uniform, the two devices used by headteachers and teachers as social control litmus paper. It is possible that the tensions these rituals are associated with may serve to focus discontents within the school, so allowing other activities to run more smoothly.

Speech days and open days

Seventy-four per cent of the schools held a speech day or open day which constituted a ritualised occasion. These occasions were slightly more common in grammar schools (89 per cent), than in modern (70 per cent) or comprehensive schools (65 per cent).

Most schools regarded pupil attendance as compulsory, although only half required all the pupils to attend. Comprehensive schools were least likely to require this; a reflection of accommodation problems in large schools.[1] In five schools only prize-winners attended. Almost half the occasions were in the evening.

The parents of all the pupils were invited to 70 per cent of these occasions, but in 15 per cent of cases the invitation was limited to prize-winners' parents. Distinguished guests were invited in all but one case, and in only two cases was there not a chief guest-speaker to award the prizes.

Almost all schools had programmes for everyone attending. These mainly contained the names of prize-winners and examination results. The latter was most common in boys' schools, least common in girls' grammar schools. A few schools listed the names and qualifications of the teaching staff. All bore those of the headteacher.

[1] Some large schools held separate junior and senior speech days.

Examination certificates were awarded on 81 per cent of occasions. This was least common in grammar schools (56 per cent), presumably because of the numbers involved. Prizes for school work were awarded on 85 per cent of occasions. The incidence of this was particularly low in comprehensive schools (55 per cent). Prizes related to good behaviour including service to the school were less common than those for school work (53 per cent of cases). Comprehensives were again least likely to have such prizes (36 per cent). Other awards made on such occasions included those for Houses and the Duke of Edinburgh's scheme.

Three-quarters of the schools included musical performances by choirs, orchestras and soloists. All the girls' schools included musical items, but not a single boys' modern school included one. We did not attempt a thorough content-analysis of the compositions recorded in the programmes, but Richard Rogers appeared to be the modern school favourite, and Thomas Arne that of the grammar schools. Dramatic performances were much less common than musical ones (14 per cent) and were confined to comprehensive schools and girls' schools. The headteacher gave a formal report or address on 90 per cent of occasions.

The uniform is the ritual of the individual pupil. The school assembly is the ritual of the membership of the school. The speech-day prize-giving is the ritual of the goals of the school. It is a celebration of school-approved success, both instrumental and expressive, to which only the successful and their kin may be invited. The low incidence of prize days and prizes in comprehensive schools may be due to their newness and their accommodation problems, but in some cases the speech day has been recognised not only as a celebration of success but also of condemnation of failure, incompatible with an egalitarian ideology, and therefore less acceptable in such schools.

Ritual as a structural variable

In their conceptual approach to the analysis of organisations Pugh and his associates (1963, 1968) distinguish six structural variables. This study uses three of those variables: standardisation, formalisation and specialisation, and adds a new one, ritualisation.[1] Ritual does appear in the Aston scheme in that symbols of office are included in the standardisation dimension of bureaucracy.

The case for considering the use of ritual to be different to other forms of the structuring of activities is based upon its expression of meaning by symbols. Symbolic interactionists regard all social acts as symbolic. (See Rose (1962).) If this is accepted then all activities

[1] Two other structure variables from the Aston scheme, centralisation and configuration are also used but only in a limited way.

are ritualised in the sense used in this study. Without denying that all activities may have subjective meaning it seems acceptable to suggest that bureaucratised activities, such as school rules, basically express fairly explicit face-meanings. In the case of school rules, they literally mean what they say. This is an element of what Weber saw as the rationality of bureaucracy. Rituals have little or no face-meaning, but non-rationally symbolise what may be called deep-meanings, which tend to be diffuse and strongly diffused with emotion. As Waller (1932) put it 'they have an emotional meaning but no intellectual content.'

5 The House system and pastoral care

House systems have their origins in the private boarding houses used by the upper middle-class pupils when they were sent to public schools, in the early nineteenth century. (See Mack (1938).) As this chapter shows, the activities of the House system in maintained secondary schools are widely variable and are often far removed from the public-school archetype.

A description of the organisation of House systems in different kinds of school leads to an analysis of the pupils' involvement in the system, and a discussion of its activities.

The section on pastoral care follows a similar pattern of presentation. The chapter concludes with a note on the organisation of school dinners.

The house system

All but two schools in the sample had House systems. The exceptions were a girls' and a mixed modern school. Most schools had four Houses, so that the size of the House was highly correlated against the size of the school (0·90). Thus the average size of a House in the modern schools was 113, in grammar schools 138, and in the comprehensives 215. In almost all cases the teachers as well as the pupils were part of the House system.

The commonest method for the allocation of pupils to Houses was to use some random technique, but this was used in only half the comprehensive schools. Nearly half of these schools attempted to distribute pupils to create Houses of equal ability composition, a method used in only one grammar and one modern school. Half the schools arranged for siblings to be placed in the same House, and in some grammar schools for children to enter their parents' House. Only one school, a boys' modern, allocated pupils by neighbourhood. Two schools allowed some pupil choice in the process, and although a fifth of schools allowed pupils to change House in special circumstances, the evidence suggests that the incidence is very low. The House-roles were therefore largely ascriptive.

Two-thirds of schools held regular House meetings and this was more common in grammar and comprehensive schools. The frequency of meetings was highest in comprehensive schools, lowest in modern schools.

The commonest form of House ritualisation was the use of House colours. House ties, flashes and flags were rare, but a third of the schools had House badges. These were much more common in girls' schools than in either mixed or boys' schools. Designated rooms sacred to particular Houses were most common in comprehensives. Pupils stood in their House groups in about a fifth of assemblies; this was most common in the comprehensives, as was the incidence of separate House assemblies.

Table 27 gives the four-item scale for the measurement of the ritualisation of the House system.

TABLE 27 *Ritualisation of House system scale*

Items	f
House colours	60
Separate House assemblies	28
Pupils stood by House in school assembly	16
House rooms	13

Mean item analysis value 0·888; mean score = 1·62 (N = 72; S.D. = 1·10).

Table 28 shows that comprehensives were the most ritualised in this respect, but boys' modern schools also score highly.

The names of Houses might be regarded as an aspect of their ritualisation. The naming of Houses after famous scientists, literary figures and heroes is to use them, as some headteachers admitted, as

TABLE 28 *Ritualisation of House system – mean scale scores*

	Boys SM	Girls SM	Mixed SM	All SM	All CS	Boys GS	Girls GS	Mixed GS	All GS
n	7	6	24	37	17	6	6	6	18
mean	2·00	1·67	1·37	1·54	2·18	1·50	0·50	1·83	1·28
S.D.	0·76	0·47	0·95	0·89	1·38	0·76	0·50	1·07	0·99

role-models and symbols of approved behaviour and endeavour. The use of local geographical locations, parishes, rivers and hills, may be seen as an attempt to establish the school in its wider social setting. Several rural modern schools named their Houses after parishes or villages, which were themselves the names of local land-owners. This could be seen as an attempt to import the local power structure into the school, and establish its legitimacy in the minds of the pupils, but there must be some doubt about how much such significances are recognised by pupils. A senior pupil guide in one school was unable to decode the House names, even though he was a senior House official.

The House system and the expressive order

Expressive activities are House-specialised when the pupils' House membership becomes a factor in behavioural control and expectations.

The principal expressive activities that become House-specialised are the use of cloakrooms, and the dining arrangements. These form the scale for the House-specialisation of expressive activities shown in Table 29.

TABLE 29 *House-specialisation of expressive activities scale*

Item Houses have different:	f
Dinner sittings	15
Dinner tables	13
Cloakrooms	13
Dinner queues	9

Mean item analysis value 0·952; Mean score 0·69 (N = 72; S.D. = 1·30).

Table 30 shows that comprehensive schools tend to score the highest together with mixed grammar schools.

TABLE 30 *House-specialisation of expressive activities – mean scale scores*

	Boys SM	Girls SM	Mixed SM	All SM	All CS	Boys GS	Girls GS	Mixed GS	All GS
n	7	6	24	37	17	6	6	6	18
mean	0·43	0·33	0·50	0·46	1·47	0·00	0·00	1·33	0·44
S.D.	1·05	0·75	1·04	1·00	1·72	0·00	0·00	1·49	1·07

The correlation between the degree of House-specialisation of expressive activities and House ritualisation is 0·65, indicating that the use of House membership as a criterion in social control tends to be aided by the use of symbols.

Judgments of pupils' behaviour, that is, their expressive performance, were often linked to the House system. More than half the House systems had a point reward scheme for general behaviour. This was twice as common in modern schools as in grammar or comprehensives. However, four comprehensives did hold detention on House basis.

The expressive activities related to the House system were sometimes ritualised. A cup or other prize was awarded to the House accumulating the highest number of behaviour reward points in a third of the schools, but its occurrence varied enormously from one type of school to another. It did not exist in any grammar schools, but did in about a third of comprehensives and half the modern schools. It was particularly high in girls' modern schools. Such events formed part of an overall House competition in one third of the schools. This was most common in the grammar schools, least common in the comprehensives. There was usually a cup or other award for the winning House.

The House system and the instrumental order

In one comprehensive the junior pupils were taught in House groups but in other schools the link between the instrumental order and the House system was usually confined to a work-mark reward system (see Chapter 7). Half the grammar schools made this connection and three-quarters of the modern schools, but the biggest distinction by type of school was based on sex composition. All the girls' schools with House systems linked it to the mark reward scheme. Fewer schools brought the results of internal examinations into the House competition. Two items form the scale for the ritualisation of House-specialised instrumental performance (Table 31).

TABLE 31 *Ritualisation of House-specialised instrumental performance scale*

Item House competition based on :	f
Work-mark reward system	43
Internal examination results	9

Mean item analysis value 1·00; mean score = 0·72 (N = 72; S.D. = 0·65).

Girls' modern schools have the highest mean score and comprehensives and boys' grammar schools have the lower scores (Table 32).

TABLE 32   *Ritualisation of House-specialised instrumental performance scale – mean scores*

	Boys SM	Girls SM	Mixed SM	All SM	All CS	Boys GS	Girls GS	Mixed GS	All GS
n	7	6	24	37	17	6	6	6	18
mean	0·86	1·33	0·71	0·84	0·41	0·17	1·17	1·00	0·78
S.D.	0·64	0·47	0·54	0·59	0·49	0·37	0·69	0·82	0·79

The House system and games

In many schools the House system functioned principally to create intra-school competitions, particularly in games. Inter-House sports competitions occurred in three-quarters of the schools. Most schools held non-sporting House-competitions also, commonly for drama and music. These were most common in girls' schools and in comprehensives.

The House system and other sub-systems

About a fifth of the schools linked the House system to the prefectorial system, usually through the creation of House prefects, some of whom were also school prefects. This was most common in the comprehensives, rare in the grammar schools.

Most of the Houses in comprehensive schools were aggregates of tutorial groups. This was rare in modern and grammar schools.

Involvement in the House system

Involvement in the House system was measured using a three-point, two-item scale (Table 33). In addition, pupils were asked to record if they held House positions of responsibility.

TABLE 33   *House involvement scale*

Item	Judges' score	per cent agreement	r item/ total score
The House system is a valuable part of the school	8·1	59	0·865
The House system gives everyone a chance to be good at something	7·7	63	0·870

Mean score = 1·2 (N = 7,457; S.D. 0·84).

Significant *social class differences* in House-involvement were found only for boys in grammar schools. In the second, fourth and fifth years of boys' and mixed grammar schools, working-class boys tended to have higher mean scores on the scale than the middle-class. This pattern was almost completely reversed in the seventh year when the mean involvement of middle-class pupils was usually the higher (Table L, Appendix C).

The younger working-class boys' higher involvement in the House system may be a reflection of the value they put upon the minor-success roles generated by the system, in House teams and as House officials, although there is no evidence for their holding these positions more often than their middle-class age mates. There were no consistent class differences in the holding of House positions.

There were no consistent patterns of *sex differences* in House involvement within mixed schools, or in the holding of House positions.

Age differences in House involvement were found for grammar school boys. In both mixed and single-sex schools there was a steady decline in mean involvement with age, although the holding of House positions increased with age (Table L, Appendix C). This pattern occurred in only one comprehensive school.

House involvement and the structure of the House system

No single structural variable was significantly correlated with involvement score. It is possible that it is the combination of structural arrangements that may be associated with differences in involvement, and a specific example will be suggested in the next section.

The use of the House system

It is clear from the structural analysis of the House system already described and the comments made by headteachers in interviews, that the House system is seen as multi-functional. Two broad conceptions appear to exist about the purpose of the House system; one stressing competition, the other, consensus.

The first sees it as a convenient way of dividing the school for the purposes of promoting intra-school competitions, and thereby creating minor-success roles that pupils of all levels can have access to. This model is held in most grammar and modern schools. The headteachers of a third of these schools considered the House system existed mainly for sporting competitions.

The second conception sees the House as an administrative unit acting as a cohesive force upon which pastoral care, discipline, careers advice and parental contact can be based. This model was characteristic of most comprehensive schools, but it did occur in some of the larger modern and grammar schools. Elements of both these ideal types did exist in particular schools, but generally one tended to predominate. It is interesting to note that schools that anticipated becoming comprehensive tended to consciously adopt or convert to the second model.

The second model was sometimes seen as a way of creating compatibility between the increasing size of schools and the notion of the school as a community. The cultural expectation that the headteacher should know all his pupils is less likely to be realised in a large school; houseteachers have become multiple headteacher surrogates in this respect.

The correlations between school size and House structural variables illustrate the relationship between size and House function (Table 34). Those related to competition are negative; those related to consensus are positive.

TABLE 34   *Correlations of House variables with school size*

	r
House specialisation of expressive activities	0·42
House ritualisation	0·20
Frequency of House meetings	0·26
Number of inter-House games	− 0·23
House-specialised expressive performance	− 0·13
Ritualisation of House-specialised instrumental performance	− 0·22

(N = 72)

The measurements of involvement show that in general the House system is made legitimate by the pupils, irrespective of the form it takes. Working-class grammar-school boys and older boys in grammar schools are exceptions. Unlike the age and sex-typing of the pupil role its House affinities are created almost entirely, and usually randomly, by the school. Allegiance to the House might be expected to arise if House groups share many activities together, as in many comprehensive schools. This may explain the maintained levels of involvement in the seventh years of such schools. In the grammar schools there existed a situation in which the boys with most responsibility in the system show the poorest disposition towards it. Perhaps the implied cynicism is compatible with the idea of service and leadership.

Pastoral care

The notion of pastoral care is very strongly related to that of the school as a community; a community cares for its members. The pastoral reference may reflect the basic authority relationship between teacher and pupil, whether the analogy is to the priest and his parish, or the shepherd and his sheep. It certainly reflects the cultural expectation that the teacher should have a wide scope of interest in his pupil, to the extent of being concerned about his happiness and other internal states of existence.

The organisation of pastoral care

In three-quarters of the schools the principal agent of pastoral care was the form-teacher, so that the unit of pastoral care was the learning unit. This was the most common in modern and grammar schools, but occurred in one third of comprehensives.

Tutors and tutorial groups occurred in 39 per cent of schools; some schools had both form units and tutorial groups, the former most commonly for the younger pupils. Tutorial groups occurred in three-quarters of the comprehensives, but in only a quarter of other schools. In almost all cases the groups were mixed for ability. (Some schools used the term tutor for the form-teacher of a mixed ability learning group.) Half the tutorial systems were also mixed by age, but not necessarily over the whole age-range of the school. In mixed-sex schools the groups were also mixed. In most cases of mixed ability and mixed age tutorial groups recruitment into the group was made to keep its composition fairly constant from year to year. Where constant composition was irrelevant pupils were allocated randomly.

Like the form unit, tutorial groups met for registration purposes, usually twice a day. In addition they usually met for a timetabled tutorial period once a week. The purpose of the meetings and the job of the tutors was to deal with all pastoral care matters including academic and behavioural problems.

In most cases each tutorial group was homogeneous in House composition and each tutor responsible to a head of House. When the tutorial system was independent of the House system, the groups were usually homogeneous for age, and the tutors were responsible to heads of years or heads of age-divisions.

In addition to the form-teacher or tutor, schools with heads of House usually allowed pupils to go to them directly for help, and virtually all schools reported that pupils could see the headteacher or senior staff with a problem. Six schools had a counsellor whose functions included the pastoral care for the whole school.

We have no estimates of how frequently these agents of pastoral care were consulted by pupils, but measurements were made of the ease with which pupils could gain access to the headteacher. Forty-four per cent of headteachers claimed that pupils could go to see them at any time. This occurred in 64 per cent of boys' schools, 50 per cent of mixed schools, but only 7 per cent of girls' schools. In a fifth of schools it was necessary for the pupil to go to the school secretary, and in 14 per cent of schools pupils could only see the head-teacher at special times. Twenty-nine per cent of headteachers only allowed pupils to consult them in their office. This was more common in grammar schools than in others.

The organisation of the pastoral care system using tutorial groups is clearly related to the size of the school, as is its association with the House system (Table 35). The notion of the school as a community is implicitly denied when schools are large and the fear that the pupils will feel lost gives rise to structural innovations which break the school into smaller units, Houses and tutorial groups, whose purpose is to act as centres of identification and interaction.

TABLE 35   *Tutorial groups and school size*

Size of school	Small	Medium	Large	Very large
Incidence of tutorial groups per cent	21	31	44	89
Tutorial group related to Houses per cent	11	27	44	67

Pupils' acceptance of the pastoral care system

A three-point, two-item scale was used for the measurement of the pupils' involvement, or acceptance, of the pastoral care system (Table 36).

TABLE 36   *Acceptance of pastoral care scale*

Items	Judges' score	Per cent agreement	r item/ total score
There is always someone to take your problems to at school	8·3	57	0·819
People care about you in this school	8·3	68	0·793

Mean score = 1·2 (N = 7,457; S.D. = 0·78).

Social class differences in satisfaction with pastoral care were found only for girls in grammar schools, where working-class girls showed the higher levels of satisfaction (Table M, Appendix C). This working-class appreciation of the pastoral care provision was not found for boys or in other types of school.

It is possible that the problems of the working-class girls differed quantitatively and qualitatively from those of the middle-class. If they had less problems or less acute problems, then this may explain their satisfaction, but they could have had more problems and more acute ones and still have been satisfied. It may be that middle-class girls were able to gain satisfaction for their problems at home, and hence were relatively less satisfied with the pastoral care of school.

There were no consistent differences in the mean scores on the scale for boys and girls in mixed schools. Presumably the needs of boys and girls, although different, were usually equally satisfied.

Only one consistent age-pattern was found. In all grammar schools except one, the mean score for the second-year pupils was higher than that for any other year-group. This held for boys and girls in both mixed and single-sex schools (Table M, Appendix C).

This tendency for older pupils in grammar schools to show a reduced satisfaction with pastoral care may have been due to their having problems particular to groups of clever children, which are not easily susceptible to amelioration, for example, anxieties about academic failure.

Satisfaction with pastoral care and pastoral care provision

There was no simple relationship between pupil satisfaction and provision of pastoral care. The problem is to decide to what extent satisfaction with the system is due to the system helping the pupil with his problems, or due to the absence of pupil problems. What can be assumed is that many different forms of provision did give rise to satisfaction.

There is no evidence that satisfaction with the pastoral care provision is lower for pupils in large schools. This may be due to the greater structuring of pastoral care in such schools, although the one very large school relying on form-teachers only did not show low mean scores.

School dinners

The provision of school dinners may be regarded as being part of the concept of the pastoral care of pupils. An analysis of the way school dinners were organised shows that they may also be considered to be a specialised aspect of the expressive order, in that particular modes of behaviour were propagated, and particular social relationships were established.

Apart from the school assembly the eating of school dinners was often the only time when (virtually) the whole school met together. The structure of the school assembly reflected the status differences within the school, and so did that of the dining arrangements. Differences in queueing, sequence of entering the dining room and seating arrangements within the room were found for pupils of different ages (Chapter 9), sexes (Chapter 11), ability groups (Chapter 8), for prefects and teachers (Chapter 10), and for different Houses (Chapter 5). When it was impossible for all the school to eat at the same sitting, the sittings were commonly divided by age (Chapter 9) or House (Chapter 5).

Pupils were usually supervised (57 per cent of schools) and this was, surprisingly, most common in grammar schools, and least common in comprehensives. Grace was usually said before or after the meal (72 per cent of schools). Two basic styles of dining were observed. *Cafeteria style* involved the pupils queueing up to receive the meal, sometimes going to eat it at any convenient table. *Family style* involved going to a particular table, and sometimes a particular seat at the table, and eating with the same group each day. The head of the family was usually a senior pupil or a teacher. The dinner was often served at the table.[1]

One undoubted function of the school dinner arrangements is nutritional, and it is interesting to note how often the pupils referred to the quality and quantity of school dinners in their free responses in the questionnaire. Not all of the comments were adverse – 'I like the school dinners. They are much better than I get at home.'

Like the school assembly it may also serve to remind pupils of the important status-relationships within the school. In a few schools there was a high table for the teachers. In one school the head-teacher sat centrally in a high-backed chair and rapped a spoon on the table to signal that the staff leftovers were available to the pupils.

Headteachers often expressed that it was a social occasion with consensual purposes – 'A community in being'. It was also seen as an opportunity for social training in good manners and politeness, although some headteachers had reservations about this. These sentiments were frequently associated with the using of family-style dining. The sentiments associated with the use of the cafeteria-style tended to be those of efficiency – 'The quickest way to do it', 'Get a good hot meal in them'.

Our observations of school dining arrangements were made at the time soon after teachers had been released from their obligation to perform dining hour duties. However, in a number of schools they

[1] Sixty-five per cent of schools had tuck shops but these seldom opened in the dinner hour.

continued to voluntarily organise and control the dining arrangements, despite the provision of dinner ladies to do the job. They did so, not only to qualify for a free meal, but because they were concerned that reasonable order should be maintained during the whole of the dinner hour. Their fear was that if order were not maintained the afternoon's work would not be done properly. Their involvement ensured a continuity of authority throughout the school day.

6 Games and out-of-school activities

Both games and out-of-school activities have a traditional place in British secondary schools. The first section of this chapter deals with the provision and organisation of games and the pupils' involvement in them. The second section presents a similar analysis of out-of-school activities.

Games

Schools varied in the extent of their provision of games and their mode of organisation.

Games provision

The average number of games provided by schools was 9·3; of these 6·3 had school teams engaged in inter-school matches. Table 37 indicates that the comprehensive and grammar schools tended to provide more games than modern schools. This was partly a matter of size; larger schools could provide more choice. The correlation between school size and the number of games provided is 0·43; for school size and the number of inter-school games, 0·52. (The correlation between the number of games and the number of inter-school games is 0·7.)

Table 37 also shows that boys are provided with a larger number of games than girls. This is true when boys and girls are compared either in mixed or single-sex schools of the same status. Boys in boys' schools tended to have more games provided than those in mixed schools of the same status.

The number of games played by both boys and girls was highest in the comprehensive schools, lowest in the modern. Our information does not allow us to estimate the extent to which these games,

TABLE 37   *Games provision – mean scores*

	Boys SM	Girls SM	Mixed SM	All SM	All CS	Boys GS	Girls GS	Mixed GS	All GS
n	7	6	24	37	71	6	6	6	18
No. games	6·6	5·4	9·0	8·0	11·5	10·5	7·2	11·5	9·7
No. inter- school	5·0	4·0	5·8	5·4	7·8	6·7	5·5	8·0	6·7
No. for boys	6·6	—	6·3	—	9·9*	10·5	—	8·7	—
No. for girls	—	5·4	5·6	—	7·7†	—	7·2	6·7	—
No. for boys or girls	—	—	2·9	—	5·5‡	—	—	4·0	—

*n = 15   †n = 16   ‡ = 14

principally tennis and swimming, are played by boys and girls together. (We have no example of PE taken in mixed classes.)

Table 38 shows that the number of games provided increases as pupils get older. It also shows that the sex gap in provision gets wider for older pupils.

TABLE 38   *Games provision and pupil age (means, all schools)*

Year	1	2	3	4	5	6+	
Boys	5·5	5·5	5·9	6·8	7·5	8·9	(n = 58)
Girls	4·8	4·7	4·9	5·4	5·7	6·4	(n = 58)

Organisation of the games system

The discussion of games provision has already indicated that the system may be specialised by both age and sex.

The system may be formalised by the use of fixture cards, and special notice boards. Table 39 shows a three-item scale for the measurement of the formalisation of the games system.

TABLE 39   *Formalisation of games system scale*

Item	f
Special notice board for games	58
Notice boards for particular games	26
Printed fixture card	26

Mean item analysis value 0·797; mean score = 1·53 (N = 72; S.D. = 0·76).

The mean scores were highest in grammar schools and boys' schools (Table 40).

TABLE 40   *Formalisation of games system – scale scores*

	Boys SM	Girls SM	Mixed SM	All SM	All CS	Boys GS	Girls GS	Mixed GS	All GS
n	7	6	24	37	17	6	6	6	18
mean	1·86	1·17	1·08	1·24	1·71	2·50	1·50	1·83	1·94
S.D.	0·64	0·37	0·76	0·75	0·67	0·50	0·50	0·37	0·62

Two factors are related to the degree of formalisation. It is positively correlated with the number of games played in the school and the average level of ability of the pupils. The correlation for formalisation against mean IQ is 0·34; against the number of games played, 0·28.

Performance in games may also be formalised when games awards and results appear on notice boards and in the school magazine. (See King and Fry (1972).) Table 41 gives a three-point scale for the measurement of the formalisation of games performance.

TABLE 41   *Formalisation of games performance scale*

Item	f
Games awards posted on notice board	8
Games awards in school magazine	18
Games results in school magazine	33

Mean item analysis value 0·926; mean score = 0·82 (N = 72; S.D. = 0·95).

As with the previous scale, high scores are associated with boys' and grammar schools (Table 42). The correlation for mean ability and the extent of this kind of formalisation is 0·40. The correlation with number of games is not significant. The two kinds of games formalisation are significantly correlated, with a value of 0·43.

TABLE 42   *Formalisation of games performance scale scores*

	Boys SM	Girls SM	Mixed SM	All SM	All CS	Boys GS	Girls GS	Mixed GS	All GS
n	7	6	24	37	17	6	6	6	18
mean	1·14	0·17	0·37	0·49	0·82	1·67	1·33	1·50	1·50
S.D.	0·83	0·37	0·63	0·72	1·04	0·94	0·75	0·96	0·90

The ritualisation of the games system was extensive. Awards, in the form of badges, ties and sashes, for playing in a school team, were given for an average of 4·5 games. Table 43 shows that this ritualisation was lowest in girls' schools and in mixed modern schools.

TABLE 43 *Number of games awards*

	Boys SM	Girls SM	Mixed SM	All SM	All CS	Boys GS	Girls GS	Mixed GS	All GS
n	7	6	24	37	17	6	6	6	18
mean	4·6	3·0	2·5	3·0	6·6	5·2	4·8	7·3	5·8

It might be expected that the number of awards was related to the number of inter-school games played, but they were not significantly correlated.

The award of a tie as a symbol of success in games occurred in 14 per cent of schools. As may be expected this symbol was most common in boys' schools (36 per cent), less common in mixed schools (2 per cent only), but surprisingly high in girls' schools (29 per cent). Sixty per cent of schools awarded badges; this was least common in modern schools.

Games successes were often incorporated into the content of school assembly. Games awards were mentioned in 58 per cent of assemblies, and in 51 per cent of schools the awards were given in a special ceremony. Both these forms of ritualisation were most common in the grammar schools, least common in the modern schools. Most schools announced games results in assembly, but a few head-teachers said that they preferred not to. In half the assemblies pupils clapped all the results announced; this was commonest in girls' schools. In four schools, three boys' grammar and one boys' modern pupils only clapped when their school won; an evaluation of success over participation. The extent of this ritualisation is measured in the scale shown in Table 44.

TABLE 44 *Ritualisation of games scale*

Item	f
Badge awarded for games success	43
Award mentioned in assembly	42
Award made in ceremony	37

Mean item analysis value 0·968; mean score 1·69 (N = 72; S.D. = 1·32).

Table 45 gives the mean scores on the scale, and shows that the degree of ritualisation was highest in grammar schools, lowest in modern schools. This is not, however, a positive or significant correlation between the number of inter-school games and the degree of ritualisation.

TABLE 45   *Ritualisation of games – mean scores*

	Boys SM	Girls SM	Mixed SM	All SM	All CS	Boys GS	Girls GS	Mixed GS	All GS
n	7	6	24	37	17	6	6	6	18
mean	1·29	1·50	1·08	1·19	2·00	2·00	2·50	2·83	2·44
S.D.	1·28	1·26	1·32	1·31	1·24	1·15	0·76	0·37	0·90

The link between the House and games systems has already been mentioned. The more games a school plays, the more form part of the inter-House games competition; the correlation is 0·33.

The school sports days were held in almost all the schools; only two girls' modern schools and one girls' grammar school did not hold one. Sports days were usually held in school time and so pupils were usually obliged to attend, and in most cases parents were invited to come. (See King (1972).)

The swimming gala was less common, probably due to problems of access to a swimming pool. Sixty-nine per cent of schools held a gala, and this was most common in grammar schools, least common in comprehensives. About one fifth of swimming galas were held out of school hours, and pupils were less likely to be obliged to attend, compared with sports days.

Nearly all schools included games in the curriculum of all pupils, and in general the only excuse accepted was that of being unwell. However, 17 per cent of schools made games optional for older pupils; this was most common in the grammar schools (39 per cent), least common in the modern schools (5 per cent). In a smaller number of schools (7 per cent) candidates for external examinations were also exempt. (Much the same policies operated in relation to PE.)

Involvement in games

Two measurements of involvement in games were used. First, the pupils' response to the question 'I like doing games', and second, the pupils' self-reported membership of school teams. The significance of this last measurement was difficult to judge because we were unable to distinguish satisfactorily between playing for the school team in school time, and playing outside of school hours, particularly on Saturdays. Schools varied in their policies; some played other schools both in and out of school time, others only in or out of school time. Some made it obligatory for team members to play out of school time, others made this optional. The voluntary commitment of a pupil to play for the school in his own time may be considered to indicate higher involvement than, for example, his recruitment into a team to play another school on games afternoons.

Social class, sex and age differences in games involvement

In single-sex schools, with the exception of boys' grammar schools, middle-class pupils were more often members of school teams than working-class pupils. This class difference was not found consistently in mixed schools, but here it was found that boys were almost always more often team members than girls (Table N, Appendix C). These sex differences are partly explained by the different opportunities available for team membership, in that there were generally more team places for boys than girls.

It is possible that in single-sex schools social class differences in rates of team membership arise in a similar way to those found for school activities (see later section), that team participation reveals the operation of class based value-judgments concerning the voluntary giving up of time, and the relative interest and importance of other activities. It is also possible that in mixed schools team membership, and perhaps sport in general, has strong masculine connotations, and so consistent class differences do not arise. This is partly supported by the rates at which the sexes agreed that they liked doing games, which in mixed schools was often higher for boys than girls (Table O, Appendix C). This sex difference tended to be wider for older pupils.

The absence of consistent class differences in team membership in boys' grammar schools may be associated with the high status given to games in such schools, although there was actually a tendency towards higher working-class participation, a trend also found for boys in the seventh years of comprehensive schools, girls in the seventh years of mixed grammar schools, and girls in the fifth year of mixed modern schools.

Team participation was only strongly associated with age in the grammar schools where it was highest in older age groups, and partly reflects the opportunities available.

Involvement in games and games provision

There was no simple relationship between the number of teams provided by a school and the percentage of pupils playing for school teams. This is probably partly due to the concentration of such teams for older pupils, and also suggests that when more teams exist the same pupils tend to join several of them.

The place of games in the school

The results of the measurements of the pupils' disposition towards games suggest that they do have important recreative functions. The games system also generates a large number of minor success roles; team member, team captain. Games may also provide opportunities for both co-operation and competition. Where the co-operation is with fellow team members and the competition is with the team of another school, then there may be consensual outcomes, reinforcing the identity of the pupil as a member of the school. School magazines contain frequent references to games successes as bringing honour to the school. (See King and Fry (1972).) Games, from this point of view, may be viewed as a part of the expressive order, concerned with the perpetuation of the image of the school as a community, and the inculcation of school-approved qualities such as loyalty, conformity, co-operation, the obeying of rules and fair play. It should be noted, however, that the provision of games for older pupils suggests that this public-school archetype is less important than it used to be. Much of the provision is for individual non-team, even non-competitive activities, such as horse riding, skating, canoeing and golf. These activities may of course be considered to engender desirable qualities but they are client-orientated rather than school-glorifying.

The provision and organisation of games is very strongly related to the age and sex of the pupils in a school. The measurements of these imply the expectation that boys will be more interested in sport than girls, and that older pupils should have more choice than younger ones. The school appears to accept the cultural notion of the sex difference in interest in games and organises according to this notion. The lower involvement of girls seems to confirm the original notion. Games clearly serve to reinforce sexual identity and the different kinds of games played by boys and girls are part of this process. To a more limited extent the age-differentiation of games provision may reinforce age-identities.

Games may provide working-class pupils with an acceptable mechanism for expressing involvement in the school. Most games are without specific social class connotations and it is possible that the high involvement shown by older working-class pupils, especially boys, is strongly supportive of their educational careers. An interesting extension of this analysis, not permitted by our results, would be to examine social class differences in participation in games with fairly specific class connotations, such as middle-class rugby and tennis.

Out-of-school activities

Provision of out-of-school activities

Most schools provided out-of-school activities. The average number provided was nearly twelve, but the number of activities varied with the type of school. Comprehensive schools provided most, modern schools least. Boys' schools provided more activities than did girls', especially among grammar schools (Table 46). The larger the school the more extensive the provision; the correlation is 0·61.

The term 'out-of-school' varies in its significance according to whether the activity is arranged in the school dinner hour, or before or after school. (The same activities were held in this or all three periods of time in some schools.) Table 46 gives their frequency by type of school. It is clear that there was no general policy to have activities at either one time or the other; the correlation between the number of activities held before or after school, with the number held in the dinner hour was 0·31. However, schools in country areas where most of the pupils travelled by school bus, were prevented from putting on clubs or societies before or after school, and held them virtually exclusively in the dinner hour, which was often extended for this purpose.

TABLE 46   *Provision of out-of-school activities – mean scores*

	Boys SM	Girls SM	Mixed SM	All SM	All CS	Boys GS	Girls GS	Mixed GS	All GS
n	7	6	24	37	17	6	6	6	18
Total no.	8·3	5·0	8·6	8·0	18·6	18·5	9·5	11·8	13·4
Held before or after school	6·6	3·6	7·4	6·7	14·2	14·8	6·3	10·0	10·4
Held in dinner hour	3·4	2·4	3·2	3·1	5·2	7·2	5·2	3·3	5·4
No. instrumental	1·0	0·6	1·5	1·3	2·8	3·3	1·2	1·4	2·0

We were unable to carry out a thorough analysis of the type of activities provided because it was clear that the name of the club or society was not necessarily a good indication of the nature of the activities that went on in them. To sort out the differences between a

Horticultural Society, Gardening Club, and Young Farmers would have required at least one visit to each. However, an attempt was made to classify activities according to their instrumental reference. An instrumental out-of-school activity was defined as one that related to a school examination subject, other than art and music. The number of these activities was highest in comprehensive and grammar schools, and more common in boys' schools than in girls' (Table 46). In some of the comprehensive schools some school subjects, especially Latin, were actually taught after school on a voluntary basis.

The provision of out-of-school activities was different for pupils of different ages and sexes. Table 47 shows the age-variation in provision. In most types of school provision increased with age, this being most marked in the grammar schools, especially the boys' grammar schools.

TABLE 47 *Age differences in provision of out-of-school activities – mean scores*

	Boys SM	Girls SM	Mixed SM	All SM	All CS	Boys GS	Girls GS	Mixed GS	All GS	All Schools
Year										
1st	5·4	3·0	6·1	5·5	9·6	11·8	6·8	7·0	8·4	7·2
2nd	5·7	3·0	6·5	5·8	9·9	11·8	7·2	7·0	8·6	7·4
3rd	6·1	3·4	7·3	6·5	9·7	12·0	7·2	7·2	8·7	7·8
4th	6·9	4·2	8·4	7·4	11·3	13·8	7·8	9·6	10·2	9·0
5th	6·0	4·0	8·5	7·3	11·3	16·4	8·2	10·2	11·4	9·3
6th	—	—	—	—	11·7	16·4	8·8	10·2	11·6	11·2

Table 48 shows the number of activities available to boys and girls in mixed schools.

TABLE 48 *Out-of-school activities in mixed schools – mean numbers*

	MSM	MCS	MGS	All schools
n	24	14	6	44
For boys	8·2	15·2	10·6	10·8
For girls	6·8	14·3	10·2	9·6

In general more activities were available for boys, and the sex gap was highest in the mixed modern schools.

In ten of the schools the term 'activity' did not strictly refer to extra-curricular activities, in that they were timetabled and took place in school time, usually Friday afternoons. Attendance of the pupils was compulsory, although they could choose from a range of activities. The activities provided were similar to those put on by schools in out-of-school hours. This kind of provision seemed to exist when participation in such activities was valued, but where there were problems in putting them on at the usual times. In the seven non-selective schools with this arrangement the problem was usually to get pupils to go to such activities voluntarily in their own time. The three grammar schools with this arrangement did so because many of their pupils could not stay after school because they had to catch the school bus for a long journey home. In both situations compulsory participation was considered better than no participation.

The organisation of out-of-school activities

The age and sex specialisation of activities was mentioned in the discussion of provision. The other organisation of activities varied greatly. Some schools had virtually no organisation, arrangements being left entirely to individual teachers and groups of pupils. In other schools, particularly large schools, there were timetables for such activities. Another kind of formalisation, the use of notice boards, forms the basis of a scale for formalisation of out-of-school activities (Table 49).

TABLE 49 *Formalisation of out-of-school activities scale*

Item	f
Special notice board for activities	27
Notice boards for particular activities	27

Mean item analysis value 1·00; mean score = 0·75 (N = 72; S.D. = 0·78).

Grammar schools tended to be most formalised, especially those for boys (Table 50).

TABLE 50 *Formalisation of out-of-school activities – mean scores*

	Boys SM	Girls SM	Mixed SM	All SM	All CS	Boys GS	Girls GS	Mixed GS	All GS
n	7	6	24	37	17	6	6	6	18
mean	0·14	0·17	0·75	0·54	0·82	1·67	0·67	1·00	1·11
S.D.	0·35	0·37	0·72	0·68	0·86	0·47	0·47	0·82	0·74

This kind of organisation was probably related to the presumed level of literacy of the pupils; the correlation of the scale scores against mean IQ was 0·32. It was also positively correlated with the size of the school (0·61) and the number of activities provided (0·30).

Involvement in out-of-school activities

Involvement in out-of-school activities was measured using the pupils' self-reported frequency of joining school clubs. Each pupil was asked to write down the names of the clubs and societies he belonged to. As was mentioned before, our pilot trials showed pupils were usually honest in their responses.

Previous research has suggested that middle-class pupils tend to take part in more out-of-school activities than working-class pupils. (See Himmelweit (1954); Holly (1965); Hargreaves (1967).) This tendency was found in many schools in the sample, although there were a few schools where this was reversed, and the working-class pupils joined more clubs than the middle-class (Table P, Appendix C).

There were few significant differences in the frequency of joining school clubs for boys and girls in mixed schools, and where they did occur it was boys who usually joined more (Table Q, Appendix C). This was the case in the seventh year of every mixed grammar school, and the second year of every mixed modern school.

The only fairly consistent age-pattern in the frequency of joining school clubs was found in grammar schools. The average number of clubs joined by seventh-year boys and girls was higher than at any other age in every grammar school except one (Table Q, Appendix C).

Involvement and provision of out-of-school activities

The correlation (rho) between the number of clubs a school provided and the average number of clubs joined was 0·39, which is significant at the 5 per cent level. This suggests that the more clubs a school provides the more pupils tend to join them, possibly because of the wider choice available.

The place of out-of-school activities

Out-of-school activities have quite clear recreative functions. The provision of such activities was related to the sex and age characteristics of the pupils. More activities were provided for boys and for older pupils. This policy may be based upon assumptions that are made about the range of interests shown by boys over girls, or older pupils over younger ones, and also upon the desirability of fostering such interests sex- and age-differentially. The higher provision for boys may be an attempt to secure general involvement in the school;

that for the older pupils a reward for voluntarily remaining within the system.

These activities also extend the boundary of the school by colonising more time and in supplementing the formal curriculum. The experience of joining clubs is expected to have outcomes in terms of the generation of lasting interests or the modification of behaviour in approved directions. But because the membership of clubs is essentially voluntary the act of joining is also seen as a commitment towards the school in the broader sense. This is made explicit in the following quotation from some notes for sixth formers by the head-teacher of a grammar school:

> Take part in many of the out-of-school activities and clubs
> and use the facilities which are so well known to you in
> this school. You are entering a competitive world. Sooner
> or later I shall be asked to write you a testimonial. I shall
> be looking for all the ways in which you have identified
> yourself with the school, responsibilities you have accepted, the
> positive impressions you have made both as a person and as a
> leader, what contributions you have made during your time at
> school. You can help yourselves best by doing the things which
> will enable me to give you a good testimonial.

Joining out-of-school activities is one way in which the school passes judgment on a pupil's behaviour; his performance in the expressive order. This is, in a sense, a moral test. The school provides activities it approves of, and tests by membership how pupils agree with the values implicit in the activities. When such assessments are used in applications for places in universities then links are made between the expressive and the instrumental, and the out-of-school activities have a selective function. These considerations also apply to the membership of school sports teams.

A further outcome of the provision of out-of-school activities in many schools is to retain more of the middle-class pupils than working-class for a voluntary period after school. Two explanations may be made of this class differential in joining clubs. First, the content of school clubs may often be more middle-class than working-class in reference and origins. Debating and dramatic societies are clear examples of this. Our information is not sufficiently detailed for this possibility to be thoroughly tested. A second explanation may be that working-class pupils have competing obligations and expectations for the time after school. One headteacher of a mixed modern school with a 78 per cent working-class composition had carried out a survey which showed that many boys over the age of thirteen had some kind of job to go to after school, and virtually all the girls had domestic obligations, such as looking after the younger childre͏r before mother returned home from work, or getting tea ready. Both explanations could be subsumed in the cultural discontinuity theory. Whether working-class pupils join school clubs less often because of their content, or because of other commitments, indicates value judgments that are different to those implied in the school system.

7 The instrumental order

The instrumental order consists of the educational knowledge transmitted by the school and the activities used in its transmission. A simple analysis is first made of the knowledge transmitted by schools, in terms of its size and content, and its relation to the contextual variables of school status and sex composition. The standardisation, formalisation and ritualisation of instrumental activities are then described. The specialisation by pupils' age, sex and ability of both educational knowledge and instrumental activities are dealt with in later chapters.

After describing the methods used in the measurement of the pupils' involvement in instrumental activities the results of the measurements are presented in a sequence similar to that used in previous chapters.

The educational knowledge transmitted in schools

The main interest in this study was in the transmission of educational knowledge, so that this discussion of the actual knowledge transmitted by schools is a simple one, which draws on relatively crude data.[1]

Weber (1948) suggested that knowledge is particularly susceptible to bureaucratisation. Most of the following comments are based on analyses of the major formalisation of knowledge in the school, the curriculum.

Curriculum and context

Table 51 relates two elements of the curriculum to the contextual variables of school status and sex composition.

[1] The term educational knowledge is being used to refer to that socially constructed by teachers. See Young (1971) and Bernstein (1971).

TABLE 51   *Curriculum and context – mean scores*

	Boys SM	Girls SM	Mixed SM	All SM	All CS	Boys GS	Girls GS	Mixed GS	All GS
n	7	6	24	37	17	6	6	6	18
Number of subjects	18·9	19·4	18·6	18·8	28·1	22·7	21·0	25·3	21·7
Languages	0·9	1·2	0·8	0·8	2·9	3·3	4·3	3·8	3·8

The differences in the size of the curriculum as measured by the total number of subjects indicate that schools for more able pupils and older pupils have a larger knowledge content than those for the less able. The correlation for size of curriculum and mean IQ was 0·24. That for size of curriculum and per cent of first-year pupils −0·25; for per cent of seventh-year pupils 0·30. The high score for the comprehensive schools indicates that the knowledge content is also related to the range of the ability of the pupils.

The mean scores for the number of languages taught are markedly higher in grammar schools than modern schools. French was taught in all the grammar and comprehensive schools, but in only 70 per cent of modern schools. Only two modern schools taught more than one foreign language. The commonest second languages were Spanish and German. All but two of the grammar schools taught Latin. Fifty-nine per cent of comprehensive schools taught Latin, but it was taught in only one modern school, to a selected group of second-year pupils 'for fun'. More languages were taught in girls' schools than boys' schools of the same status.

The variation in the specialisation of knowledge is most clear for the sciences. All the grammar schools and most of the comprehensives taught the separate sciences of chemistry, physics and biology. One third of the grammar schools made a further specialisation into botany and zoology. (This occurred in only one comprehensive.) General science was taught in almost all modern and comprehensive schools, but in only three grammar schools. Biology was taught in 56 per cent of modern schools, physics in 41 per cent and chemistry in 19 per cent. No girls' modern school taught chemistry or physics as a separate science. Human biology, often a vehicle for sex education, was taught in 20 per cent of modern schools, none of them for boys only.

These simple analyses indicate that the knowledge transmitted to pupils is related to at least two of their salient characteristics; sex and imputed ability. Girls learn more languages than boys and are often assumed to be more verbally fluent. Special female knowledge may be transmitted to them in preparation for marriage and mother-hood. Boys encounter more science than girls. They are thought to be more interested in 'things' rather than people, compared with girls, and they are more often expected to take up occupations which utilise scientific concepts. More able pupils receive a more specialised education than the less able; they are likely to enter high status occupations via the examination system, both of which entail the possession of specialised knowledge.

At the level of cultural transmission these differences mean that more able pupils are given access to forms of consciousness that are wider in space and time, and more detailed in structure than that allowed to the less able. The study of foreign languages gives access to other cultures. Latin, even if it is the last remnant of medieval initiation rite (see Campbell (1968)), gives access to a culture which exists only ideationally. The specialised study of science provides access to forms of explanation that imply the mastery of nature and some control of the destiny of man. Thus the able pupils who have most likelihood of gaining middle-class status encounter knowledge most likely to engender what Kluckholn and Strodtbeck (1961) consider to be some of the value-orientations of the middle class.[1]

The organisation of instrumental activities

Apart from summarising the educational knowledge transmitted the curriculum also structures the activities used in its transmission. A written curriculum existed in all schools and so is an example of formalisation of instrumental activities, as are the syllabuses and examinations which are related to it. This use of paper control is congruent with the principal methods used in the transmission of knowledge which also involve paper: reading and writing. However, instrumental activities were also standardised and ritualised.

Examinations

Examinations have several bureaucratic purposes. They are clearly an example of the formalisation of instrumental performance, but they also tend to standardise the instrumental activities themselves.

All schools had internal examinations, usually one set a year, and all entered candidates for external examinations, principally the GCE and CSE. These public examinations were preceded by a mock internal examination in 88 per cent of schools, which was, in about half the cases, a qualifying examination for the external examination.

Schools of different types had different policies in relation to external examinations, in terms of which they used, their level of provision and the proportion of the annual intake entered.

[1] The correlation between curriculum size and per cent of working-class children is -0.32.

A-level was virtually confined to grammar and comprehensive schools (where they had sixth forms), but a few modern schools did enter small numbers of candidates for a limited range of subjects, usually art or history. The average grammar-school entry was about half of the annual intake, compared with about 10 per cent for the comprehensives. Science and arts/science combinations were more common in the grammar schools, arts only in the comprehensives. Grammar schools were able to offer an average of 14·7 A-level subjects compared with 8·4 for comprehensives. Grammar-school policy was to allow a maximum of three or four subjects to be taken; this was more commonly three in comprehensives.

Every grammar and comprehensive took O-level examinations, compared with half the modern schools. Virtually every pupil was entered in the grammar schools, about half of the intake in the comprehensives, and in modern schools taking the examinations, about one fifth. The number of subjects taught at this level was very similar for grammar and comprehensives, with averages of 19·8 and 18·9 respectively. Modern schools averaged 4·6, with girls' schools providing more than boys' (6·8 compared with 3·7). A maximum of eight or nine subjects to be taken at one time was set by the grammar and comprehensives, six most commonly by the modern schools. The minimum in grammar schools was commonly two; in the non-selective schools one could often be taken.

All the modern and comprehensive schools prepared candidates for CSE, compared with only 58 per cent of grammar schools. Of the modes of CSE Mode One was most common, Mode Two the least. Mode Three was twice as common in comprehensive as in modern schools; it occurred rarely in grammar schools. It is clear the grammar schools regarded CSE as suitable only for their less able pupils. They entered about a third of their intake, a similar proportion to that in modern schools, but less than comprehensives with nearly sixty per cent. Candidates were usually entered in only two or three subjects, which was usually the number taught for CSE. The average number of CSE subjects taught in comprehensive schools was 19 compared with 13 in modern schools. The usual maximum entry in these schools was eight subjects in one sitting, but a few modern schools allowed less than two to be taken, as did half the comprehensives.

The practice of double entries for external examination was most common in comprehensive schools (Table 52), and relates to an ideology of providing wide educational opportunities.

It is quite clear that grammar schools had the highest degree of involvement with external examinations; virtually all pupils took them compared with a minority in most modern schools. Certification does not cover the whole range of ability, and excludes all who

TABLE 52   *Double entry examination policies (per cent incidence)*

Individual pupils make take:		Modern	Compre- hensive	Grammar	All
	n	37	17	18	72
CSE and GCE in same sitting		46	94	61	61
CSE and GCE in same subject		35	76	28	43
GCE of different boards		8	59	17	19

Note. Only two schools entered individual pupils for the GCE of different boards at the same sitting in the same subject. Both schools were comprehensives.

leave school at fifteen to enter semi-skilled and unskilled manual occupations with a non-certificated entry.

Standardisation of instrumental activities

Homework was the principal method of standardising instrumental activities. It was set in all schools, but it was compulsory for all pupils in only 69 per cent of schools. It was set over the weekend in 90 per cent of schools, over half-term in 46 per cent, and during the holidays, often in the form of projects, in 43 per cent. The five-point scale derived for this dimension is given in Table 53.

TABLE 53   *Standardisation of instrumental activities scale*

Item	f
Homework diaries checked by signing	14
Homework set over holidays	31
Homework set over half-term	33
Homework set at weekends	65

Mean item analysis value 0·914; mean score 1·99 (N = 72; S.D. = 1·16).

The mean scores on the scale are given in Table 55. Higher scores are associated with modern schools and with boys' schools, perhaps a reflection of the kind of pupils the teachers think need their noses kept to the grindstone. These scale figures could be misleading in that the items may not apply to all pupils in the schools concerned. Whereas every pupil in every grammar school did homework, this rule was relaxed in a few comprehensives and existed in only half the modern schools.

TABLE 54   *Standardisation of instrumental activities – mean scores*

	Boys SM	Girls SM	Mixed SM	All SM	All CS	Boys GS	Girls GS	Mixed GS	All GS
n	7	6	24	37	17	6	6	6	18
mean	2·57	2·17	1·92	2·08	2·06	2·00	1·17	2·00	1·72
S.D.	1·18	0·90	1·32	1·26	1·26	0·82	0·37	1·00	0·87

Standardisation of instrumental performance

A great many methods were used in assessing how well pupils were learning. The regular collection of homework marks occurred in a third of schools. The regular collection of marks for tests and school work occurred a little more often than this, and assessments for effort a little less so. In most cases a percentage or grade was calculated in each subject for each pupil. Positions and effort assessments in each subject were calculated in about half the cases, as were the pupils' overall positions, and score or grade in all subjects.

Intra-school competitions based on marks gained for school work were run in 61 per cent of schools. In 57 per cent these were based upon assessments of effort, and in a quarter of these schools marks could be deducted for poor effort. In 56 per cent of schools the basis of the competition was achievement in work rather than effort. (Some schools had both criteria.) Here again, in a fifth of cases marks could be deducted for poor work. Half the schools put pupils into detention for persistent poor work or effort.

These work competition schemes were often run as part of the House system, or sometimes within year-groups or particular classes. They thus varied in whether it was a group or individual score that led to success. Grouping was most common, but in one girls' grammar school the competition decided which girls in each form received a speech-day prize.

The five-item scale for the measurement of the standardisation of instrumental performance is given in Table 55.

TABLE 55   *Standardisation of instrumental performance scale*

Item	f
Pupils' overall position calculated	14
Homework marks regularly collected	23
School work marks regularly collected	30
Test marks regularly collected	31
Pupils' score (per cent, grade) calculated in each subject	34

Mean item analysis value 0·980; mean score 1·83 (N = 72; S.D. = 2·05).

The mean scores on the scale (Table 56) show that high standardisation is associated with grammar schools, especially mixed and boys'. Girls' schools in all categories scored lower than boys' on average, possibly indicating a different degree of importance placed on success in school work for the sexes.

TABLE 56   *Standardisation of instrumental performance mean scores on scale*

	Boys SM	Girls SM	Mixed SM	All SM	All CS	Boys GS	Girls GS	Mixed GS	All GS
n	7	6	24	37	17	6	6	6	18
mean	2·17	1·17	1·25	1·51	1·67	3·00	1·33	3·67	2·67
S.D.	1·83	1·86	1·71	1·85	2·06	2·24	1·89	1·70	2·19

The incidence of the use of competitive mark systems for school work is shown in Table 57.

TABLE 57   *Competitive mark systems for school work (per cent incidence)*

	Boys SM	Girls SM	Mixed SM	All SM	All CS	Boys GS	Girls GS	Mixed GS	All GS
n	7	6	24	37	17	6	6	6	18
Based on effort	86	100	67	76	53	0	33	17	22
Based on achievement	51	83	67	70	47	0	67	33	33

It is particularly associated with modern schools. Where such systems are used in grammar schools they tend to be based more on assessments of achievement rather than effort. This may be related to the assumption that clever pupils will manifest effort without reward, and that their effort is measured by their achievement. The lower level of incidence among comprehensive compared with modern schools may be ideological, in that the belief in equal opportunities for all pupils may be thought to be fostered by reducing or delaying personal or group competition between pupils.

Formalisation of instrumental activities

The major methods of this kind of a structuring form the items of the scale constructed to measure this organisational dimension. All the items refer to homework.

TABLE 58 *Formalisation of instrumental activities scale*

Item	*f*
Homework done in special exercise books	14
Homework diaries	16
School rules refer to homework	28
Homework timetable	57

Mean item analysis value 0·804; mean score 1·60 (N = 72; S.D. = 0·95).

High mean scores on the scale (Table 59) are associated with grammar schools, and are part of the general tendency of grammar schools to use formalisation, which is associated with high levels of pupil literacy. This analysis is confirmed by the correlations between the scale score and mean IQ, which is 0·27, and the correlation with the percentage of manual-workers' children, which is −0·27. Every grammar school had a homework timetable compared with 88 per cent of comprehensives and 65 per cent of modern schools.

TABLE 59 *Formalisation of instrumental activities – mean scores*

	Boys SM	Girls SM	Mixed SM	All SM	All CS	Boys GS	Girls GS	Mixed GS	All GS
n	7	6	24	37	17	6	6	6	18
mean	1·29	1·83	1·21	1·32	1·82	2·00	1·67	2·17	1·94
S.D.	1·16	0·69	1·04	1·04	0·86	0·00	0·75	0·69	0·62

Formalisation of instrumental performance

The major formalisation was the use of school reports, which were issued in every school usually twice a year. Four other methods form the scale for the measurement of this dimension (Table 60). In addition to these, the results of external examinations were reported in the speech- or open-day programme in 65 per cent of schools, and in the local newspaper in 46 per cent.

TABLE 60 *Formalisation of instrumental performance scale*

Item	*f*
Marks or test results displayed on list	16
Examination results in school magazine	17
Examination results displayed on list	22
Work or test results reported to parents	38

Mean item analysis value 0·822; mean score 1·29 (N = 72; S.D. = 1·16).

Low mean scores on the scale for formalisation of instrumental performance are associated with girls' schools and comprehensives (Table 61). The sex difference is another index of the relative importance of academic success to boys and girls. The low comprehensive score may have an ideological basis. Too many signals of success are thought to discourage the unsuccessful.

TABLE 61 *Formalisation of instrumental performance – mean scores*

	Boys SM	Girls SM	Mixed SM	All SM	All CS	Boys GS	Girls GS	Mixed GS	All GS
n	7	6	24	37	17	6	6	6	18
mean	1·57	1·17	1·33	1·35	0·94	1·83	0·83	1·83	1·50
S.D.	1·18	1·07	0·99	1·05	1·16	1·21	0·90	1·46	1·30

The frequency of school reports was higher in the grammar schools than in others; two or three a year compared with one or two.

Ritualisation of instrumental performance

Bernstein suggested (1966b) that it is the expressive order that was particularly susceptible to ritualisation. This suggestion is broadly true, but the instrumental order is ritualised too. In most cases the school work competition led to a trophy being presented to the winning group. Most speech-day programmes included a ritualised presentation of prizes for attainment in school work and external examinations (see Chapter 3). One in ten schools had plaques of scholarship winners in the school hall. The scale derived from these items is given in Table 62.

TABLE 62 *Ritualisation of instrumental performance scale*

Item	f
Cup or prize for school examination competition	10
Cup or prize for school work competition	38
Attainment prizes presented at speech or open day	45

Mean item analysis value 0.968; mean score 1·29 (N = 72; S.D. = 0·89).

The mean scores on the scale (Table 63) indicate high scores for girls' schools compared with boys', a reflection of the same sex difference in the ritualisation of expressive activities.[1] The low score for comprehensives is probably due to their ideological rejection of rituals as traditional practices especially where they relate to attainment.

TABLE 63   *Ritualisation of instrumental performance – mean scores*

	Boys SM	Girls SM	Mixed SM	All SM	All CS	Boys GS	Girls GS	Mixed GS	All GS
n	7	6	24	37	17	6	6	6	18
mean	1·43	2·17	1·33	1·49	0·65	1·00	1·67	1·83	1·50
S.D.	1·05	0·69	0·75	0·86	0·68	0·58	0·75	0·90	0·83

In a few cases it was possible to see evidence not just of the low levels of ritualisation in comprehensive schools but of actual de-ritualisation. One form of ritual that does not appear in the scale is the existence of plaques of scholarship winners in the hall. Not surprisingly these were never found in modern schools, but occurred in one comprehensive and a third of grammar schools. In one comprehensive, pale rectangular patches on the wall were due to the actual removal of such plaques, which referred to the grammar school which had become part of the school and shared its name.

The organisation of instrumental activities in different types of school

A rough index of the degree to which instrumental activities were structured or organised is obtained by the addition of the scores for the five-item analysis scales already discussed (Table 64).

TABLE 64   *Degree of structuring of instrumental activities*

	Boys SM	Girls SM	Mixed SM	All SM	All CS	Boys GS	Girls GS	Mixed GS	All GS
n	7	6	24	37	17	6	6	6	18
score	9·57	8·51	7·04	8·24	7·14	9·83	6·67	11·50	9·33

High scores are associated with both boys' grammar and boys' modern schools, although the score for mixed grammar schools is the highest.

[1] The correlation between the degree of ritualisation of expressive activities and the ritualisation of instrumental activities was 0·41, significant beyond the 1 per cent level.

Relationships between structural variables

The correlation between the scores for the standardisation and formalisation of instrumental activities is 0·38, which is significant beyond the 1 per cent level. This possibly indicates that when schools are concerned about keeping the pupils working hard they tend to use several different forms of bureaucracy to structure the situation. A similar explanation is possible for instrumental performance (how well pupils are working). The correlation between its standardisation and formalisation is 0·56.

The purpose and legitimacy of the instrumental order

The two major purposes of the instrumental order, or 'school work', considered by headteachers in their letters to parents, in school brochures and speech-day reports, were, first, to satisfy the interests and aptitudes of the pupils, and, second, to assist in the occupational placement of pupils, often via the examination system. 'We make every effort to give a child a course suitable to his/her aptitudes, interests and future career.' (Notes for parents, comprehensive school.)

The reference to assistance with occupational placement was most common in modern schools, and least common in grammar schools, a reflection of the extent to which leavers from these schools made a direct entry into the labour market (Table 65).

TABLE 65   *Leavers' destinations as percentages of annual intake*

	Modern	Compre-hensive	Grammar
n	37	17	18
University	0	2	18
College of Education	0	3	11
Other full-time education	12	3	17
Occupation	88	92	54

Modern schools often made specific references to career opportunities for which the school was, implicitly, the route.

OPPORTUNITIES – the employment situation in . . . is generally satisfactory for girls. Jobs fall into three main groups according to ability and aptitude
1. Office and clerical work
2. Sales assistants and shopwork

3. Factory work, including training as a skilled machinist, in a wide variety of factories.

(Notes for parents, girls' modern school)

References were often made to career opportunities available through post-school education. In grammar schools the principal reference was to the universities. Lists of undergraduate former pupils were common in speech-day programmes and school magazines. The grammar school/university route to occupational placement was echoed in some modern schools in their references to technical colleges. 'Many of our leavers go on to the Technical College to take academic and vocational courses.' (Letter to new parents, mixed modern school.)

Comprehensive schools celebrated the range of opportunities open through the school.

Last year 57 pupils went on to Colleges of Further Education and one won an Open Organ Scholarship to Oxford University. We have already sent students to Cambridge and 15 other universities. Other Sixth Form pupils take up careers in Banking, Civil Service, Insurance and Computer Work. (Prospectus, comprehensive school).

The sources of legitimacy of the instrumental order of the school clearly include the occupations and higher order educational institutions which its leavers enter. The evidence of other research suggests that parents are also an important source of legitimacy,[1] and the content of much of the literature sent to parents, as in the examples quoted, indicates that many schools foster this.

Much of this legitimacy is concerned with the ends of the instrumental order, occupational placement, and not with its content, what is taught. Most grammar schools referred to 'the grammar school curriculum', modern schools to 'a sound general education'; clearly the use of tradition as a source of legitimacy.

Although the Young Leavers Report indicated that teachers, and more especially headteachers, do place an intrinsic value on learning, few mentions of this appear in the documents. As the same survey indicated a strongly calculative orientation to school work on the part of parents (and more importantly pupils), it may be assumed that any references teachers make to schoolwork are partly made to meet the parents' expectations.

Careers' guidance

A more detailed account of the careers' guidance systems of the schools has appeared elsewhere. (See King and Easthope (1971).)

[1] See, for example, Schools Council Enquiry No. 1.

This brief description is made to complement the discussion on the purpose of the instrumental order.

Every school made provision for careers' guidance. Most schools had specialist careers teachers, but although these existed in all boys' schools 29 per cent of girls' schools and 18 per cent of mixed schools were without one. In these schools headteachers and senior staff were more likely to take on this function.

All schools gave careers' talks, and these were commonly time-tabled in non-selective schools. All schools provided careers' information in the form of displays of pamphlets and booklets, but this was more common for boys' schools than girls'. Visits to work places occurred in most non-selective schools, but in less than half the selective. However, visits to institutions of higher and further education were common in both comprehensives and grammar schools, but rare in modern schools.

It is clear that the structure of careers' guidance was related to the presumptions that schools make about the educational and occupational destinies of their pupils. Girls' career choices are considered less important than boys', largely because of their presumed stronger orientation towards marriage. Less able pupils are presumed to make a direct entry into occupations rather than transfer to a higher level of education.

It would be a mistake to assume that it was only the pupils' work performance that was taken into account in these advisory and allocative processes. Both instrumental and expressive performances were taken into account in that behavioural ratings were also used. In one modern school the assessment was formalised on a rating sheet, made out for all fourth- and fifth-year pupils, and included teachers' estimates of co-operation and obedience. It has already been suggested that the pupils' participation in out-of-school activities, membership of school teams and occupancy of official school positions may all be used as tests of approved behaviour and orientation, and may therefore also be used in the careers' guidance and allocative processes of the school.

Instrumental involvement

Two methods were used to measure the pupils' involvement in the instrumental order of the school; one attitudinal, the other, indirectly, behavioural.

The figures for the six-item scale for instrumental involvement are given in note 2, p. 103.

The second measurement was the pupils' self-reported expectation of receiving any kind of post-school education. Such an expectation was taken to imply that the instrumental activities of the school were valued as a means to a desired end, since most post-school courses require certain levels of academic attainment.

Social class differences in instrumental involvement

It is well established that the actual rates at which pupils proceed to post-school education is higher for the middle class than the working class.[1] The measurements of the expectation of post-school education tend to follow the same pattern. Higher percentage expectations for the middle class are particularly associated with non-selective schools and with the early years of secondary schooling (Table R, Appendix C). Fewer class differences were found in the fifth and seventh years, probably partly due to the dropping out of the less ambitious working-class pupils. There was no general tendency for the mean scores on the involvement scale to be higher for the middle-class pupils within individual schools, comparing pupils of the same age and sex.

Pupils of different social classes do not appear to vary significantly in their orientation towards school work, but the middle class appear to place greater relevance upon it in terms of their educational, and probably, therefore, their occupational destinies, compared with the working class.

Sex differences in instrumental involvement

There were no consistent sex differences in the percentages of pupils expecting post-school education within mixed schools, keeping age and social class constant (Table R, Appendix C).

In the second year of most mixed schools, girls had higher mean scores than boys on the instrumental involvement scale. This is probably part of the sex-typing of the good-pupil role that has been suggested to occur in the early years of mixed schools (Table S, Appendix C).

[1] See, for example, the Robbins Report, *Higher Education* (1963).

[2] *Instrumental involvement scale*

	Judges' score	Per cent agreement	r Item/score total
Passing exams is the way to get on	6·4	88	0·410
You must do homework if you want to do well in exams	6·9	82	0·769
School work is usually interesting	6·3	79	0·749
Doing homework is important	7·4	79	0·647
The point of working hard is to pass exams	7·3	77	0·664
I enjoy learning new things	8·2	97	0·757

Mean score = 5·0 (N = 7,457; S.D. = 1·22)

Age differences in instrumental involvement

Two patterns are apparent in the age differences for expectation of post-school education (Table R, Appendix C). For boys of both social classes in non-selective schools, a steady rise in expectation is generally found with increasing school age. This pattern may be partly due to the experience of school enhancing ambitions, and the rise from the fourth to the fifth year partly due to the early leaving of the less ambitious.

Pupils of both social classes in single-sex grammar schools tended to show a lower level of expectation of post-school education in the fourth year compared with the second, and a higher level in the fifth than the fourth. Seventh-year pupils almost always had higher expectations than others in comprehensive schools, but not necessarily so in grammar schools. This is partly related to the high levels of expectation found generally in grammar schools.

The most common pattern for the mean scores on the involvement scale was to find a fall in the fourth year followed by a rise in the fifth (Table S, Appendix C). This was particularly common in single-sex modern schools and comprehensives, and was generally true for both social classes. The fourth- to fifth-year rise may again be due to the loss of low involvement early leavers.

Instrumental involvement and the organisation of instrumental activities

No significant correlations were found between levels of instrumental involvement and the degree and type of organisation of instrumental activities as measured on the item-analysis scales. Thus, for example, the use of a work-mark reward scheme is not always associated with high levels of pupil involvement and aspiration. This kind of result does not necessarily indicate that the organisation of school work does not affect involvement, but that organisation does not determine involvement.

8　Ability-specialisation

Every school in the survey showed some degree of ability-specialisation in the form of their grouping of pupils for teaching purposes. This chapter examines the variety of teaching/learning groups found in schools, and relates these to levels of ability-specialisation of both instrumental and expressive activities, and the ability-specialisation of knowledge.

A second section relates the involvement of pupils to their membership of two different kinds of learning groups, streamed and non-streamed.

Learning groups

The creation of learning groups is fundamental to the organisation of all but very small schools. Several problems were found in attempting to establish what kind of grouping schools were using. The written information provided by the questionnaire was often quite unreliable and confusing; one school claiming, for example, both streaming and non-streaming in the same year-group. Eliciting the actual arrangements was often the most difficult part of the interview with the headteacher. One element of the problem was semantic confusion. Different meanings were placed on terms such as non-streaming, banding and options. Another was the noticeable tendency for some headteachers to regard a report of 'non-streaming' as a socially acceptable response. Hence several cases of banding were called non-streaming. Related to this was a certain defensiveness about the reporting of the use of streaming. 'We *still* stream them.'

As a preliminary to the inquiry an attempt was made to frame definitions of the principal kinds of grouping.

Streaming was defined as the allocation of pupils to groups homogeneous for both age and imputed ability, there being only one group for each ability-status.

Banding is the allocation of pupils to groups homogeneous for both age and imputed ability, there being more than one group for some ability-statuses. Many patterns of banding occur as these examples illustrate:

(i) Six groups three bands; two equal-status top-band groups, two equal-status middle-band groups, two equal-status bottom-band groups.

(ii) Three groups two bands; *either,* two equal-status top-band groups, one bottom-band group, *or* one top-band group, two equal-status bottom-band groups. (These situations were sometimes referred to as streaming with non-streaming.)

Non-streaming (unstreaming, homogeneous groupings), is the allocation of pupils to groups homogeneous for age but heterogeneous for ability. Each group has the same ability-status.

Setting refers to the grouping of pupils homogeneous for age, for the teaching of individual subjects. Sets may be homogeneous or heterogeneous for ability in the subject.

Options refers to the grouping of pupils for particular subjects that they have chosen to study. Limitations may be placed on the number of subjects available for choice, the number of subjects to be chosen, and the combinations of subjects possible. Subjects may also be offered at a number of different levels.

Streaming was most common in incidence, and most extensive through the year-groups of modern schools, least common in comprehensives (Table 66). It was also more common in girls' and mixed schools than in boys'. It occurred most frequently in the fifth year of comprehensives, and in the third and fourth years of other schools.

TABLE 66   *Extent of streaming*

	Boys SM	Girls SM	Mixed SM	All SM	All CS	Boys GS	Girls GS	Mixed GS	All GS
n	7	6	24	37	17	6	6	6	18
Per cent occurrence in:									
Year									
1st	13	50	54	46	23	0	0	0	0
2nd	28	83	54	54	35	0	17	33	17
3rd	43	83	71	68	33	0	17	66	28
4th	57	50	58	57	36	17	33	50	34
5th	43	16	42	38	56	33	50	50	44
Mean extent in years	1·9	2·8	2·8	2·6	1·8	0·5	1·2	2·0	1·2

Banding was most common and most extensive in comprehensive schools, least common in girls' modern and mixed grammar schools (Table 67). In the non-selective schools it was found mainly in the first three years, but like streaming it did not occur in the first year of any grammar school.

TABLE 67   *Extent of banding*

	Boys SM	Girls SM	Mixed SM	All SM	All CS	Boys GS	Girls GS	Mixed GS	All GS
n	7	6	24	37	17	6	6	6	18
Per cent occurrence in:									
Year									
1st	43	17	29	30	59	0	0	0	0
2nd	43	0	29	27	47	50	50	17	39
3rd	43	0	25	24	53	50	50	17	39
4th	29	17	17	19	29	33	17	17	22
5th	14	17	8	11	18	17	17	17	17
Mean extent in years	1.7	0·5	1·1	1·1	2·1	1·5	1·3	0·7	1·2

Non-streaming occurred most commonly and most extensively in grammar schools, where it was found in every first year (Table 68). Half the comprehensives used non-streaming, usually confining it to the first two years. Among modern schools it was most common in boys', least common in mixed schools, and was also largely confined to the early years. The high incidence of non-streaming in grammar schools indicates that its use does not necessarily relate to the acceptance of a comprehensive ideology, as some commentators have implied.

TABLE 68   *Extent of non-streaming*

	Boys SM	Girls SM	Mixed SM	All SM	All CS	Boys GS	Girls GS	Mixed GS	All GS
n	7	6	24	37	17	6	6	6	18
Per cent occurrence in:									
Year									
1st	43	33	17	24	35	100	100	100	100
2nd	49	17	17	19	29	33	33	50	39
3rd	14	17	4	8	18	33	33	17	28
4th	14	17	4	8	12	17	33	33	28
5th	29	17	0	8	12	17	17	33	22
Mean extent in years	1·3	1·0	0·4	0·7	1·1	2·0	2·2	2·3	2·2

Setting was common in all schools, but most common in the comprehensives (Table 69). In all schools its frequency increased with the age of the pupils. We were unable to obtain reliable data on the number of subjects setted. This was mainly because when setting was used with streaming or banding, the streams or bands were often setted to different extents and in different subjects.

TABLE 69   *Extent of setting*

	Boys SM	*Girls SM*	*Mixed SM*	*All SM*	*All CS*	*Boys GS*	*Girls GS*	*Mixed GS*	*All GS*
n	7	6	24	37	17	6	6	6	18
Per cent occurrence in:									
Year									
1st	57	83	33	46	41	0	50	17	22
2nd	71	100	58	68	59	50	100	33	61
3rd	86	83	63	70	76	50	100	50	67
4th	57	83	67	68	83	50	100	83	78
5th	71	83	58	65	88	67	100	83	83
Mean extent in years	3·4	4·3	2·8	3·2	3·5	2·2	4·5	2·7	3·1

Other forms of grouping were much less common. Much of the streaming in the fourth and fifth years of non-selective schools was in the form of course or examination specialisation. Top streams were prepared for CSE, middle streams for quasi-vocational examinations particularly in commercial subjects, and the bottom-stream pupils were non-examinees. Arts and science specialisation was virtually confined to schools with sixth forms, although it did occur in one modern school in the fifth year. Team teaching, to a limited degree, existed in three modern schools and three comprehensives. Options were largely confined to the fourth and fifth years and were in practice very difficult to distinguish from setting.

The organisation of remedial teaching in the non-selective schools varied with the size of the school. In larger schools a separate remedial form usually existed in the first two years. In smaller schools the remedial pupils were usually placed in the bottom stream and withdrawn for special provision in certain subjects, especially English and mathematics. This procedure was also used in some non-streamed schools.

The orientation of headteachers towards their remedial groups was interesting. They often omitted to mention their existence in the questionnaire, and even in the interview until prompted. The impression given is that remedial pupils were not regarded as being part of the general educational process of the school, but that the one or two years of remedial treatment helped them into the mainstream (albeit often the low stream).

It is clear from the analysis so far presented that individual schools use several different grouping methods. It is rare to be able to talk about the streamed school; and there is no case of a truly non-streamed school.

The commonest form of organisation in modern schools was streaming in the first four years. In small modern schools the fifth year often consisted of one class, usually an extension of the fourth-year top stream. In some very small modern schools fifth year and top-stream fourth years were taught together for some subjects. The commonest form of organisation in comprehensive schools was banding throughout the first five years. The commonest grammar-school pattern was non-streamed in the first year followed by banding till the fifth year. In all three types of school the older year-groups were progressively more setted.

The different kinds of internal organisation represent different degrees of ability-specialisation. We were unable to construct a very sophisticated scale for its measurement because of the complexities of combining different grouping in the same year, e.g. streaming and setting, sometimes setting for only some streams. However, a five-point ordinal scale which could adequately classify the first four years of most schools was evolved (Table 70).

TABLE 70 *Ability-specialisation by grouping scale*

Score	Grouping
0	non-streaming
1	non-streaming with separate remedial group
2	non-streaming with setting
3	banding
4	streaming with or without setting

The mean scores on this simple scale are given in Table 71.

TABLE 71 *Ability-specialisation by grouping – mean scores*

	Boys SM	Girls SM	Mixed SM	All SM	All CS	Boys GS	Girls GS	Mixed GS	All GS
n	7	6	24	37	17	6	6	6	18
Year									
1st	2·6	3·0	3·0	2·9	2·6	0·0	0·7	0·3	0·4
2nd	3·1	3·7	3·1	3·2	2·7	2·2	2·7	2·2	2·4
3rd	3·4	3·7	3·6	3·6	3·1	2·2	2·8	3·5	2·9
4th	3·6	3·5	3·4	3·5	3·3	3·0	2·8	3·0	3·0

For all types of school ability-specialisation increased with age. The degree of specialisation at each age was lowest for grammar schools, highest for the modern. This is clearly related to the ability-range of the pupils, which is narrowest in the grammar schools, although it is interesting that the comprehensives with a wider range than the modern schools had a lower level of specialisation.

Initial allocation to learning groups

Schools used many different methods to allocate pupils to their first-year learning groups. The methods may be categorised according to whether or not they take into account imputed ability. Ability is taken into account when schools use eleven-plus results (used by 42 per cent of all schools), school-administered tests (18 per cent), or primary-school reports (42 per cent). Every school with streaming or banding in its first year used one or more of these methods, but they were used in only half the schools with first-year non-streaming (with or without remedial grouping), and a third of the schools with first-year non-streaming with some setting.

Ability is not taken into account when schools use a random distribution (22 per cent), the age of pupils (3 per cent), primary school of origin (8 per cent) or pupil choice (one case only). Such methods were used in half the schools with first-year non-streaming (with or without remedial group or setting) but never by schools with first-year streaming or banding. Only three schools used a combination of the two types of method; all three used non-streaming with some setting.

These results indicate that use of estimates of imputed ability increases with the degree of initial ability-specialisation.

Ability-specialisation

As the preceding section on grouping indicates, every school made some differentiation between pupils according to their imputed ability at school work. This ability-differentiation or specialisation was measured using four scales, described in the following section.

The ability-specialisation of instrumental activities

The grouping system was used to establish in each school a simple able/less able distinction among the groups of pupils. If, at a given age-level, only non-streaming was employed, no organisational distinction was being made between the able and the less able as groups, only differences between individuals within groups.

Four differences in the control of instrumental activities were common between able and less able groups. The less able were commonly setted less or excluded from the setting system. They often had a different curriculum and did less homework. These last two differences were wider for older pupils until the fifth year when the less able tended to leave (Table 72).

TABLE 72   *Ability-specialisation of instrumental activities – all schools (per cent incidence ($N = 72$))*

Year	1st	2nd	3rd	4th	5th
Less able group(s):					
Excluded from setting	14	18	14	15	7
Setted less	10	13	14	11	7
Have different curriculum	34	46	51	55	35
Do less homework	27	27	32	38	18

A simple scale to measure the extent of the ability-specialisation of instrumental activities was derived from the addition of the incidence of the four possible differences for years one to five. Table 73 gives the mean scores for schools of different kinds.

TABLE 73   *Ability-specialisation of instrumental activities scale – mean scores*

	Boys SM	Girls SM	Mixed SM	All SM	All CS	Boys GS	Girls GS	Mixed GS	All GS
n	7	6	24	37	17	6	6	6	18
mean	7·4	5·8	7·5	7·2	9·9	2·2	2·5	2·8	2·5
S.D.	4·2	1·7	4·4	4·1	3·5	2·3	1·8	1·3	1·9

The degree of this kind of ability-specialisation was clearly related to the ability-range of the school. Comprehensives, with the widest range, specialised most; grammar schools, with the narrowest range, specialised least. Girls' modern schools specialised less than boys'.

The ability-specialisation of instrumental performance

Three differences were commonly found in the way schools assessed school work performance among pupils in different ability groups. The less able were often set different internal examinations (related to their different curricula, mentioned above). Work-marks and examination results were usually calculated by ability-groups and not by age-groups. The frequency of these differences, and the degree of specialisation they represent, increased until the fifth year, as with the specialisation of instrumental activities (Table 74).

TABLE 74   *Ability-specialisation of instrumental performance – all schools (per cent incidence (N = 72))*

Year	1st	2nd	3rd	4th	5th
Ability groups have:					
Different exams	29	36	40	45	30
School marks by group	15	21	25	25	20
Exam results by group	33	45	50	52	42

A simple scale for the degree of ability-specialisation of instrumental performance was obtained by the addition of the frequency with which the three differences occurred in the five age-groups (range 0–15) (Table 75).

TABLE 75   *Ability-specialisation of instrumental performance scale – mean scores*

	Boys SM	*Girls SM*	*Mixed SM*	*All SM*	*All CS*	*Boys GS*	*Girls GS*	*Mixed GS*	*All GS*
n	7	6	24	37	17	6	6	6	18
mean	8·6	8·8	7·3	7·8	7·4	3·7	3·8	6·5	4·7
S.D.	4·7	2·7	3·9	3·9	4·5	3·7	2·2	3·3	3·4

Unlike the ability-specialisation of activities, the specialisation of performance does not relate strongly to ability-range. The comprehensives did tend to have high scores, but at much the same level as those of modern schools. Grammar schools were less specialised but mixed grammar schools scored higher than single-sex schools. There was, however, a significant correlation of 0·27 between the degrees of ability-specialisation for instrumental activities and performance.

The ability-specialisation of expressive activities

Few differences were found in the expressive sphere in the treatment of pupils by ability-groups. Sixty-four per cent of schools registered pupils in ability-groups. This happened in the large majority of modern and grammar schools but in only two comprehensives. Seventeen per cent of schools allocated cloakrooms by ability-group. These two differences form the items of a short three-point item-analysis scale (mean item analysis value 1·00, mean score 0·81 S.D. 0·70). The mean scores for different kinds of school are given in Table 76.

TABLE 76   *Ability-specialisation of expressive activities scale –*
            mean scores

	Boys SM	Girls SM	Mixed SM	All SM	All CS	Boys GS	Girls GS	Mixed GS	All GS
n	7	6	24	37	17	6	6	6	18
mean	0·71	0·83	0·96	0·89	0·29	1·11	1·33	0·83	1·11
S.D.	0·45	0·69	0·58	0·56	0·57	0·69	0·34	0·69	0·81

The low mean score of the comprehensive schools is possibly related to their ideology of equality, just as the higher scores for grammar schools, especially the single-sex ones, may reflect a meritocratic ideology.

The ritualisation of ability-specialised expressive activities

In 53 per cent of schools the pupils' positions in assembly reflected their ability-status: A stream commonly behind B. The ceremonials of entry and exit were also stratified in this way (43 per cent and 53 per cent incidence respectively).

These three items form a four-point item-analysis scale (mean item analysis value 1·00, mean score 1·49, S.D. 1·42). Table 21, Chapter 4, gives the mean scores on the scale. The low score of the comprehensives reflects similar low scores for other uses of ritualisation in these schools.

The correlation between the ability-specialisation of expressive activities and the ritualisation of such activities is 0·69. This high value suggests that when schools relate behaviour to ability it is structured by both bureaucracy and ritual.

Ability privileges

Very few privileges were distributed to the more able pupil groups compared with the less able. In six modern schools examination candidates in the top stream were excused games and in five schools excused PE. There may be some doubt as to whether these were privileges. Only one school allowed the A stream to receive dinner before the B.

Learning groups and structural variables

The structural variables referring to ability-specialisation have been related to types of school. They are now related to the two principal forms of learning group, streaming and non-streaming. Table 77 shows the correlation coefficients between the extent of streaming and of non-streaming with each variable.

TABLE 77 *Correlations of the extent of learning groups with structural variables* ($N = 72$)

	Extent of streaming	*Sig. %*	*Extent of non-streaming*	*Sig. %*
Ability-specialisation of:				
Instrumental activities	0·43	1	−0·36	1
Instrumental performance	0·41	1	−0·44	1
Expressive activities	0·19	NS	−0·34	1
Expressive ritualisation	0·29	5	−0·43	1

These correlations indicate that the use of streaming is associated with a great many organisational differences between the levels of ability it defines. The less able are taught a different, less specialised curriculum and do less homework. The examinations they do are different and their work assessed at a standard particular to their group. The differences between the streams is often further marked by arrangements for dinners, cloakrooms, registration and assembly.

Ascription of membership of learning groups

Studies of streaming in primary schools suggest that it is operated in a fairly rigid way with few transfers between streams, which implies that a pupil's stream-status is highly ascriptive. (See Douglas (1964); Jackson (1964).) We were unable to obtain accurate information about the rate of transfer between learning groups, but we were able to obtain information about the criteria used when transfers did occur, and about the existence of an automatic review of group composition.

About half the schools automatically reviewed learning group compositions at the end of the first and second years. This rose to 65 per cent at the end of the third year when allocation to examination streams occurred in many non-selective schools and setting became commoner in the grammar schools. The frequency fell to 28 per cent for reviews at the end of the fourth year.

The most common criterion for transfer was academic performance (89 per cent of all schools). Its incidence was, however, very low in comprehensives; only two schools used it. Behaviour was a criterion in 14 per cent. This was much more common in boys' schools than girls' (29 per cent compared with 7 per cent). Only four schools used estimates of effort as criteria for transfer.

114

There is no strong evidence to suggest that streaming is more ascriptive or less flexible than non-streaming. The correlation for the extent of streaming against the number of years when automatic reviews of composition were made is 0·14; that for non-streaming −0·14. Neither correlation is significant, nor is the difference between them.

The ability-specialisation of educational knowledge

The existence of differences in curriculum for pupils of different ability, as defined by their learning groups, has already been mentioned. The nature of the differences varies with the type of school.

In the grammar schools the most common curriculum difference between ability-groups was the second foreign language, commonly Latin or German usually taken only by the higher ability-groups. In non-selective schools a similar distinction was made using French, often taught only to higher ability-groups.

The results presented in the previous sections indicated that the ability-specialisation of instrumental activities increased with pupils' age up to the fourth year. The evidence suggests that the educational knowledge transmitted by these activities also became more specialised. The splitting of general science into chemistry, physics and biology was very common.

The most striking examples concern the curriculum of fourth-year pupils in non-selective schools who were not being prepared for external examinations. Many of the special schemes for this group of pupils were organised with the raising of the school leaving-age in mind, and many drew ideas and legitimacy from the Newsom Report. The pupils were often called the Newsom group. (In one school an apparently genuine mishearing by pupils had led to their being known as 'nuisance' children.) Some schools had Newsom Departments.

The curriculum for the potential early leavers was often quite different from that of the potential examination candidates. The following quotations give an indication of the kinds of knowledge transmitted; non-academic, vocational, local and domestic.

> Opportunity is given to those pupils leaving at the end of their fourth year to learn, in their final year, about social services, employment opportunities, working conditions and the obligations and rights of citizenship, as well as to gain some appreciation of the wider background of life. This approach is backed up by visits from outside speakers drawn from a wide range of occupations. (Prospectus, mixed modern school)

> We throw overboard the academic subject divisions: English,

History and Geography depart to become an integrated course
which we call 'This World of Ours', Mathematics becomes
'Money and Machines'; Religious Education becomes 'Meeting
Point'. We offer every boy a course in Cooking, Homemaking,
Horticulture, Handyman, Animal Care and Car Mechanics. We
offer every girl Homemaking, Handywoman, Family Care,
Floral Art and Typing. (Account of a comprehensive school by
headteacher)

The purpose and legitimacy of ability-specialisation

The purpose and legitimacy of ability-specialisation, as expressed in
academic learning groups, may be studied through the comments
made by headteachers and the operation of the system.

One purpose commonly suggested for ability-specialisation was 'to
suit the needs of all types of children'. (Prospectus, comprehensive
school). This was often elaborated to include a reference to the
pupils' occupational destinies. 'We make every effort to give a child
a course suitable to his/her aptitudes, interests and future career.'
(Notes for parents, comprehensive school.)

Ability-specialisation is often mediated through the external
examination system. External examinations represent a point of
articulation between the school and the occupational structure. Thus
both the examination system and ability-specialisation are seen to
be made legitimate by the occupational structure. This is illustrated
in the following quotation: '. . . qualifications much in demand by
local employers who offer good apprenticeships and who provide
opportunities leading to permanent careers in skilled and responsible
work'. (A reference to CSE – prospectus, comprehensive school.)

The stratified nature of the occupational structure therefore is
reflected in the ability-stratification within the school.

the fourth year will be split into three broad bands. The first
band to be primarily academic and to include all borderline
'O' level candidates, the second band to be primarily technical
(skilled and semi-skilled artisans, not high grade technologists,
who will come from the first band) and band three will be
primarily general. (Notes on school organisation for teachers,
comprehensive school)

This is an explicit recognition of the selective and allocative
functions of ability-specialisation. (They are also recognised in
offering careers' advice.) In most modern industrialised societies it is
assumed that certain levels of attainment and kinds of knowledge are
prerequisites to the satisfactory performance of an occupation, and
that in general the higher the societal status of the occupation the

higher is the prerequisite educational level. (See Davis and Moore (1945).)

Secondary schools allocate pupils to learning groups according to the relationship between the pupils' imputed ability and the presumed prerequisites of occupational placement and performance. Thus membership of a high-status learning group implies a high (relatively speaking) social-status destiny.

Not all courses or examinations constitute terminal education, but may have transfer purposes, and so high-order educational institutions are used as sources of legitimacy for specialisation.

the more able academic pupil may well achieve a sufficiently high standard in 'A' level to be able to enter the various forms of higher education, e.g. Teacher Training Colleges, Specialist Colleges of one sort or another, Colleges of Advanced Technology, and Universities etc., etc. (Notes on the sixth form, comprehensive school).

Many different forms and degrees of ability-specialisation were justified in terms of the needs of individual pupils. Streaming, early non-streaming, banding and setting were all considered to be means to this same end in different schools. Mention has already been made of a certain defensiveness on the part of headteachers using streaming, and of the existence of an educational respectability for non-streaming. Headteachers seldom attempted to justify the use of streaming; perhaps an example of the use of tradition for legitimation. Justifications were fairly common for other forms of ability-grouping and these often took the form of a condemnation of streaming.

The justification and legitimacy of the special schemes for the non-examined pupils follow the lines I have suggested elsewhere (1969b), that the innovations were a response to what was seen as a problem of the social control of pupils whose education received little legitimacy from their parents or from their potential employers. In these circumstances the pupils were sought as sources of legitimacy.

a watered down version of our approach to academic children was both ineffective and unacceptable. Though unsuccessful in teaching them very much we were succeeding in boring them. Bored, frustrated youngsters could only damage the general tone and atmosphere of the school. In view of these considerations it seemed essential that courses should be designed for these young people which would be relevant to their needs and which would be plainly seen by them to be relevant. ('Work Experience', comprehensive school booklet)

John White (1968) has suggested that some of these schemes are covertly intended to produce a docile, local-orientated, workforce of semi-skilled and unskilled manual workers. It is, however, possible that work-experience schemes make the prospect of work less attractive to pupils who may then stay on at school. One girls' modern school abandoned its scheme because it was considered that it exacerbated rather than alleviated the transition from school to work.

The composition of learning groups

Each learning group has an ability, sex and social class composition. The variations in these social compositions are presented for streamed and non-streamed groupings at three age-levels. The streamed/non-streamed distinction is used very broadly in that supplementary setting has been ignored and banding is included with streaming. Most of the data refers to the sub-sample of schools used in the pupils' survey.

Sex composition of learning groups

Studies of streaming in primary schools indicate that girls are sometimes over-represented in the top streams of mixed schools. (Douglas (1964); Jackson (1964); Lunn (1970).)

In general there is little evidence for this effect in the schools of the sub-sample. In one comprehensive boys were over-represented in the top stream of the fourth year, and the same effect was found in the top stream of the fifth year in one modern school. Both probably reflect the operation of pupil choice in opting to take examination courses.

The sex composition of non-streamed groups of the same age within individual schools did not usually vary significantly. Mixed schools tended to keep the sex composition of their grouping reasonably even as a matter of policy. However, some mixed schools did create single-sex groupings. One modern school had a top-stream for boys banded with a top stream for girls, a mixed middle band of one group, and two single-sex equal-status groups in the bottom band. A comprehensive school recently formed by the amalgamation of separate boys' and girls' schools taught the first year in mixed non-streamed groups. Boys and girls were taught separately in years 4 to 5, boys in streams, girls in non-streamed groups. The sixth form were taught together. The arrangement was an attempt to allay the women teachers' anxieties about teaching older boys. The plan was to allow the mixing of groups to increase year by year.

Ability composition of learning groups

Streaming is an attempt at ability-stratification, and it would be expected that the mean ability of pupils would decline with stream-status. This was true in nineteen of twenty-one schools using streaming in the second year; the two exceptions were grammar schools. The proportion fell from 90 per cent of cases in the second year to 70 per cent in the fourth year. Of twenty-three schools with fourth-year streaming sixteen showed the decline, seven did not, and in one case, a mixed grammar school, the mean score in the second stream (of two streams) was significantly higher than that for the top. Of fourteen schools with fifth-year streaming only nine (64 per cent) showed the pattern.

The general distribution of mean-measured ability by stream is not surprising considering the methods used in the allocation of pupils to streams (see previous discussion), although it should be pointed out that there were overlapping scores between every stream. The falling proportion of cases in the older age-groups probably reflects the mobility between streams.

There were no significant variations in the mean scores of pupils in non-streamed groups of the same age in the same school, so that the intention to create mixed ability-groups was probably realised. Thus, although only half the schools used ability-estimates in the allocation of pupils to non-streamed groups, equally effective distributions were obtained using other methods.

Social composition of learning groups

Studies of streaming in primary schools by Jackson (1964) and Lunn (1970) and in secondary schools by Holly (1965), Hargreaves (1967) and Lacey (1970), have found that middle-class pupils tended to be over-represented in the top streams.

Of twenty-one schools with second-year streaming only five (24 per cent) had middle-class pupils significantly over-represented in the top stream. Of these, three were modern schools, one comprehensive and one grammar. There were no examples of working-class over-representation in the top streams.

Of twenty-three schools with fourth-year streaming eight (35 per cent) showed the middle-class over-representation effect. Four were modern schools, three comprehensive, and one grammar. No cases of working-class over-representation were found.

Of the thirteen schools with fifth-year streaming only one, a modern school, showed the pattern, and there were no reversals.

The over-representation of middle-class pupils in top streams is therefore not a common phenomenon, but it must be regarded as more than a chance effect since no cases of working-class over-representation were found. The social class differences in social compositions between the streams may be partly explained by the relationship between social class and measured ability although there is no evidence to suggest that social selection occurred, keeping ability constant, as Douglas (1964) suggests happens in the primary school. There is no relationship between the incidence of middle-class over-representation in the top stream and the method of allocation to the streams.

The fall in the incidence of the phenomenon with age is a reflection of stream mobility and the fallout of proportionally more working-class early leavers in the fourth year.

There were no significant differences in the social compositions of non-streamed groups in the same age-category within individual schools, indicating that the intention to achieve a social mix in such groups was achieved using many different allocation procedures.

Streaming and involvement

The extensive literature of streaming suggests that a pupil's stream-status is related to his or her orientation towards many aspects of the school. For this reason the general involvement scale was used as the important dependent variable in the analysis of grouping and involvement. The basic hypothesis derived from previous research is that involvement is proportional to stream-status. This was tested by comparing the mean scores in the general involvement scale for pupils in different streams in the same school.

Of twenty-one schools with second-year streaming, twelve (57 per cent) show the expected pattern.[1] Two schools showed the reverse pattern; the bottom stream had the highest scores (Table T, Appendix C).

Of twenty-three schools with fourth-year streaming, nine (39 per cent) showed the pattern, with three reversals (Table U, Appendix C).

Of fourteen schools with fifth-year streaming, seven (50 per cent) showed the pattern, and there were no reversals (Table V, Appendix C).

It is clear that in only about half the cases were top-stream pupils on average more involved than lower-stream pupils.

The phenomenon, however, was more common for boys than for girls. Among ten mixed schools with second-year streaming, six showed a decline in mean involvement for boys with stream-status, but only one showed this for girls (Table T, Appendix C). In seven mixed schools with fourth-year streaming, two showed the pattern

---

[1] Groups with the same band status would be expected to have the same mean scores. This did not always occur. The figures for expected pattern include schools where the mean scores of all higher status banded groups exceed those of lower status banded groups.

for boys and two for girls (Table U, Appendix C). The pattern was shown twice for boys and once for girls in the five cases of fifth-year streaming (Table V, Appendix C).

A similar sex difference is found when single-sex schools are compared. Ignoring age-status, fifteen sets of streams were found in boys' schools, nine of which (60 per cent) showed the declining pattern. This was most common in boys' grammar schools where it occurred in all but one case. Eleven sets of streams were found in girls' schools, of which only three (27 per cent) showed the effect (Tables T, U and V). It is interesting to note that most of the streaming studies of secondary schools have been in boys' schools, where, according to these results, the involvement differences between the streams are more likely to be found. (For example, Hargreaves (1967); Lacey (1970); King (1969a).)

In the second years of mixed schools girls tended to be more involved than boys in the same stream, irrespective of stream-status (Table T). In the fourth year this sex difference was only found in the bottom stream, where in nine cases out of ten the girls had a higher mean score than the boys (Table U).

It is important to note that there were few consistent differences in the mean involvement scores of middle-class and working-class pupils in the same stream. This confirms the results of my previous study of a boys' grammar school.

Before discussing the social significance of these results it is necessary to examine the theory implicit in the hypothesis that involvement would be related to stream-status. The theoretical propositions are: that pupils are aware of status differences between the streams, that high-status pupils in the top streams legitimate the status system and this approval is extended to the school in general. Low-status pupils in the low streams do not legitimate the status system and their approval of the school is generally low.

This study, unlike my previous case study (1969a) and that of Hargreaves (1967), did not investigate the pupils' perception of their own ability-status. It is possible that where mean involvement was found not to be related to stream-status some pupils show a lack of sensitivity to the implications of stream-status. This would be most likely in the second year.

It is also possible that pupils in low streams were aware of their status but legitimated the system, that is, they agreed with the school's definition of them as less able, and considered this an acceptable one. This may explain the higher incidence of declining involvement with declining stream-status for boys. The implications of low or high ability for boys are more profound than for girls because of the relationship between school performance and occupational placement, and the stronger orientation of girls towards marriage compared with that of boys. The effect is perhaps most acute in the boys' grammar schools where the school's status has defined the pupils as being able, but where the stream system denies this to the low-stream pupil.

Two other possible explanations could be checked. It is possible that when streaming is supplemented by setting then stream-status is less apparent, and so its effect on involvement is reduced. It is also possible that special programmes for fourth-year leavers from non-selective schools do sustain pupil involvement. Supplementary setting was not related to the incidence of the pattern in the second year. Of the nine schools that showed the pattern in the fourth year, three (33 per cent) had supplementary setting. Of the fourteen not showing the pattern twelve had supplementary setting (86 per cent). Thus the suggestion that supplementary streaming blunts stream-status is only partly supported. Of non-selective schools with special programmes for fourth-year leavers, half showed the effect. This result may reflect the nature of the organisation and content of such programmes.

Another index of involvement that was analysed by stream-status was the pupils' expectation of post-school education. Our resources limit this discussion to the second year only. The hypothesis would be that the proportion of pupils expecting post-school education would be directly related to stream-status. In the boys' schools this pattern was found in five out of six cases. For boys in mixed schools this occurred in six out of ten cases. However, in girls' schools the pattern occurred in only one case out of five, and for girls in mixed schools, five cases in ten (Table W, Appendix C).

These results illustrate the stratification of educational expectation associated with streaming. The higher relevance of stream-status for boys is also shown in the sex differences in the frequency of this pattern.

Neither these results nor those for the mean scores for general involvement establish any causal connections between streaming and involvement. The relationship between streaming and involvement may be partly due to the pupils' experience of streaming; the experience of the high stream enhances involvement, that of the low stream reduces it. My previous research (1969a) in a single boys' grammar school presented some evidence for this, and it is interesting to note the high incidence of stream-related involvement in the boys' grammar schools in this investigation. Another possible explanation is that the process of allocation to streams results in the placement of highly involved pupils in the top streams and less involved ones in the bottom stream, i.e. streaming selects for involvement, rather than alters it. It is not possible to test this explanation using the data from this research.

Non-streaming and involvement

Non-streamed groups of the same age-level have the same ability-status. If ability-status is an index of involvement it would be expected that there would be little variation in the mean scores on the general involvement scale for non-streamed groups. This expectation was sometimes met, but it was also common for significant differences in mean involvement to exist between non-streamed groups. Since these groups have been shown not to vary significantly in sex, ability or social class composition within schools, the variations in involvement must be related to non-organisational factors, of which pupil/teacher interaction in the teaching situation is probably one.[1]

There were no significant differences in the levels of involvement of pupils of different social classes within non-streamed groups. However, in the second year girls were the more involved in twelve cases out of fifteen in mixed schools (Table X, Appendix C). This sex difference had disappeared by the fifth year.

Non-streamed groups were heterogeneous for ability but there was no simple relationship between the measured ability of pupils and the level of involvement within groups. Sometimes the mean scores decreased with ability, sometimes it increased, in most cases the relationship was nearly random. One of the purposes of non-streamed grouping was to retain or promote the involvement of the less able pupils, and this was sometimes being achieved.

The instrumental order, grouping, conflict and consensus

A pupil's sex and age identities are mainly established independently of the educational system. Identity as a mentally able person is only crudely established outside the educational system. As Sarason and Gladwin (1958) have documented, most societies have a cultural definition of the mentally sub-normal, but the educational systems of individual societies through their selective and allocative activities, make much finer differentiations than these simple normal/sub-normal ones, indeed, most of the indices of ability, such as certificates and diplomas, have their origins in educational systems.[2] The secondary school thus creates and establishes a new identity for each of its pupils, an ability one, which in the case of modern and grammar schools has already been crudely shaped by the eleven-plus.

In the streaming system ability-identity is distributed on a group basis; high ability is a shared characteristic of top streams, low ability a shared characteristic of low streams. This ability-stratification can be associated with social conflict in that involvement

---

[1] This is suggested by the results of Lunn's investigation of primary school grouping.
[2] This is sometimes referred to as the creation of talent.

sometimes becomes related to stream-status, particularly for boys whose ability-identity has important life-long implications in terms of eventual occupation. Ability-specialisation therefore tends to be divisive within the school. Ultimately the divisions are not between groups of like situated pupils, but between individual pupils. Success in the instrumental sphere, school work, is generally individuated. Despite the incidence of projects, pupils do not enter for public examinations in groups.

The expressive order, projected through the notion of the school as a discrete community, attempts to promote consensus within the school. The activities of the expressive order tend to be intrinsically valued, its morality is held out to all the members of the school. The instrumental order, and the ability-specialisation it gives rise to, divides pupils and sets them in competition against one another for the largely extrinsically valued prizes of examination success and desired occupations. There is therefore a tension between the expressive and the instrumental orders of the school, the one drawing pupils together, the other pulling them apart.

This tension is likely to be greater in schools using streaming rather than non-streaming. In non-streaming the attempt and the outcome is to create equal-status learning groups with similar ability, sex and social compositions to one another, and, just as importantly, to that of the whole school. Thus the non-streamed group is an isomorph of the school except for its age composition, and the same principles of community and consensus may be used in the group as in the school.[1] Streaming creates groups which often differ from one another in their ability and social composition, and, just as importantly, differ in these respects from the whole school. Streaming therefore tends to deny the notion of the school as a community.

The use of multiple setting and options may be seen as a device to allow ability-specialisation to exist, but in such a way as not to give rise to group conflict. Unlike streaming, setting can be an individuated form of ability-specialisation. A pupil does not share his ability level with others in the same stream, but as a member of several sets holds a particular, even unique, ability-status, which is much less visible, and the effects of which are borne alone. As Bernstein (1966b) has pointed out, controlling the sentiment in streaming is shame, the exposure of failure, which may be shared. In the setting situation, and possibly in the non-streamed group, guilt, the individual's feeling of having failed, may be more important.

[1] One reason given for the introduction of non-streaming in boys' modern schools was to avoid the concentration of difficult pupils in the bottom streams.

9 Age-specialisation

This chapter is mainly concerned with the ways in which the age of pupils is given organisational meaning. Both instrumental and expressive activities may be specialised for pupils of different ages, and the specialisation may take the organisational form of ritualisation or formalisation. The age-specialisation of games and out-of-school activities was discussed in Chapter 5, and the relation of pupil age to power within the school appears in the section on prefects in Chapter 10.

Previous chapters have already noted age variations in involvement. A short second section relates these to the age variations in the organisation of activities described in the first section.

Age-specialisation of expressive activities

Five age variations in the organisation of the expressive order were measured.

Age-specialisation of expressive activities

Age is an important organisational factor in pupil behaviour and in many activities differences are made on the basis of pupils' age. Most registration groups in school were homogeneous for age (see Chapter 5). Sixty-one per cent of dinner-sittings were age-separated, and in half the schools the pupils sat at the dinner table with their age-mates. The age-specialisation of cycle parking, playground entrances, playground areas, entrances to school, corridors and stairs, and cloakroom areas, all form parts of the seven-item scale for the measurement of the age-specialisation of expressive activities which appeared in Table 3, Chapter 1.

The mean scores on this scale (Table 78) show that this kind of age-specialisation was much higher in grammar and comprehensive compared with modern schools, and this may be attributed to their having sixth-form pupils. The correlations between the scale score and the percentage of first- and seventh-year pupils are -0.34 and 0.36 respectively.

TABLE 78   *Age-specialisation of expressive activities scale – mean scores*

	Boys SM	Girls SM	Mixed SM	All SM	All CS	Boys GS	Girls GS	Mixed GS	All GS
n	7	6	24	37	17	6	6	6	18
mean	1·86	1·67	1·54	1·62	3·88	3·67	4·00	2·67	3·44
S.D.	0·83	0·75	0·87	0·85	2·05	0·75	1·15	1·70	1·38

Formalisation of age-specialised expressive activities

Three expressive activities in which paper was used as a form of control were age-specialised and form the scale to measure this dimension (Table 79).

TABLE 79   *Formalisation of age-specialised expressive activities scale*

Item	f
Older pupils register themselves	20
Notice board for pupils of particular ages	20
School rules for particular ages	30

Mean item analysis value 0·867; mean score = 0·97 (N = 72; S.D. = 1·00).

As with the previous scale, high scores were associated with comprehensive and grammar schools (Table 80).

TABLE 80   *Formalisation of age-specialised expressive activities scale – mean scores*

	Boys SM	Girls SM	Mixed SM	All SM	All CS	Boys GS	Girls GS	Mixed GS	All GS
n	7	6	24	37	17	6	6	6	18
mean	0·14	0·83	0·50	0·49	1·76	1·17	1·33	1·17	1·22
S.D.	0·35	0·69	0·76	0·72	1·00	0·90	0·94	0·90	0·92

Ritualisation of age-specialised expressive activities

All of the items forming the scale for the measurement of this dimension refer to school assembly (Table 81).

TABLE 81   *Ritualisation of age-specialised expressive activities scale*

Item	f
Pupils stand in age-groups in assembly	63
Pupils enter assembly in age-groups	43
Age-groups conduct assembly	27

Mean item analysis value 0·927; mean score 1·85 (N = 72; S.D. = 0·94).

The mean scores on this table do not follow the same pattern as for the previous two scales. High scores were associated with single-sex modern schools and girls' grammar schools (see Table 21, Chapter 5).

Age differences in school uniform occurred in 46 per cent of schools. This varied from older pupils not having to wear a cap or beret, to their not having to wear a uniform at all (22 per cent of schools).

Age-specialisation of expressive performance

In schools with a mark-reward scheme for behaviour it was common for older pupils to be outside the system. In some schools that held detentions older pupils were not punished in this way. These observations probably indicate that schools have higher expectations of the behaviour of their older pupils. A short scale to measure the degree of this age-specialisation is shown in Table 82.

TABLE 82   *Age specialisation of expressive performance scale*

Item	f
Older pupils outside mark-reward system	20
Older pupils not put in detention	22

Mean item analysis value 1·00; mean score 0·58 (N = 72; S.D. = 0·72).

High scores on this scale were associated with comprehensive schools and girls' grammar schools (Table 83).

Age privileges

Goffman (1961) has called the privilege system of the total institution the 'alleviation of deprivations'. Unlike the boarding school, the

TABLE 83   *Age-specialisation of expressive performance scale –*
            mean scores

	Boys SM	Girls SM	Mixed SM	All SM	All CS	Boys GS	Girls GS	Mixed GS	All GS
n	7	6	24	37	17	6	6	6	18
mean	0·29	0·17	0·33	0·30	1·06	0·33	1·33	0·50	0·72
S.D.	0·45	0·37	0·55	0·51	0·73	0·47	0·94	0·50	0·80

day school cannot be considered to be a total institution, but some
of the privileges given to older pupils in schools were really relaxations
of the controls used with the younger ones. Being allowed to stay in
the formroom at dinner-time or break-time are such examples.
In 36 per cent of schools older pupils could enter the school before
the younger ones, and in 18 per cent of cases enter the classroom
before the teacher. Dinner-time privileges were fairly common.
Older pupils had first sitting for dinner in only three schools and
were first in the dinner queue in only three cases, but they were
exempt the dinner queue in more cases. They were frequently the only
ones allowed to leave school during the dinner-break, and often the
only pupils allowed to bring sandwiches.

Whether exemption from PE or games is considered a privilege
is a matter of opinion, but this happened for older pupils in 8 per
cent and 17 per cent of schools respectively.

Five of these items form the age privilege scale (Table 84).

TABLE 84   *Age privileges scale*

Item	f
Only older pupils:	
May bring sandwiches	8
Exempt dinner queue	14
May leave school in dinner-hour	25
May stay in formrooms in dinner-hour	44
May stay in formrooms in break-time	47

Mean item analysis value 0·864; mean score 1·92 (N = 72; S.D. = 1·42).

The mean scores on the scale are highest for grammar and comprehensive schools, but girls' modern schools also score highly
(Table 85). The correlations of the scale scores with the percentage of
first- and seventh-year pupils are $-0·13$ and $0·27$ respectively, indicating that it is especially the existence of a sixth form that is associated with extensive privileges.

TABLE 85   *Age privileges scale – mean scores*

	Boys SM	Girls SM	Mixed SM	All SM	All CS	Boys GS	Girls GS	Mixed GS	All GS
n	7	6	24	37	17	6	6	6	18
mean	1.00	2·17	1·54	1·30	2·82	2·17	2·67	2·17	2·33
S.D.	1·07	1·21	1·28	1·21	1·54	1·21	0·94	0·90	1·05

Two age privileges exclusive to girls are being allowed to wear make-up and being allowed to wear stockings or tights (as distinct from socks). These were most commonly granted in girls' grammar schools.

Age-typing of transmitted modes of behaviour

The results of the analysis of the age-specialisation of the expressive order imply the transmission of a specific sixth-form model of approved behaviour, more autonomous, more responsible, and more approved than that for younger pupils. This is confirmed in the documents obtained from schools.

It [the sixth form] will be composed of young adults. Adult demands will be made upon you and adult responsibility will be expected from you. ('Why stay on for the Sixth', pamphlet, comprehensive school)

Let me say that the staff and I wish to treat you all as adults. How you are treated depends on how you respond to that privileged position which you are about to enter. I look to you to help in the smooth running of the school and to show, by example, that you actively support your staff and Headmaster. ('Entering the Sixth Form', letter, mixed grammar school)

Age-specialisation of the instrumental order

Both knowledge and the activities used in its transmission may be age-specialised.

Age-specialisation of knowledge

The size of the curriculum was generally larger for older age-groups (Table 86). This does not indicate that individual older pupils learn more subjects, but that they become more specialised in their studies. Age- and ability-specialisation are therefore linked, as was indicated in the discussion in Chapter 8.

129

TABLE 86   *Mean number of subjects taught by age*

Year	1st	2nd	3rd	4th	5th	6th
	14·8	15·7	16·9	19·2	18·0	20·1

At the subject-level, sciences tended to be taught separately for the older age-ranges. Languages were introduced sequentially: French first, followed by German, Latin or Spanish. Russian and Greek were virtually confined to the sixth form.

Age-specialisation of instrumental activities

In almost all schools (93 per cent) older pupils were set more homework than younger ones during the school week. In addition they were more often set work over the weekends, half-terms and holidays. Three of these items form a four-point scale for the measurement of this specialisation (Table 87). Clearly older pupils were expected to work harder than younger ones.

TABLE 87   *Age-specialisation of instrumental activities scale*

Item	f
Older pupils:	
Do more homework during the week	62
Do homework over half-term	28
Do homework during holidays	31

Mean item analysis value 0·954; mean score = 1·68 (N = 72; S.D. = 1·00).

The mean scores on the scale are highest for modern schools (Table 88). The older/younger pupil distinction was greatest between the fifth and fourth years in these schools, and the differences in homework policy represented by the scores also reflects the high ability-status of the fifth-year pupils who voluntarily stay on to take examinations.

TABLE 88   *Age-specialisation of instrumental activities scale –
mean scores*

	Boys SM	Girls SM	Mixed SM	All SM	All CS	Boys GS	Girls GS	Mixed GS	All GS
n	7	6	24	37	17	6	6	6	18
mean	2·14	2·17	1·83	1·95	1·24	1·50	1·33	1·83	1·56
S.D.	0·99	0·69	1·07	1·01	0·94	0·76	0·75	0·90	0·83

Age-specialisation of instrumental performance

Although the previous results suggest that older pupils were expected to work harder than younger ones, their school work was generally less assessed, an indication of an expectation of self-motivated rather than school-motivated learning. Table 89 shows seven age differences in this respect which form a scale for this specialisation.

TABLE 89   *Age-specialisation of instrumental performance scale*

Item	f
Older pupils:	
Not given homework marks	7
Not given marks for school work	7
Not given overall effort marks	7
Not given effort marks in subjects	7
Not given test marks	8
Not given per cent or score in subjects	10
Not in mark-collection scheme	12

Mean item analysis value 0·983; mean score 0·81 (N = 72; S.D. = 2·04).

The mean scores on the scale (Table 90) are highest for grammar schools, and indicate an expectation that sixth formers need fewer school rewards for, and assessments of, their work progress. The correlations of the scale scores against age composition are −0·26 for the percentage of first-year pupils and 0·28 for the percentage of seventh-year pupils.

TABLE 90   *Age-specialisation of instrumental performance scale – mean scores*

	Boys SM	Girls SM	Mixed SM	All SM	All CS	Boys GS	Girls GS	Mixed GS	All GS
n	7	6	24	37	17	6	6	6	18
mean	0·86	0·00	0·50	0·49	0·65	1·17	1·17	2·50	1·61
S.D.	2·10	0·00	1·50	1·54	1·64	2·61	2·61	3·20	2·89

Formalisation of age-specialised instrumental activities

The two items of the scale for this dimension (Table 91) also indicate less control of older pupils' school work. They had homework time-tables and homework diaries less often than younger pupils.

TABLE 91   *Formalisation of age-specialised instrumental activities scale*

Item	*f*
Older pupils do not have homework timetables	28
Older pupils do not have homework diaries	10

Mean item analysis value = 1·00; mean score = 0·53 (N = 72; S.D. = 0·67).

The mean scores on the scale (Table 92) indicate high values for grammar schools and comprehensives. The correlations for the scale scores against age composition are −0·22 for the percentage of first-year pupils and 0·27 for the percentage of seventh-year pupils.

TABLE 92   *Formalisation of age-specialised instrumental activities scale – mean scores*

	Boys SM	Girls SM	Mixed SM	All SM	All CS	Boys GS	Girls GS	Mixed GS	All GS
n	7	6	24	37	17	6	6	6	18
mean	0·43	0·00	0·17	0·19	1·00	0·50	0·83	1·00	0·78
S.D.	0·49	0·00	0·37	0·39	0·77	0·50	0·37	0·82	0·63

Overall age-specialisation

A crude index of the degree of age-specialisation is obtained by the summation of the scores of the eight relevant scales (Table 93). High degrees of age-specialisation are associated with comprehensive and grammar schools.

TABLE 93   *Degree of age-specialisation – mean scores*

	Boys SM	Girls SM	Mixed SM	All SM	All CS	Boys GS	Girls GS	Mixed GS	All GS
n	7	6	24	37	17	6	6	6	18
mean	9·01	9·84	8·08	8·31	14·00	11·84	15·33	13·34	13·49

Correlations between forms of age-specialisation

Table 94 shows eight zero-order correlations between pairs of scale variables which are statistically significant. These correlations imply that when schools differentiate the pupils' behaviour by age, they

132

use more than one method of organisation, but tend to use only one method for the age differentiation of school work. (There were no significant correlations between the instrumental scales.) The use of privileges may be used to tie together the instrumental and expressive age differences. The age-specialisation of behaviour and school work are rewarded together.

TABLE 94   *Correlations between age-specialisation scales (N = 72)*

	r	Sig. %
Expressive activities/formalisation of expressive activities	0·24	5
Expressive activities/privileges	0·42	1
Expressive performance/formalisation of expressive activities	0·33	1
Expressive performance/privileges	0·25	5
Expressive performance/formalisation of instrumental activities	0·28	5
Formalisation of expressive activities/privileges	0·35	1
Privileges/instrumental performance	0·24	5
Privileges/formalisation of instrumental activities	0·25	5

Age differences in involvement related to age-specialisation

Previous chapters have reported differences in the mean scores on a number of involvement scales for pupils of different ages. In this chapter a number of scales to measure the degree of age-specialisation of the structure of schools have been shown to be related to the age composition of schools. It is possible that a relationship may exist between age differences in the involvement of pupils and the degree and type of age-specialisation of the organisation of the school they attend.

All the tau correlations between the difference in mean involvement scores on all relevant scales for pupils in different pairs of age-groups, e.g. second and fourth, matched and unmatched for sex and social class, with the scores on the eight relevant scales, were of no statistical significance.

This does not necessarily mean that the organisational structure of the school is not an influence in producing the differences in involvement shown by pupils of different ages, but it is clear that the structure does not determine those differences.

Age-specialisation in schools

The results presented in this chapter indicate that all schools are conspicuously age-stratified. Only rarely, as in the use of family

133

grouping in primary schools, are teaching groups heterogeneous for age. Most societies are also age-stratified. In modern British society age differences are embodied in the law, including the law of education. At the cultural level age is given a great deal of meaning, because, in addition to occupation and sex, it gives an important clue to a person's manner and life-style. (See Abrams (1971).)

Eisenstadt (1956) has suggested that age-grades arise from the basic socialisation relationship of child to adult: 'The function of differentiated age-definitions is to enable the individual to learn and acquire new roles . . .' Compliance with authority, co-operation with status equals, and the ultimate assumption of authority are all assisted by the age-differentiation of roles. Age-differentiation is a feature of what Eisenstadt calls universalistic achievement societies. As it is these societies, such as our own, that tend to provide mass education, it is not surprising that the schools incorporate the principle of age-differentiation in their organisational processes. Here the basic adult–child socialisation relationship is transformed into the teacher–pupil relationship. It is the existence of the teacher as a specialised representative of the adult world that distinguishes education from other socialisation processes, and schools from other organisations.

There are many ways in which age is given organisational meaning within the school, as this chapter has shown. One of the principal ideologies in modern education is that of development; what Bernstein and Davis (1969) call the horticultural view of the child, and Goslin (1965), the farming view. Although most common in primary schools it existed, explicitly and implicitly, in the secondary schools studied here. 'We aim to provide each pupil with an education suited to his age, aptitude and ability.' This paraphrase of the 1944 Education Act was very common in the documents. The ideology of development views the age-specialisation of the school as primarily associated with the adaptation of the presumed psychological, and to some extent physiological, learning potential of the child, to the various skills, knowledge and behaviours considered important.

Age-differentiation of specialisation, both in societies and schools tends to stratification. Most schools are conspicuously age-stratified in that older pupils are given more honorific status than the younger ones. However, the pupil-role is a self-extinguishing one and in most systems the acquisition of higher status is automatic. This research confirms two uses of this age-stratification suggested by my previous research (1969a): the use of older pupils as role-models, and allowing them to enter the formal social control processes of the school as prefects (see Chapter 10). It may also retain the involvement of younger pupils who may look forward to the higher status, with its attendant privileges and power, possibly inducing them to stay beyond the age of compulsory attendance.

The age-typing of the pupil-role is a reflection of the age-typing of roles in society. Unlike his ability-identity, a pupil's age-identity is not basically created by the school, but by society. The school mainly confirms, perhaps slightly modifies, cultural age definitions. This may explain why there were no important relationships between the age-specialisation of the organisation of schools, and age differences in involvement. Both age-specialisation and age differences in school involvement arise largely from the general cultural context, and their likely relationship is illustrated in the paradigm shown in Figure 2.

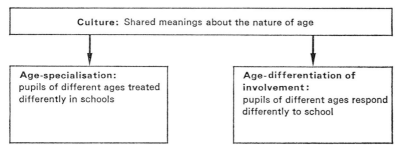

FIGURE 2

10   Authority relationships

Four important sets of authority relationships are explored in this chapter. Those between headteacher and pupils, teachers and pupils, prefects and other pupils, and those associated with school councils.

The headteacher

It was not intended to study the role and status of the headteacher in a detailed way. Our interest was confined to the organisational position of the headteacher as it was visible to the pupils, and thus virtually excludes headteacher–teacher relationships.

The organisation and presentation of the headteacher confirms his or her position as the holder of most formal authority. The ritualisation of the headteacher in the school assembly has already been mentioned in Chapter 4, and a five-item scale for its measurement is given in Table 95.

TABLE 95   *Ritualisation of the headteacher's role scale*

Item	f
Pupils stand especially for entry into assembly	15
Teachers stand especially for entry into assembly	20
Headteacher wears gown in assembly	33
Headteacher leaves assembly separately	58
Headteacher enters assembly separately	60

Mean item analysis value = 0·866; mean score = 2·58 (N = 72; S.D. = 1·35).

The mean scores for different kinds of school (Table 21, Chapter 4) indicate higher degrees of ritualisation in grammar schools, especially single-sex ones, compared with other schools, although girls' modern schools do have a high mean score.

The correlation between scale score and mean IQ of pupils is 0·28, indicating that the more intelligent pupils encounter a ritualised presentation of authority more often than the less intelligent.

The ease of access to the headteacher has already been mentioned in the discussion of pastoral care (Chapter 5). The headteacher was usually the only member of staff to whom pupils could not go directly, partly because he was sometimes the only one with an exclusive room. This was usually known as the headteacher's room, but also as his study or office. The term study was common in grammar schools, especially those for boys (67 per cent of cases), but rare in non-selective schools. This may indicate the projection of an image of the headteacher as an academic figure. The term office was confined almost entirely to modern schools. The more bureaucratic connotation of this term might have lead to supposing it to be most common in the large comprehensives where headteachers are supposed to have more managerial functions. However, the doors of headteachers' rooms in comprehensives did bear the title 'headteacher' less often than in either modern or grammar schools. Perhaps the greater remoteness of the headteacher in the large comprehensives is indicated in the higher frequency with which they had their names on the door. Only four headteachers had their academic qualifications on the door; all had them on their letter headings.

All the pupils' non-ritualised encounters with the headteacher confirm his authority. He was the one most likely to cane them. In a third of schools he had a part in offering careers advice. (See King and Easthope (1971).) If there was a school council he was usually a member of it. He convened House meetings in a third of schools, controlled the content of assembly in three quarters of them. He was the major selector of the prefects, and the source of testimonials.

Teachers

It was not our intention to make a general study of the role or status of the teachers in the sampled schools. Our interest was confined to the part teachers played in the organised processes of the school which were visible to the pupils. Thus, teacher–teacher, and teacher–headteacher relationships were virtually excluded.

Teachers in the organisation of the school

Much of the interaction between teachers and pupils is non-organisational. The teacher's authority over the pupils is derived more from his professional status than from his status as an employee in a particular school. Much of what he does is 'up to the individual teacher' and not 'up to the school'.

Teachers in British schools are professionals working in an organisational setting; the analogy to doctors in hospitals is reasonably apposite. However, the organisation of the school does limit the teachers' autonomy, and the use of staff handbooks, syllabuses and curricula may be examples of this. Since teachers are the major judges of pupils' behaviour and work-performance, the standardisation of these procedures controls not only the pupils but also, to some extent, the teachers. If the school rule is that pupils must walk down the left-hand side of the corridor, the expectation is that the teachers will see that this rule is obeyed.

Similarly the formalisation of pupils' activities also controls the teachers. It is they who fill in the reports and write most of the notices. Homework diaries may function not only to ensure that pupils do their homework, but also to ensure that teachers set it.

Teachers are also organisationally specialised. The commonest basis is by subject taught; this is instrumental specialisation. Expressive specialisation takes the form of tutors and House-staff. To a more limited extent teachers may be specialised by the characteristics of the pupils they teach. The PE staff are usually sex-specialised. Heads of department in some schools take only senior classes; they are age-specialised. Remedial teachers are an example of ability-specialisation.

Pupil age, sex and ability-status may also form the basis of what Bernstein (1966b) calls the *personalised control* of pupils by teachers. Unlike the use of bureaucracy or ritual, personalised control is non-organisational in that it is generated by the individual teacher, but the following authentic examples show that some of the principles behind all the three forms of control are similar.

(a) *Age reference control* Teacher to fifth-year pupils showing interest in the arrival of an observer: 'Alright now. Stop behaving like a set of silly first years. Get on with your work.'

(b) *Sex reference control* Teacher doing question-and-answer work with a mixed class: 'Come on boys, don't let the girls do all the work.'

(c) *Ability-status reference control* Teacher to class not responding correctly to his questions: 'What's the matter with you today? I thought this was 2A not 2D.'

It would be wrong to assume that the organisation of the school always reduces the teachers' autonomy; it may also preserve and even create it. The timetable may do so. Although it constrains a teacher to teach a certain subject to a certain set of pupils, in a certain place, at a certain time for a certain length of time, it may also

138

create the conditions that allow the exercise of his professional autonomy in choosing the content of the lesson, and the methods of teaching and social control. Specialisation, too, may create more and not less autonomy for teachers. The contrast between the high degree of control that the primary-school headteacher may have over the curriculum taught by a staff of largely non-specialists, and the much lower level of curriculum control exercised by the secondary-school headteacher over his staff of specialists, illustrates the point.

Teachers and pupils

It is in the areas outside the classroom that pupil–teacher relation-ships tend to become most organised. Eighteen per cent of schools had special entrances to the school grounds for teachers. In six per cent of school they had exclusive access to a part of the school grounds. Thirty-nine per cent of schools had entry doors for the exclusive use of teachers. Thirty-five per cent had exclusive corridors or stairs. Teachers in many schools had special tables at lunch (lunch for teachers, dinner for pupils). In three-quarters of the schools the teachers had a separate dining area, and often a different style of dining to that of the pupils; cafeteria style was rare. The extent of this pupil–teacher differentiation is measured by a four-item scale, Table 96.

TABLE 96   *Pupil–teacher differentiation scale*

Item	f
Teachers have special corridors or stairs	25
Teachers have different dining style	27
Teachers have special dining area	54
Teachers have special dining tables	64

Mean item analysis value 0·928; mean score 2·36 (N = 72; S.D. = 1·10).

Table 97 shows that the extent of this differentiation was highest in grammar schools and lowest in modern schools. The low compre-hensive score is partly reflected in the correlation of the scale scores with school size, which is −0·29. The extent of these differences was greatest when the pupils were most like the teachers. The correlation with mean IQ is 0·26, with the percentage of manual-workers' children −0·14, with the percentage of first-year pupils 0·23, with seventh-year pupils −0·26. It is the older, cleverer, middle-class pupils who are most differentiated from their teachers in this way.

139

TABLE 97   *Pupil–teacher differentiation scale – mean scores*

	Boys SM	Girls SM	Mixed SM	All SM	All CS	Boys GS	Girls GS	Mixed GS	All GS
n	7	6	24	37	17	6	6	6	18
mean	2·14	2·17	2·62	2·46	1·65	2·83	2·67	3·00	2·83
S.D.	1·12	1·07	1·03	1·08	1·13	0·90	0·47	0·58	0·69

The staffroom (the usual term in non-selective schools) or common room (the grammar school term) varied in its permeability to pupils. In three schools the pupils were not even allowed to knock on the door, more commonly they were forbidden to knock at certain times, usually during the dinner/lunch hour. In some schools they could knock in emergencies only, but in over a half they could do so at any time. In 40 per cent of the schools the pupils were never allowed in the common room, but in half they could go in to do duties such as clearing away and washing up cups. In about a third of schools pupils could be invited into such rooms. A few schools allowed pupils to walk in after knocking. Only one allowed them in without knocking.

Mixed schools had the most impermeable staffrooms. This may have been due to the teachers' wish to avoid being seen by their pupils as men and women. Many mixed schools have strong taboos on the public demonstration of even the mildest non-professional relationship between teachers of different sexes. Teachers themselves often feel vulnerable about these things, and there are authentic cases of couples being secretly engaged without anyone, either staff or pupils, suspecting even a friendship. Keeping the staffroom door firmly closed to pupils avoids their accidental witnessing of the banter that characterises the informal relationships between teachers, as men and women.

The ritualisation of teachers in the school assembly was mentioned in Chapter 4. The three-item scale for its measurement is given in Table 98.

TABLE 98   *Ritualisation of teachers scale*

Item	*f*
Teachers on platform in assembly	21
Teachers sit whilst pupils stand in assembly	22
Teachers process out of assembly	31

Mean item analysis value 0·901; mean score = 1·03 (N = 72; S.D. = 1·07).

Table 21, Chapter 4, shows that the mean score for grammar schools is higher than for non-selective schools. That for boys' grammar schools is the highest, but the girls' modern schools' score is also high.

The level of this ritualisation is related to the ability of the pupils. The correlation between the scale score and mean IQ is 0·25. As may be expected, the higher the percentage of working-class pupils the lower the degree of ritualisation tends to be. The correlation is −0·32. The level of ritualisation is also higher when there are more older pupils in the school; the correlation with the percentage of first-year pupils is −0·32, with seventh-year 0·22. Thus the pupil–teacher ritualisation tends to be highest when the teachers and pupils share most characteristics, in terms of ability, age and social class.

The degree of this ritualisation is positively correlated with the degree of which non-ritualised differences are made between teachers and pupils. The correlation with the scale for pupil–teacher differentiation is 0·26. Ritualisation of the headteacher role also correlated significantly with that for teachers, 0·35.

The prefectorial system

Prefects may be defined as pupils who have formal authority over other pupils. Four schools in the sample claimed not to have prefects. They had been abolished either because they were considered undemocratic, or because it was considered unfair to give a few pupils the privilege of being a prefect. These schools did, however, have pupils who had formal authority over other pupils. Usually a whole year-group, the fifth year in a modern school or the seventh year in a grammar school, had some control over all younger pupils. In effect these schools had only removed the title of prefect, and this was confirmed during the visits to the schools when the pupil guides confirmed that the older pupils thought of themselves as prefects, and younger pupils referred to them as prefects. This is a good illustration of the conservatism of pupils. The free responses in the questionnaire often included criticisms of any kind of organisational change. In one school the prospect of the abolition of the prefectorial system provided many adverse comments from existing and aspiring potential prefects.

The selection of prefects

Age was the most important criterion for prefect eligibility. It was usually the oldest age-group or groups in the school that formed the selection group, although in a few modern schools the fourth year were made prefects rather than the fifth in order to allow the latter,

who had been prefects, to concentrate on examination preparation.
In some schools, particularly girls' schools, all the pupils in a
given age-group were ascribed as prefects. In most schools, however,
there was a finer selection procedure. It was difficult to get a precise
description of the mechanism of selection in most schools; who may
propose candidates, whose opinion is sought, who decides, and so
on. What is clear is that the headteacher is always involved, and the
teachers nearly always. In a fifth of schools the outgoing or existing
prefects were involved in selecting the new ones. In only four schools
did younger pupils play any part in the process.

The number of prefects created depended on the size of the school;
the correlation was 0·45. The proportion of prefects created could be
calculated in terms of all the pupils in the school or the selection
group of eligible pupils. Table 99 gives both of these indices of
prefectorial éliteness.

TABLE 99   *Percentage of pupils made prefects*

	Boys SM	Girls SM	Mixed SM	All SM	All CS	Boys GS	Girls GS	Mixed GS	All GS
n	7	6	24	37	17	6	6	6	18
of those eligible:	30·1	64·0	48·6	47· 6	45·1	50·0	70·4	35·2	53·0
of whole school:	5·1	6·2	8·7	7·7	4·7	7·8	7·9	5·0	7·0

When éliteness is measured by the percentage of eligible pupils
made prefects, boys' modern schools and mixed grammar schools
had the more élite system, whereas girls' schools, both modern and
grammar, show the least élite systems. These trends are reflected in
the measurement for the proportion of prefects in the whole school,
except for the comprehensives which tend to have comparatively
small sixth forms as the selection group. This is reflected in the
correlation between school size and this measure of prefectorial
éliteness, which is −0·29.

Prefectorial duties

The prefects' basic duty was to act as a general agent of social
control in the school. In addition they acted as guides to visitors,
were stewards at school functions, supervised other pupils on their
way to assembly and their entry into assembly, read the lesson in
assembly, supervised other pupils on the school buses and, more
rarely, in detentions. Sometimes they rang the bell or buzzer for the

change of period. The extent of these duties was measured using a five-item scale (Table 100).

TABLE 100 *Prefectorial duties scale*

Item	f
Ring bell or buzzer	9
Supervise entry into assembly	12
Read lesson in assembly	20
Steward at functions	51
Guides to visitors	56

Mean item analysis value 0·860; mean score = 2·06 (N = 72; S.D. = 1·22).

The mean scores on the scale (Table 101) show that grammar-school prefects usually had more duties than those in other schools, especially in boys' grammar schools, although the average duty expectation was also high in girls' modern schools.

TABLE 101 *Prefectorial duties scale – mean scores*

	Boys SM	Girls SM	Mixed SM	All SM	All CS	Boys GS	Girls GS	Mixed GS	All GS
n	7	6	24	37	17	6	6	6	18
mean	1·29	2·50	1·75	1·78	1·82	3·50	2·83	2·17	2·83
S.D.	0·70	0·50	0·92	0·90	1·15	0·96	1·46	1·67	1·50

In general the more able the pupils in a school the more duties the prefects perform. The correlation between scale score and mean IQ is 0·43. The number of duties is also related to the age composition of the school. The correlation between scale score and the percentage of first- and seventh-year pupils is −0·39 and 0·37 respectively, indirectly indicating that older prefects are given more duties than younger ones.

The control of prefectorial duties, what was to be done, when and by whom, was in the hands of the headteachers in 18 per cent of schools. This was most common in boys' schools (29 per cent) but never occurred in girls' schools. The deputy head or a senior teacher had control in 38 per cent of schools. When the prefectorial system was linked to the House system, the head of House usually controlled the system. In half of the schools the senior prefect or prefects were in control. This was common in the grammar schools (78 per cent), less common in comprehensive and modern schools (53 per cent and 35 per cent respectively).

143

Prefects' sanctions

The most common of pupil punishments given by prefects was the writing of lines. This occurred in 35 per cent of schools, and was most common in grammar schools. The power to give detentions was available to prefects in 29 per cent of schools. This too was much more common in grammar schools with a 61 per cent incidence, compared with 19 per cent in non-selective schools. In only one school were they allowed to give or take away merit marks for the assessment of other pupils' behaviour.

The other sanctions available to prefects consisted of being able to refer a pupil to a member of staff. This was usually the headteacher, but it also often included the deputy head, or duty teacher. House teachers and tutors were also involved in some schools.

Prefects' privileges

A few schools did make distinctions between prefects and their age mates with regard to cloakrooms and dinner arrangements. The most common was that they were exempt the dinner queue, or were first in the queue. They were sometimes allowed to enter school early without waiting in the playground, sometimes through a special entrance. They occasionally had exclusive pupil access to certain stairs or corridors within the school. In two schools they had their own exclusive entrance to the playground and reserved area of the school grounds. In some schools they were the only pupils of their age allowed to remain in the formroom during the break or lunch hour, and the only ones to be allowed to leave the school in the lunch hour. The most prized privilege, an exclusive prefects' room, occurred in 15 per cent of schools, most commonly in grammar schools with a 28 per cent incidence, compared with 11 per cent in non-selective schools.

The extent of these privileges is measured in the scale shown in Table 102.

TABLE 102 *Prefects' privileges scale*

Item	*f*
Only prefects:	
Allowed in formroom at break	7
Allowed in formroom at dinner time	7
Enter school before bell	11
Exempt dinner queue	17

Mean item analysis value 0·901; mean score = 0·58 (N = 72; S.D. = 1·01).

The mean scores on the scale (Table 103) show large variations by type of school, the highest scores being for boys' modern schools, the lowest for girls' grammar schools.

TABLE 103   *Prefects' privileges scale – mean scores*

	Boys SM	Girls SM	Mixed SM	All SM	All CS	Boys GS	Girls GS	Mixed GS	All GS
n	7	6	24	37	17	6	6	6	18
mean	1·57	0·17	0·83	0·86	0·18	0·83	0·00	0·33	0·39
S.D.	1·29	0·37	1·21	1·21	0·38	1·07	0·00	0·47	0·76

Formalisation of the prefectorial system

The use of paper in connection with the prefectorial system was fairly common. A list of prefects appeared on a notice board in 58 per cent of schools, it appeared in the school magazines in 15 per cent of schools, and in the speech-day programme of two schools. A prefects' duty list was prepared in most schools and they sometimes had a special section of the school rules devoted to them.

The five-item scale for the measurement of this formalisation of the system is given in Table 104.

TABLE 104   *Formalisation of prefectorial system scale*

Item	f
Section on prefects in school rules	9
List of prefects in school magazine	11
Prefects have own notice board	25
List of prefects displayed on a notice board	42
Prefects' duty list drawn up	61

Mean item analysis value 0·825; mean score = 2·06 (N = 72; S.D. = 1·19).

Table 105 gives the mean scores for different types of school, and shows low mean scores for comprehensive schools and girls' schools.

TABLE 105   *Formalisation of prefectorial system scale – mean scores*

	Boys SM	Girls SM	Mixed SM	All SM	All CS	Boys GS	Girls GS	Mixed GS	All GS
n	7	6	24	37	17	6	6	6	18
mean	2·29	1·83	2·21	2·16	1·76	2·83	1·67	1·83	2·11
S.D.	1.48	0·69	1·12	1·15	1·21	1·46	0·75	0·90	1·20

The extent of prefects' privileges is positively and significantly correlated with their formalisation ($r = 0.34$).

Ritualisation of the prefectorial system

The office of prefect was often marked by emblems, commonly badges or ties, the latter being most common in grammar schools. Special sashes or girdles were sometimes awarded in girls' schools. The short scale for this form of ritualisation is shown in Table 106.

TABLE 106   *Emblemic ritualisation of prefectorial system scale*

Item	f
Prefects have special ties	15
Prefects have special badges	54

Mean item analysis value 1.00; mean score 0.96 ($N = 72$; S.D. $= 0.48$).

The mean scale scores (Table 107) show low emblemic usage in comprehensive schools and girls' grammar schools. The low score for comprehensives probably accounts for the negative correlation between school size and ritualisation ($r = -0.32$).

TABLE 107   *Emblemic ritualisation of prefectorial system scale – mean scores*

	Boys SM	Girls SM	Mixed SM	All SM	All CS	Boys GS	Girls GS	Mixed GS	All GS
n	7	6	24	37	17	6	6	6	18
mean	1.00	1.17	0.94	1.03	0.82	1.17	0.67	1.00	0.94
S.D.	0.00	0.69	0.62	0.93	0.38	0.69	0.47	0.58	0.62

The ritualisation of the prefectorial system in the ceremonials of assembly were mentioned in Chapter 4. Table 108 gives the short scale for its measurement.

TABLE 108   *Ceremonial ritualisation of prefectorial system scale*

Item	f
Prefects' duty to participate in assembly	14
Prefects have special positions in assembly	32

Mean item analysis value 1.00; mean score 0.64 ($N = 72$; S.D. $= 0.67$).

Table 21, Chapter 4, shows that high scores are associated with boys' and mixed grammar schools.

The extent of this ceremonial ritual is positively correlated with the extent of the prefects' duties (r = 0·29).

A third kind of ritualisation of the prefectorial system is also a ceremonial, that of induction. Sixty-five per cent of schools held such a ceremony, usually during a school assembly, and in four schools it was the focus of a special assembly. In most cases the passing of the headteacher's authority to the prefects was symbolised by their shaking hands, and by the presentation of the symbols of office (tie or badge). In a small number of schools the prefects swore an oath of allegiance to the school, and in two schools they signed a special prefects' book.

Table 109 gives the five-point scale for the measurement of the extent of this ceremonial.

TABLE 109   *Prefects' induction ceremony scale*

Item	f
Ceremony incidence	47
Ceremony in normal assembly	41
Headteacher shakes hands with prefects	41
Headteacher gives prefects symbols of office	41
Prefects take oath of allegiance	7

Mean item analysis value 0·939; mean score = 2·46 (N = 72; S.D. = 1·87).

Table 110 shows that high scores are associated with modern and comprehensive schools rather than grammar schools.

TABLE 110   *Prefects' induction ceremony scale – mean scores*

	Boys SM	Girls SM	Mixed SM	All SM	All CS	Boys GS	Girls GS	Mixed GS	All GS
n	7	6	24	37	17	6	6	6	18
mean	2·71	2·83	2·54	2·62	2·71	1·83	2·00	1·83	1·89
S.D.	0.70	0.50	0·92	0·90	1·15	0·96	1·46	1·67	1·50

The extent of this ritualisation was positively and significantly correlated with the extent of the use of prefects' emblems (r = 0·29) and with the degree of formalisation of the system (r = 0·28).

The head-prefect

Eighty-eight per cent of schools had a senior pupil with the title of head-prefect or school-captain. This position existed in every grammar school, and was least common in mixed non-selective schools. In

147

mixed schools there were usually two such positions, one for each sex.

The head-prefect position was often ritualised. The most common emblem of the office was a special badge. A special tie existed in four schools. In some cases there was a special induction ceremony, distinct from that for other prefects. The extent of this ritualisation was measured by a two-item scale (Table 111).

TABLE 111   *Ritualisation of head-prefect scale*

Item	f
Special induction ceremony	28
Special symbol of office	44

Mean item analysis value 1·00; mean score 1·00 (N = 72; S.D. = 0·80).

The mean scores on the scale show high degrees of ritualisation particularly associated with girls' schools (Table 112).

TABLE 112   *Ritualisation of head-prefect scale – mean scores*

	Boys SM	Girls SM	Mixed SM	All SM	All CS	Boys GS	Girls GS	Mixed GS	All GS
n	7	6	24	37	17	6	6	6	18
mean	1·00	1·67	0·67	0·89	1·18	0·50	1·50	1·17	1·06
S.D.	0·76	0·47	0·62	0·73	0·92	0·50	0·76	0·69	0·78

The most common duty of the head-prefect was to organise the other prefects. They were also commonly expected to make public speeches in welcoming guests, and in representing the school at the former pupils' association meetings, and to read the lesson in assembly on special occasions, especially the end and/or beginning of the school year and terms. In four grammar schools and one comprehensive the head-prefect had effective charge of the pupils entering and leaving the school assembly.

The extent of the head-prefects' duties was measured with a three-item scale shown in Table 113.

TABLE 113   *Extent of head-prefects' duties scale*

Item	f
Read lesson on special occasions	16
Make public speeches	42
Organise other prefects	55

Mean item analysis value 0·956; mean score 1·57 (N = 72; S.D. = 0·98).

The mean scores on the scale (Table 114) indicate extensive duties associated with grammar schools, and among the non-selective schools, boys' modern schools.

TABLE 114 *Extent of head-prefects' duties scale – mean scores*

	Boys SM	Girls SM	Mixed SM	All SM	All CS	Boys GS	Girls GS	Mixed GS	All GS
n	7	6	24	37	17	6	6	6	18
mean	2·00	1·83	1·00	1·32	1·29	2·50	2·17	2·33	2·33
S.D.	0·93	0·69	0·82	0·93	0·89	0·76	0·69	0·75	0·75

As may be expected the extent of these duties correlates positively with the mean IQ of the school, 0·49, and negatively with the percentage of manual-workers' children, $-0·47$. The extent of the duties was also related to age composition; the more older pupils there are the more duties occurred. The correlation between scale score and per cent of first-year pupils was $-0·45$, for per cent of seventh-year pupils, 0·44.

The correlation between the extent of duties and the ritualisation of the prefectorial system by ceremonials is 0·30. The more duties prefects had, the more duties the head-prefect had; the correlation is 0·40. The extent of the head-prefect's duties also correlated significantly and positively with the extent of prefects' privileges, 0·25.

The degree of ritualisation of the head-prefect also positively correlated with the number of head-prefect duties ($r = 0·25$), the formalisation of the prefectorial system ($r = 0·23$), the ritualisation of teachers ($r = 0·23$), and the ritualisation of the headteacher ($r = 0·27$).

Sixty-eight per cent of schools also designated a vice-captain or deputy head-prefect.

The purposes of the prefectorial system

I have previously suggested that prefects have two major purposes (King, 1969a), to be agents of social control and to act as role-models. These suggestions are confirmed by the comments of head-teachers on the purpose and importance of the prefectorial system and the structural analysis already presented.

The prefect as role-model was mentioned the most often by head-teachers, and was expressed in phrases such as 'act as an example to younger pupils', 'set a standard', 'set the tone of the school'. These sentiments were expressed most strongly in modern schools, and are possibly a reflection of concern about pupil behaviour.

149

The use of prefects as agents of social control was explicitly stated in the commonly used phrase, 'help maintain order'. This was more commonly expressed in grammar schools, and the wide range of prefects' duties in these schools reflects this. Modern-school head-teachers often pointed out that the age difference between their prefects (fifteen- to sixteen-year-olds) and the most troublesome pupils (thirteen- to fifteen-year-olds) was too narrow for the prefects to be very effective in dealing with them.

In some schools prefects were viewed as agents of pastoral care in helping younger pupils and acting as a liaison between other pupils and staff. This was a common view in comprehensive schools and may reflect their general concern about pastoral care.

Some headteachers held clear images of the prefects' special qualities. The composite picture is of the prefect acting in an adult manner with tact, politeness, tolerance, common sense and humanity. Prefects were chosen because they were thought to have these qualities, or have them in potential, and the indices of their existence were good behaviour, good performance in school work and games. Only a few headteachers thought that being a prefect fostered desired character traits.

The extent of prefects' privileges and their ritualisation indicates that being made a prefect was often a reward for good performance in the pupil-role, in both its instrumental and expressive aspects. Being a prefect also has an implied advantage in getting a place in higher education or a job, as applicants and headteachers are often asked about the holding of the office.

School councils

Katz and Kahn (1966) define the democratisation of organisations by the extent to which all members share in the decision-making processes. The school council is sometimes seen as a democratic institution. Thirty-nine per cent of schools in the sample had a school or pupil council of some kind. Many headteachers claimed to have had one, but that it had lapsed. Others had plans to create one. This evidence suggests that these councils are gaining social acceptance in secondary schools, but they tend to be rather ephemeral. They were found more often in comprehensive schools (59 per cent) compared with grammar (33 per cent) and modern schools (32 per cent).

Structural aspects of school councils

The councils met an average of 3·5 times a term, but there was wide variation between types of school. Comprehensives, although most likely to have a council, usually had meetings only once or twice a year (the average is 0·47 a term). Modern schools met two or three times a term (mean 2·46), and grammar-school councils met most frequently with a mean of 3·3 times a term.

Only a third of councils had a written constitution or an agenda for meetings, but most kept minutes of meetings. Table 115 indicates that grammar-school councils were the least formalised, an interesting reversal of the general trend for formalisation to be highest in such schools. Not a single grammar-school council had a written constitution.

The degree of formalisation of the council was related to the number of officers serving it. Fewer grammar-school councils had a chairman and secretary than those in non-selective schools.

The chairman was just as likely to be a pupil as a teacher. When it was a pupil it was almost always the head-prefect. A staff chairman was commonly the headteacher or one of the senior staff. Only one council elected its chairman.

In most cases the secretary was a pupil. A pupil secretary was most common in modern schools, but half the secretaries in comprehensives were teachers. The secretary was usually elected in modern schools, appointed in the comprehensives.

The incidence and extent of the use of elections and voting form two related indices of democratisation. The election of council officers has already been mentioned. Some of the other members of the council (but never all of them) were elected in most schools. These were usually pupils' representatives. The representatives covered all the age-groups in less than half the councils; it was always the younger pupils who were under-represented. The grammar school councils received the broadest range of representatives by age.

Voting was allowed in most councils, but was least common in grammar schools (Table 115). In almost all schools the headteacher could use the veto whether or not he was a council member.

Headteachers, senior staff or other teachers were *ex-officio* members of about half the councils. Every council received at least one *ex-officio* staff member. The extent of this kind of membership was highest in grammar schools, lowest in comprehensives. All prefects were *ex-officio* members in about a fifth of councils. In a further quarter they had representatives only. Both kinds of representation of perfects were higher in modern schools. The head-prefect was an *ex-officio* member of about half the councils. This was most common in grammar schools, least common in the comprehensives.

TABLE 115   *Structural features of school councils (percentage incidence)*

	Modern ($n=12$)	Compre-hensive ($n=10$)	Grammar ($n=6$)	All ($n=28$)
Formalisation				
Agenda	25	60	17	36
Minutes	75	70	17	61
Written constitution	33	40	0	29
Officers				
Chairman	92	100	33	82
Secretary	58	90	17	61
Democratisation				
Some members elected	75	70	83	71
All ages represented	42	40	83	43
Voting allowed	67	70	50	64
Head holds veto	75	90	100	86
Ex-officio members				
Headteacher	42	50	50	46
Senior staff	58	30	83	46
Other teachers	67	30	83	54
All prefects	33	10	17	21
Prefects' representatives	42	10	17	25
Head-prefect	58	30	83	54
Matters discussed				
School rules	75	90	67	82
Uniform	75	90	67	82
Assembly	50	70	50	57
Future policy	42	30	33	36
Cases of misbehaviour	50	20	17	32
Syllabus	9	50	33	29

Matters discussed at council meetings

School rules and uniform were the most common matters discussed in school councils. The school assembly was discussed in half the councils, the syllabus, future policy and cases of misbehaviour in about a third of councils. Unfortunately school dinners were omitted from the precoded responses to the interview question, 'What things are most frequently discussed?' The number of free responses referring to it indicates that it was probably quite important; indeed one council seemed to be almost entirely devoted to it.

We were unable to obtain accurate information to distinguish between what was discussed and what was decided at council meetings. This distinction was further clouded by the use of the meetings to pass on information, which may have been about previous discussions or which gave rise to discussion. The impression gained was that most things could be discussed except individual teachers, that the things actually discussed were usually limited in range within a given council (one functioned entirely to arrange dances), that the number of decisions made was limited, and related mainly to the school uniform. Recommendations made by the council about other matters were sometimes embodied in decisions made by other bodies or persons within the school.

The use of school councils

This largely structural analysis of a small number of school councils does not permit a thorough discussion of their activities. This would require periods of observation in meetings, and an analysis of their activities over a period of time.

The major value of the councils in the headteachers' opinion, is for the passing of information. Related to this is the opinion expressed by some headteachers, particularly in comprehensive schools, that it enables pupils to suggest valuable ideas about the running of the school. (Compare with the study by Chapman (1971).)

Another common suggestion was that the council allowed pupils to bring their discontents into the open, so preventing the growth of ill-feeling. This suggestion must be qualified in two respects. The free responses in the pupils' questionnaire were often complaints about particular teachers; such complaints were seldom if ever discussed in council meetings. A second qualification is that where the discussion of grievances is not linked to the power to decide what to do about them, then the situation may be made worse. Discussion without decision is as likely to be exacerbating as either ameliorative or cathartic. This may explain the short lives of some councils.

Consensual purposes of the council were implied when headteachers said that its value was to make the pupils feel involved in the school, and help the process of 'living together'. The relatively high incidence of school councils and of those sentiments in comprehensive schools is another indication of their concern about the creation of a feeling of community in a large school.

The suggested benefit of the school council for pupils is that it gives them responsibility and experience in helping to run the school, and an introduction to the methods of democracy. Clearly the low level of democratisation of some councils (no election of officers or representative, no voting powers, and a veto) operates against this being fulfilled.

153

Pupils and power

Pugh *et al.* (1963) use the term *centralisation* to describe the distribution of legitimate authority in an organisation. Although this study has not included the relationships between teachers it is clear that in most British schools power is highly centralised.

The headteacher's formal authority, in Peabody's (1962) usage, authority inherent in office, is extensive as he is legally responsible for the curriculum, organisation and discipline of the school. (See King (1968).) This legal basis is likely to constrain most headteachers in allocating power to others, and the amount he is likely to allocate to those he is legally responsible for, his pupils, is small. As the study of prefects shows, their powers are usually not much more than tokens. In addition, the professional authority of teachers limits the pupils having much direct power over the detailed curriculum and pedagogy.

Attempts to democratise schools seem to be limited exercises. School councils do not present many opportunities for pupils to play democratic roles, although they may allow pupils to play at such roles. This may explain why the school council was least common in grammar schools, and when it did occur, was usually the least democratic in its form. Older, more intelligent pupils, are the most likely to perceive the difference between discussion and decision, between consultation and power.

It has already been suggested in the discussion of the school assembly that the conception of authority transmitted by schools tends to be strongly hierarchical and implicitly eternal. This rather draconian analysis can be put into perspective by remembering Waller's (1932) observation, that the teacher's exercise of power rests ultimately with the consent or legitimacy of their pupils. The measurements of pupil involvement made in this study show that in terms of their evaluative and affective dispositions most pupils do legitimate most of the processes of the schools they go to. However, most teachers recognise that the control of their pupils is partly an exercise in bluff. Every classroom in every school could be empty if the pupils so decided. It could be a feeling of this kind of power that helps them to accept that of the school over them.

11 Sex-specialisation

This chapter is mainly concerned with the ways in which the organisation of mixed school differs for boys and girls. Some of these sex-differentiations have been mentioned already in the chapters dealing with uniform, school assembly, games and extra-curricular activities.

Sex-specialisation of the expressive order

It has already been suggested that different cultural expectations of behaviour exist for boys and girls. In the mixed school this is reflected in the sex-specialisation of expressive activities and in its ritualisation.

Sex-specialisation of expressive activities

Throughout the length of the school day boy and girl pupils were organisationally separated, their activities were sex-specialised.

When they travelled by school bus or coach in many cases they had separate seating. In 14 per cent of schools they parked their bicycles separately, and in a quarter of cases entered the playground by separate entrances. Fifty-seven per cent of mixed schools had separate play areas for boys and girls. About half had separate entry doors for the sexes, and about a fifth had sex-exclusive stairs or corridors. Separate cloakrooms were common, particularly in grammar schools. Separate dinner sittings were less common, although the queues for dinner were usually separated, and girls and boys sometimes sat at separate tables.

Prefects usually only dealt with pupils of their own sex in a quarter of schools, but this did not occur in the grammar schools.

The extent of this sex-specialisation of expressive activities is measured by a six-item scale (Table 116).

155

TABLE 116 *Sex-specialisation of expressive activities scale*

Item	f
Sexes have separate:	
Dinner sittings	5
Corridors or stairs	10
Dinner tables	12
Entry doors	20
Cloakrooms	25
Queues for dinner	26

Mean item analysis value 0·783; mean score = 2·23 (N = 44; S.D. = 1·16).

Table 117 shows that mixed modern schools tend to have the highest scores, comprehensives the lowest.

TABLE 117 *Sex-specialisation of expressive activities scale–mean scores*

	Mixed modern	Mixed comprehensive	Mixed grammar
n	24	14	6
mean	2·67	1·50	2·17
S.D.	1·62	1·35	1·46

The formalisation of sex-specialised expressive activities was rare. Twenty-three per cent of schools had some school rules which applied to only one of the sexes, or to relationships between the sexes, usually forbidding entry into the other's cloakrooms.

Ritualisation of sex-specialised expressive activities

The sex-differentiating ceremonials of the school assembly were mentioned in Chapter 4. The scale for its measurement is given in Table 118.

TABLE 118 *Ritualisation of sex-specialised expressive activities scale*

Item	f
Sexes enter assembly separately	17
Prefects separated by sex in assembly	23
All pupils separated by sex in assembly	27

Mean item analysis value 0·91; mean score = 1.52 (N = 44; S.D. = 1·14).

Table 21, Chapter 4, shows that the level of the mean scores follows those for the previous scale for sex-specialisation, a high mean score for modern schools, low for comprehensives.

Only two schools held separate assemblies for the sexes. Both were cases of recent amalgamation, one a modern school, the other a comprehensive. It is interesting to note that other schools formed by the amalgamation of a boys' with a girls' school used the separate buildings to create mixed junior and senior departments.

Sex-specialisation of the instrumental order

Some of the differences in the subjects taught to pupils in schools of different sex composition were discussed in Chapter 7. This section reports on such differences found *within* mixed schools.

Table 119 shows the mean number of subjects taught separately to boys and girls, these were commonly RE and PE, and the number of subjects taught exclusively to boys, usually handicrafts, and exclusively to girls, usually homecrafts.

TABLE 119   *Sex-specialisation of the instrumental order – mean numbers of subjects taught to age groups 1–5*

	Mixed modern	Mixed compre-hensive	Mixed grammar	All mixed
n	24	14	6	44
Subjects taught separately to boys	3·4	3·4	2·3	3·2
Subjects taught separately to girls	3·5	3·5	2·5	3·3
Subjects exclusive to boys	1·8	1·2	0·8	1·4
Subjects exclusive to girls	1·6	1·1	1·0	1·4

It is clear that the degree of this sex-specialisation was highest in the non-selective schools. There was also a trend in each type of school for the extent of the specialisation to decrease with the age of the pupils.

Sex-specialisation of the instrumental order is therefore associated with younger, less able pupils, as the correlations in Table 120 confirm.

Sex differences in involvement related to sex-specialisation

This and other chapters have reported the sex-specialisation of pupils' activities. In previous chapters sex differences in the levels of certain kinds of involvement were reported for mixed schools.

TABLE 120   *Sex-specialisation – correlations (N = 44)*

Mean number of subjects:	Mean IQ	% 1st Year	% 7th Year
Taught separately to boys	– 0·29	– 0·04	0·00
Taught separately to girls	– 0·28	– 0·01	0·00
Exclusive to boys	– 0·40	0·29	– 0·28
Exclusive to girls	– 0·32	0·31	– 0·26

The levels of acceptance of the school assembly and school uniform were higher for girls than boys in the same school. Second-year girls showed the higher levels of general and instrumental involvement. In some, but not all, mixed schools, boys joined more school clubs than girls.

It is possible that relationships may exist between the sex differences in the involvement of pupils and the degree and type of sex-specialisation of the organisation of the schools they attend. All of the tau correlations between the differences in the mean scores of the sexes matched by age, with the score on the various relevant scales were of no statistical significance.

This does not necessarily mean that the organisational structure of the scheme is not a factor in creating differences in involvement of boys and girls, but it is clear that the structure does not determine these differences. Sex as an organisational factor is analogous to age. Cultural notions about the nature of sexuality give rise to sex-specialisation in the school organisation. These same meanings give rise to sex differences in involvement. These relationships are summarised in the paradigm shown in Figure 3.

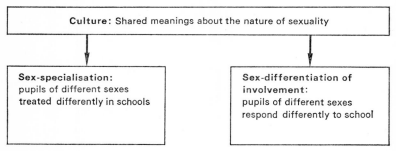

FIGURE 3

Sex-specialisation in schools

'One does not have to be a Freudian to insist that sex makes a difference, even for organisational behaviour.' Gouldner's (1959) observation is probably more true of schools than most other organisations. Although the biological sex difference is given widely different kinds of social meaning in different cultures, the basic model in Western industrialised societies is that of the man as the principal economic-provider and the woman as the principal child-rearer and domestic controller. (Mead (1949); Parsons and Bales (1956).) It is this man–woman relationship that is the external source of sex-specialisation in schools, as it is assumed that a congruence should exist between a pupil's education and his or her presumed, eventual adult role.

Sex is an important factor in defining the primary boundary of a school. Single-sex schools are a reflection, perhaps in modern Britain a rather dated one, of the different social positions of men and women in society. Parsons (1954) has pointed out that age is considered to be a more important social factor than sex when children are young, but that the role of the older child becomes more heavily sex-typed. In Britain most primary schools are mixed, but nearly half the secondary schools are single sex.

Within mixed schools societal sex differences are given organisational meaning. Boys and girls learn different things, are controlled in different ways. The outcome of this organisational sex-specialisation appears to be to confirm the pupils' sexual identity rather than modify it. Thus schools vary in the degree to which the sexes are taught separately, but there is no related sex difference in involvement level. In particular schools it could be seen that reduction of sex-differentiation may have actually enhanced sexual identity. When girls in one school were allowed to do metal work they all chose to make pieces of personal jewellery.

It is, however, possible that the experience of the mixed school context may influence sexual identity as compared with the experience of single-sex schools. (See Dale (1969).) This is implied in results that show differences in levels of involvement of boys or girls in mixed and single-sex schools, for example, girls in girls' grammar schools had lower levels of acceptance of the school assembly than those in mixed grammar schools.

The Crowther Report (1959) showed that the proportion of girls studying science in the sixth forms of grammar schools was higher in girls' grammar schools than in mixed. This may be an example of sex composition influencing subject choice. In mixed schools science may have masculine connotations, possibly mediated through a predominance of male science teachers. We were able to investigate this phenomenon in the grammar schools in our sample in terms of A-level entries. (The numbers in comprehensive schools are too small for inclusion.)

The results (Table 121) indicate that boys were the more likely to do science A-levels, and that the tendency was greater in mixed schools. Girls were more likely to do arts A-levels, and this tendency was stronger in mixed schools. If the explanation of this phenomenon is sex composition then the proportion of science entries for boys in every mixed school should be higher than that in every boys' school, and the proportions of arts entries for girls in every mixed school should be higher than those in every girls' school. In only one of the six boys' grammar schools was the percentage of science studies higher than that for boys in any of the six mixed schools. Two of the six girls' grammar schools entered proportionally more arts candidates compared with any of the mixed schools. The suggestion that the sex composition of the school influences subject choice, and possibly sexual identity, is therefore partly confirmed by these results.

Another purpose of sex-differentiation in mixed schools is the control of pupil sexual liaison. Holding hands was only approved between girls. Apart from the possibility of sexual misbehaviour, the fear seems also to be that such affectively based relationships may

TABLE 121   *A-level entries in grammar schools*

Boys in boys' schools				*Boys in mixed schools*			
	n	% Science	% Arts		n	% Science	% Arts
School				School			
No. 2	66	39	27	No. 8	28	54	36
No. 9	18	44	44	No. 13	41	29	49
No. 28	71	37	49	No. 27	12	67	17
No. 60	69	49	42	No. 59	40	60	23
No. 63	49	47	4	No. 65	44	68	32
No. 64	16	0	69	No. 67	36	53	31
Total	289	45	39	Total	201	54	33

Girls in girls' schools				*Girls in mixed schools*			
	n	% Science	% Arts		n	% Science	% Arts
School				School			
No. 17	40	13	58	No. 8	27	4	70
No. 18	57	33	49	No. 13	35	26	57
No. 61	61	36	64	No. 27	17	12	88
No. 62	63	25	64	No. 59	29	17	48
No. 66	39	18	62	No. 65	33	9	91
No. 69	36	11	72	No. 67	42	17	71
Total	296	25	61	Total	183	15	70

Note. Combinations of science and arts subjects have been excluded from the table.

distract the partners from the educational process, and if the couple occupy different age- or ability-statuses the whole basis of the distribution of honorific status is seen as threatened. In particular the effectiveness of the prefectorial system may be thought to be jeopardised by a friendship between a boy prefect and a younger girl.

One interesting difference between sex as an organisational factor compared with age and ability, is that although the sexes were always differentiated in schools there was never sex-stratification. The implicit value judgment in the age-stratification pattern is that older is better than younger; an acceptable one as younger pupils do become older. Ability-stratification implies that being good at school work is better than being less good at it. It is difficult to see how any school could completely deny this. To stratify sex differences implies that being a boy is better than being a girl or vice versa. This seems unacceptable because the basic sex roles are highly ascriptive. The only sex privileges observed in schools did not strongly imply high or low status for the recipients, only that they were different, as for example, when boys allowed the girls to leave the classroom first.

12 School organisation and pupil involvement

This study has been concerned with the answering of three important questions about secondary schools. Answers to these questions have been suggested in the previous chapters. This chapter collates those answers in an attempt to give a unity to the whole research.

A concluding section discusses a number of possible educational implications which arise from the research.

School organisation

This discussion of the organisation of pupil learning and behaviour is made under two headings representing the how and the why of the situation. The how of the organisation concerns the actual structuring of activities of the school. The why concerns the actions of those who create and sustain the organisation, the teachers and, more importantly, the headteachers.

The organisational configuration of schools

The structure of the school has been analysed along the dimensions of standardisation, formalisation, specialisation and ritualisation. Each of these has been presented in relation to particular activities within the school, for example, the standardisation of instrumental activities. The addition of the scale scores for all kinds of standardisation, formalisation, specialisation and ritualisation, gives an index of the degree to which schools were structured in these ways. The extents of sex- age- and ability-specialisations were discussed in previous chapters. Their extents and those of standardisation, formalisation and ritualisation were calculated as percentages of the

162

total possible scores for all relevant scales, and are presented in histogram form (Figures 4a and 4b). These histograms present the *configuration,* or organisational shape in Pugh's (1963) use of the term.

Standardisation by the use of rules, regulations and similar procedures was highest in boys' modern schools, and lowest in girls' grammar schools.

Formalisation, the use of written forms of control, was higher in grammar and comprehensive schools than in modern schools, and was highest in boys' grammar schools.

Ability-specialisation was highest in modern schools and lowest in grammar schools.

Age-specialisation was highest in grammar and comprehensive schools.

Sex-specialisation was highest in mixed modern schools.

Ritualisation was highest in girls' modern schools and lowest in comprehensives.

The configuration of some individual schools

These results and most of those reported in previous chapters have referred to type of school, classified by status and sex composition. There is, however, a cultural expectation that every school has, or should have, its own special, even unique, characteristics, and these may include forms of organisation. This expectation is fulfilled when the organisational structures of individual schools are compared.

Table 122 gives the scores on a number of the item-analysis scales

TABLE 122 *Selected scale scores for six schools*

School no.	Modern 11	Modern 36	Compre-hensive 14	Compre-hensive 42	Grammar 13	Grammar 65
Scale						
Formalisation of expressive performance	0	1	3	4	0	1
Prescription of uniform (boys)	6	8	7	2	7	8
Prescription of uniform (girls)	2	4	5	1	5	5
Standardisation of instrumental performance	5	0	4	0	4	5
Sex-specialisation of expressive activities	6	2	1	0	1	5
Formalisation of prefects	4	2	2	1	1	3

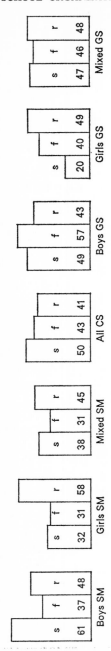

FIGURE 4a   *Organisational profiles – degrees of standardisation, formalisation and ritualisation in types of school*

Legend. s = standardisation; f = formalisation; r = ritualisation. Numbers refer to percentage score.

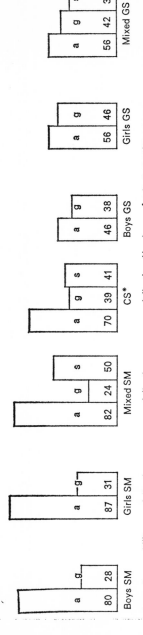

FIGURE 4b   *Organisational profiles – degrees of ability-, age- and sex-specialisation in types of school*

Legend. a = ability-specialisation; g = age-specialisation; s = sex-specialisation. Numbers refer to percentage score.

* All CS for a and g. Mixed CS for s.

for three pairs of schools: one pair of mixed modern schools, one of mixed grammar schools, and one of mixed comprehensives. Each pair is matched as closely as possible for size. The variations in the scores of any pair are therefore reasonably independent of the contextual variables of status, size, age, sex and ability composition.

The organisational profiles, or configurations, of these six schools in terms of their overall standardisation, formalisation, specialisation by age, sex and ability, and ritualisation are shown in Figures 5a and 5b. The indices used were the same as those used in the report for types of school, that is, summated scales as a percentage of total possible score.

The variation between the pairs of matched schools indicates the limitations of the generalisations about types of school. The source of the variation is difficult to establish. Other contextual variables such as social composition and recent social history may be suggested. The high level of sex-specialisation in grammar school no. 65 may be related to its having been formed by the amalgamation of two single-sex schools only a few years previously. The high levels of autonomy allowed to headteachers in the organisation of their schools may also be a source of variation between schools.

School size and organisation

The size of schools, as measured by the number of pupils in the school, has appeared in the analysis of school structure in earlier chapters. In view of the great interest in the size of organisations in general and school in particular (see Campbell (1965)) a summary is now made of the relationship between school size and organisation. The elevation of size to a major independent variable in this way leads to an ignoring of variations in school status, so that it is important to bear in mind that smaller schools tended to be modern schools, and larger ones comprehensives.

The expectation that bureaucratisation increases with organisational size is well established in sociology. Studies of teachers may well confirm this expectation in schools, but that of the pupils does not do so in any striking way.[1] Table 136 gives the significant correlations between size and structural variables, and shows that in some cases the degree of bureaucratisation actually decreases with increasing size.

It is interesting to note that no scales for general standardisation or formalisation correlate positively with size. The increase in the number of rules and set procedures and the increased use of paper

[1] My former colleague, Gary Easthope, is preparing a doctoral thesis which presents evidence of a positive relationship between school size and the bureaucratisation of teacher activities.

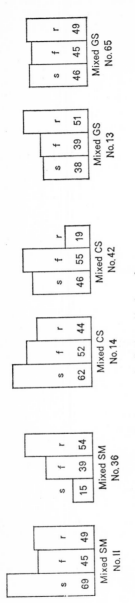

Legend. s = standardisation; f = formalisation; r = ritualisation. Numbers refer to percentage score.

FIGURE 5a *Organisational profiles – degrees of standardisation, formalisation and ritualisation in individual schools*

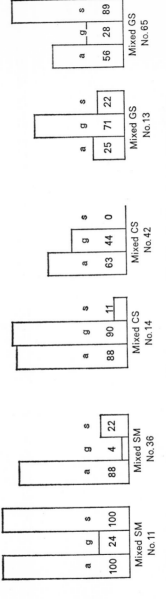

Legend. a = ability-specialisation; g = age-specialisation; s = sex specialisation. Numbers refer to percentage score.

FIGURE 5b *Organisational profiles – degrees of ability-, age- and sex-specialisation in individual schools*

166

TABLE 123 *Correlations of size and structural variables* ($N = 72$)

	r
Ability-specialisation of instrumental activities	0·39
Age-specialisation of expressive activities	0·52
Age-specialisation of expressive performance	0·41
Formalisation of age-specialised expressive activities	0·33
Formalisation of age-specialised instrumental activities	0·27
Age-specialisation of instrumental activities	− 0·22
Ability-specialisation of expressive activities	− 0·31
Pupil–teacher differentiation	− 0·29

are clearly not functional requisites of large schools, as is commonly thought.

The social construction of school organisation

The discussion so far has been concerned with how schools are organised. What follows is an attempt to understand why schools are organised in the way they are.

The occasional use of the term function in parts of previous discussions, the explanations of school organisation made here are not consciously functionalist. The idea of function has sometimes been used as method of analysis. This follows Homans's (1964) distinction between functional analysis as a way of answering how questions, and functional theory, used to answer why questions. In addition, the use of the term school in phrases such as 'the school expects' does not pose the school as a superordinate impersonal entity, but follows the common usage in such contexts where school usually refers to the headteacher and teachers.[1]

The approach used to explain why schools are organised in the way they are is basically an action one, where the idea of action follows that of Weber (1948), 'all human behaviour when and in so far as the acting individual attaches subjective meaning to it'.

It is not intended to rehearse the discussion of functionalist versus action theories in relation to sociology in general or the analysis of school in particular. A critique of functionalist approaches to organisations and the case for an action approach has been lucidly put by David Silverman (1970). Without accepting all the arguments he makes, the explanations made in this study do tend to follow his basic premise that sociology is concerned with understanding action rather than observing behaviour. That action

---

[1] Such reifications are also an indication of the extent to which headteachers identify with their schools. Headteachers are often judged by the success of *their* school. Its failure is their failure. A case of *l'école c'est moi.*

arises from meanings that define social reality. Positivistic explanations, such as those made by some functionalists, which suggest that action is determined by external social forces, such as functional requisites or social needs, tend to deny the human basis of social life.

The meaning of school organisation to two sets of actors must be considered. First, the meaning to those who establish and maintain the organisation, the teachers and especially the headteachers, who are legally responsible for the organisation of their schools. (See King (1968).) Some of the variations in organisation between individual schools are a reflection of the high degree of autonomy headteachers have in these matters. Second, the meaning of the organisation to those whose behaviour it is intended to control, the pupils. This section deals mainly with the headteachers' purposes in running their schools in the way they did. The later section on pupil involvement discusses their perspectives.

The basic method used in making such interpretations of meanings is that of *Verstehen*, or simply, understanding. The attempt to understand the meanings that headteachers' give the actions they take in organising a school draws on a number of sources. First, the interview with each headteacher which included a number of questions about their purpose in organising the school in the way they did. Second, the examination of documents provided by the school, including in some cases written statements of aims or philosophies. The headteachers of comprehensive schools were most likely to make explicit statements of this kind, perhaps a reflection of their Utopian position in Mannheim's (1936) sense of having to propagate a new ideology.

As with all of this kind of data, such statements must be considered to be face or public ones, and regard must be paid to the audience to which they were addressed, mainly pupils and parents. What is often required is what Berger (1966) calls an unmasking to reveal the covert intentions of those making the statements.

A third method of understanding was to make inferences from the analysis of organisational structures. This direct understanding of action does not necessarily assume that the action is rational, although headteachers often suggested that their organisation was a rational one.

A final method of understanding was based upon experience. The personal experience of having been a teacher and a pupil, and the pooled experiences of many teachers revealed in seminars on courses held at the Exeter Institute of Education.

An important limitation on this last method, and it has been argued, the general use of *Verstehen* analysis, is that it may lead to mere expressions of personal opinion. As Diane Leat (1972) has pointed out, this is a criticism of the sociologist and not the method itself. I am not in a position to suggest which elements in the explanations given here are personal. The attempt has been to keep them as impersonal as possible. At this point, I am acutely aware of the trap that Merton (1959) suggests all sociologists may be caught in. If their explanations confirm conventional wisdom they may be judged to have wasted their time in pointing out the obvious. If their explanations deny conventional wisdom, no one believes them.

It has already been suggested that pupil specialisation arises from cultural assumptions about the nature of age and sex, and the relationship between ability at school work and occupation. This method of expressing the matter implies a vague process of social osmosis. Made more explicit it suggests that the forms of specialisation are propagated by headteachers and teachers because they share certain cultural meanings about the social characteristics of their pupils.

It is assumed that boys and girls have different needs, interests, sensitivities and amenability to discipline, and have different social destinies. Within mixed schools the response is to teach them different things and to have different expectations of their behaviour, which are expressed in the organisation as sex-specialisation. The degree of sex-specialisation does vary from school to school. Thus in some schools boys may learn cookery and girls do woodwork. But the extent to which the basic sex differences are taken for granted is indicated when a consideration is made of the likelihood of a school allowing only boys to do cookery and only girls to do woodwork.

It is also assumed that pupils of different ages have different needs, interests, amenability to discipline and capacity to learn. The response is to teach them different things in separate groups, with different privileges, all aspects of age-specialisation. The extent of age-specialisation varied from school to school and was generally greater in schools with wide age-groups. But the extent to which age differences are part of what teachers take for granted in the school situation can be tested by considering the possibility of first-year pupils being made prefects with authority over older pupils.

Sex and age are characteristics that pupils bring into the school situation, but a pupil's ability identity is created within the school. Headteachers and teachers tend to accept the assumption that ability to do school work, ultimately expressed in examination success, is a prerequisite for entry into high-status occupations. Underlying this assumption is the belief that high ability is necessary for the adequate performance in a high-status occupation.

The proposition of this belief forms an important part of Davis and Moore's (1945) functionalist theory of social stratification, although as Anderson (1961) and others have pointed out, educational success is not the only criterion in occupational placement. Personal qualities and kinship may often be more important. However, the headteacher's general acceptance of the selective and allocative purposes of the school is indicated in the existence in every school of forms of ability-specialisation.

A reference has already been made to the way in which time is used in the justification of school organisation by headteachers. Time is transcended by bringing the present and the future together. The use of sex-specialisation and ability-specialisation is justified in terms of the needs of the pupils now and the presumed requirements of their eventual social positions in the future. Thus girls do needlework because they are interested in making things to wear, and because such skills will be useful when they are married. Less able pupils are not taught science because it does not interest them, and because it will be of no use to them in the semi-skilled and unskilled manual occupations they are expected to take up.

It is very difficult to estimate the extent to which the meanings teachers place upon the social origins of their pupils give rise to particular forms of organisation.[1] This is partly because of the relationship between measured ability and social class. Are the broad organisational differences between grammar and modern schools related to the differences in their ability compositions or their social compositions? Attempts to answer this are made more difficult when it is recognised that most grammar-school pupils are potentially middle-class, and most modern-school pupils potentially working-class, whatever their social class of origin.

However, it can be suggested that the extensive use of formalisation as a method of control in grammar schools is related to the teachers' expectations that their pupils, characteristically more able, more middle-class and older than those in other schools, will read, understand and act upon what they have read on notice boards and elsewhere. This assumption is not made in modern schools, particularly those for boys, where notice boards are rare and information tends to be passed directly from teacher to pupils.

The use of formalisation implies a particular kind of authority, impersonal, unquestionable and permanent (consider the fuss made when a notice is defaced in a school). Such paper control allows information to pass in one direction only, from teacher to pupil. In general, the teacher has limited direct knowledge of the pupils' reception of the information.

[1] The pupils' social class origins were given a clear organisational meaning in those nineteenth-century public schools where the free-place charity pupils were taught separately from the fee-paying upper-class pupils. See Simon (1965). Race may sometimes be given organisational meaning. A modern school not in this study, had forms 1P and 2P, referring to the learning groups, first-year Pakistani and second-year Pakistani.

The high levels of standardisation in modern schools, especially those for boys, partly arises from the teachers' perceptions and experience of controlling less able pupils from mainly working-class homes. The ritual used in these schools is that of the symbolic reward of good work and good behaviour, two aspects of pupil behaviour considered most precarious in such schools.

The explanations posed so far could be called cultural determinism: teachers share cultural meanings which lead to their organising schools in the way they do. However, teachers and headteachers do share sets of ideas, values and beliefs about the nature of their pupils and the process of education which are fairly particular to them. These ideologies are used to justify and legitimate their actions in organising the school, and are therefore assertive ideologies in the sense used by Archer and Vaughan (1972) in referring to the ideology of a dominant group which is used to produce willing conformity rather than reluctant compliance in others.

These school ideologies are to some extent related to the kinds of educational ideologies discussed by Archer and Vaughan and held by dominant groups, mainly outside the school, and used to promote and resist educational change. Another set of ideologies is held by subject specialist teachers, and is used to justify and legitimate the existence of their subject in the curriculum. These subject ideologies are outside the scope of this particular discussion.

Age-specialisation within schools is justified by the ideology of development (see Chapter 9). It occurred most commonly in non-selective schools. 'Our prime duty is to see that every individual child should have an opportunity to develop fully and happily. (Letter to parents, girls' modern school.)

However, the ideology of development is relatively unimportant in secondary schools compared with primary schools. Learning groups in the secondary school are based on age-groups but, particularly in the older age-range, also on imputed ability. The pupils defined as less able are not kept in school until they develop to the levels of the most able. Academic development, although acknowledged in secondary schools, is made finite.

The ideology of child-centredness or paediocentricity is closely related to that of development, and both have their origins in the current conception of childhood which stresses the individuality and intrinsic worth of children. Many activities within the schools were justified in terms of their meeting the needs of individual pupils. Virtually every form of grouping was justified in this way. The presumed needs of individual pupils, and what are seen to be the exigencies of creating learning groups (numbers of pupils, teachers, classrooms and so on), are made one.

Compared with primary schools paediocentricity was relatively unimportant in the schools. This was partly because pupils cease to be children in secondary schools. The only pupils who had a curriculum that was at all paediocentric were the less able older pupils in some non-selective schools, for whom the traditional subject-centred curriculum was considered unsuitable, or for which they were considered to be unsuited (both arguments were used).

It is interesting to note that few schools made references to their sex composition as a part of a stated ideology. This may be a reflection of the dissensus about mixed versus single-sex secondary education in this country. However, some mixed comprehensive schools did see the reduction of sex differences in the school as part of the ideology of equality (see later discussion), and expressed this in reducing the level of sex-specialisation, particularly in the curriculum, and attempting to reduce the sex-typing of such subjects as woodwork and cookery.

The six denominational schools in our sample did not possess special organisational features that could be related to their religious affiliations, although it is quite probable that the nature of what was transmitted to the pupils had a definite sectarian element, particularly in the case of Catholic schools. The ideologies of such schools may therefore have had a specifically religious component, which was sometimes explicit. 'To give a sound practical knowledge of their Catholic Faith, so that pupils may become loyal, practising Catholics in their parishes and good citizens in the general community.' (One of three written aims of a Catholic modern school.)

A much more important set of ideologies is related to the organisation of the instrumental order and the way it may provide access to high-status occupations through examination success. The most common form was the meritocratic ideology, which expresses the belief in the provision of educational opportunities for all who are considered to have the ability or merit to take advantage of them. This was used to justify many different forms of learning groups and examination policies.

The meritocratic ideology was expressed most commonly by headteachers of comprehensive schools who justified the existence of their schools mainly in terms of the wider educational opportunities they provided and, implicitly or often explicitly, the wider occupational opportunities. They could even celebrate the large size of their schools instead of being defensive about it: 'it is the very largeness of the school and its staff that enables it to offer a wide variety of courses.' (Notes to fourth- and fifth-year pupils, comprehensive school.)

Arising from this was a variant of the meritocratic ideology found only in some comprehensives which treats the pupil as a customer: 'next you have to choose your course' (ibid.).

An ideological element found only in modern schools was an ameliorative one. It was the attempt to revive the pupils' self-esteem, despite the low status of their school, and the provision of external examinations was presented as a second chance of success.

> I think it important, therefore, that you should be fully aware although not selected for a grammar school, your child has a full range of opportunities, academic, social and vocational, for which the school makes full preparations. (Letter to new pupils' parents, modern school)

> Our aim is to make parents glad their children came to our school and to forget that such things as 11-plus and 13-plus selection tests ever existed. (Handbook, modern school)

The origins of this meritocratic ideology and its variants are in the notion of equality of opportunity in education, which is an aspect of the more general political ideology of equality. This in turn is related to what must be regarded as a British cultural trait, that of fairness. The bipartite system of grammar and modern schools was once regarded as fair. The comprehensive movement derives in part from a new conception of fairness in education, and part of the legitimacy of examinations in modern schools is that they correct unfairnesses in a divided system.

Only a few headteachers of comprehensives expressed what Dennis Marsden (1969) has called the egalitarian ideology. This views the school as an agent of social change in producing a better, more just society. 'The comprehensive school is designed towards the desirable, if not completely attainable, classless society.' (Comprehensive school headmaster's account of his educational ideas.)

The mechanism of this change is to reproduce in the school the conditions of the desired for society, yet another example of the transcendence of time. 'Here children not only of widely differing social backgrounds, but also of widely differing intellectual ability, mingle and live together, valuing, we hope, each other's varying qualities' (ibid.).

One of the most important ideologies expressed by headteachers in virtually all schools is concerned with the nature of the school itself. That it is, or should be, a community. The ideology of community was used to justify and explain the rituals of uniform and school assembly. In large schools, particularly the comprehensives, the fear that community feeling would be lost often led to the reform of the House system to provide smaller units of identification, and the introduction of elaborate systems of pastoral care.

Members of communities have wide obligations and expectations. This is expressed in the scope of interest that teachers are expected to have in their pupils, in the diffuseness of the teacher's role and the idea of teaching as a vocation. Loyalty to the school community is an important element in social control, shown in appeals not to let the school down. It is also expressed in the importance of pupils representing the school in team games, and in the teachers' voluntary involvement in games and other activities out of school hours. The idea is also congruent with the conception of the headteacher's role as a community leader and moral exemplar.

The ideology of community is used to justify and legitimate all of these aspects of the school, its morality and the whole of the expressive order of which they form a part. It is used to imply consensus among the members of the school, and therefore obtain the compliance of the pupils to the authority of the teachers.

It has already been suggested that teachers and headteachers view the control they have over their pupils as being tenuous. It is not suggested that order had broken down in any of the schools studied, but that the generation and maintenance of order are seen as essentially mysterious, and therefore the subject of slight, but chronic anxiety.

The evidence from the pupils' survey suggests that with the exception of school uniform and assembly most pupils do legitimate what goes on in the school. The irony about the use of what are intended to be the community-propagating rituals of assembly and uniform is that they are not associated with consensus but conflict. The conflict is contained because to reject the assembly or uniform would be seen as a rejection of the ideology of the school as a community, and therefore a challenge to the authority of the group who propagate that ideology, the teachers and headteachers.

The ideology of community was less commonly expressed in those schools where the social control of pupils was considered to be an important problem. These were mainly boys' secondary modern schools, which did not generally stress the school uniform and had few out-of-school activities. Here were found expressions of a custodial ideology, although this was never made explicit, perhaps because that would be to admit failure in producing an ordered community. The high levels of standardisation and the prevalence of corporal punishment were justified as being the means to the end of containing unwilling pupils between the hours of nine and four each day.

One origin of the community ideology is historical; the example of the nineteenth-century public schools which has formed the archetype of so much in secondary education. (See Banks (1955); Mitchell (1964).) The setting up of public schools as communities in remote country areas was partly to isolate their delinquent upper-class pupils from the temptations of town life, and later in the century to prepare them for the kind of social isolation associated with their destinies as army officers and civil servants, often in remote parts of the Empire (See Weinberg (1967); Wilkinson (1966); Mack (1938).)

A few comprehensive schools in the sample had inverted this original idea. Instead of using the school community to isolate pupils from the neighbourhood, they attempted to include the neighbourhood within the community of the school. The educational colonialism of these community schools was propagated by the opening up and sharing of the school's plant and resources, so that, for example, the distinction between out-of-school activities for pupils and evening institute activities for young adults was often hard to define.

Another source is the educational experience of school teachers. They are mainly former pupils of grammar schools, where the community ideology is often strongly adhered to. On leaving school they either went to colleges of education (largely residential 'communities'), or to universities ('communities of scholars').

In addition, there is a strong attachment to the general idea of community life in Britain, often powerfully suffused with a nostalgia for a mythical past that is now lost, or the romanticism of social engineering for the future.

Pupil involvement

The results presented in previous chapters have shown that the mean levels of pupil involvement within individual schools do vary for different aspects of the school, and for pupils of different social characteristics.

Etzioni (1961), in his scheme of organisational analysis, proposes that the basic kind of involvement pupils manifest in schools is moral involvement, that is, positive involvement at a high level of intensity. The principal orientation of this kind of involvement is towards the normative power of the teachers in the school. Normative power is defined as 'allocation and manipulation of symbolic rewards and deprivations through the employment of leaders, the manipulation of mass media, allocation of esteem and prestige, administration of ritual and influence over the distribution of "acceptance" and "prestige response". '

In this study the level of pupil involvement in expressive activities, which represents something very close to Etzioni's normative power, was indeed generally very high, but with two exceptions. These were the ritualised aspects of uniform and assembly. It is clear that pupils may respond to different aspects of the normative order in different ways.

Etzioni also proposes that pupil involvement will also contain an alienative element related to the school's use of coercive power. He

175

defines coercive power as the use of physical sanctions or the deprivation of 'basic needs'. In school these may include corporal punishments, detentions, written compositions and ostracism from school activities. However, in some schools caning is a ritualised ceremony. It takes place in the headteacher's sacred study, and is administered by an emblemic cane. The number of strokes is traditionally one, two, four or six, seldom three or five. The atmosphere is solemn and a moral sermon may be given by the headteacher. Is this coercive power or moral power?

Within every school there was a small minority of pupils who had low expressive involvement. However, it would be wrong to assume that the pupils' experience of coercive power, assuming it can be precisely defined, is associated with low involvement. It is quite possible that punished pupils may actually legitimate their receipt of punishment.

In Etzioni's scheme calculative involvement is associated with the use of remunerative power. As remunerative power is defined as the allocation of material rewards, including money, benefits, services and commodities, this kind of involvement should be rare in schools. However, 94 per cent of pupils in this study agreed that, 'The main reason for working hard is to get a good job.' This high level of what could be called calculative involvement has been reported in other studies of secondary-school pupils. (See Schools Council Enquiry No. 1 (1968); King (1969a).)

The secondary school has no immediate material rewards to confer on its pupils, but pupils do perceive that school success in passing examinations is a major route to high-status, high-remuneration occupations. Thus schools do use a kind of deferred remunerative power. As the examples given in previous chapters have shown, this is often made explicit in careers advice and guidance, in the allocation to learning groups and in the display of examination opportunities.

Pupils live in a time world in which they make perceptions of their future states of existence, particularly their occupational destinies. When they aspire to high-status occupations, using high in a relative sense, and they also perceive the relationship between occupation and educational success, then a principal form of involvement in the school is as a means to this end. This form of involvement may be powerful enough for many pupils to put up with the resented school uniform and the boring school assemblies.

The nub of Etzioni's approach to organisations is in his hypothesis of compliance; that organisations 'shift' in such a way that the kind of involvement of the subordinates becomes related to the kind of power used by the superordinates, because these congruent types are more effective. His three congruent types are alienative involvement with coercive power, calculative involvement with remunerative power, and moral involvement with normative power.

The schools in this study were therefore mainly incongruent. Moral involvement in the ritualised normative power was low, and calculative involvement high in the absence of direct remunerative power.

Pupils did not only respond to different aspects of the school in different ways but also according to their age, sex and social class of origin.

Age differences in mean levels of involvement within individual schools were found in relation to many different activities. Sex differences were particularly associated with the ritualisation of the expressive order, with girls generally showing higher involvement in school assembly and uniform.

Social class differences in involvement hinge on the idea of relevance. At the attitudinal level the working-class pupils' disposition towards most aspects of the school was as favourable as that of middle-class pupils in the same school. However, these positive sentiments and high evaluations had less relevance for some working-class pupils. This is implied in the lower rates at which they join school clubs and their lower expectations of post-school education, both behavioural measures of involvement.

For working-class children, particularly those of average and below average ability, school is a pleasant or unpleasant experience that has few apparent future consequences, and does not relate to their world outside the school. For middle-class children, school is a pleasant or unpleasant experience, which has implications for their future, and relates more closely to their world outside the school.

These age, sex and social class differences in involvement indicate that the pupils' experience of school is not completely determined by the exposure to school, but is partly created from meanings that they bring into the situation. These cultural roots of pupil involvement are summarised in the following simple paradigm.

CULTURE	PUPIL INVOLVEMENT
Shared meanings about the qualities of age	Varies by age
Shared meanings about sexuality	Varies by sex
Social class sub-cultural meanings about the relevance of education	Varies by social class

The theoretical significance of these measurements of pupil involvement is to create doubts about Etzioni's basic proposition that the lower participant's involvement is principally directed towards the kind of power used to control them.[1]

[1] Similar doubts have been raised by Harris (1969) in relation to church membership, and Musgrove (1971) in relation to schools.

177

In Etzioni's school the pupils are locked in the here and now. They have no existence outside the school, they have no recollection of the past and no anticipation of the future.

School organisation and pupil involvement

The variations in school organisation have been shown to be related to cultural notions about the nature of childhood, sex, ability and occupational prerequisites often mediated through ideologies held by teachers. The variations in the involvement of pupils in school have also been shown to relate to some of these same cultural notions. However, with the important exception of the use of streaming in some schools, the variations in organisation are not directly related to the variations in pupil involvement. Thus, for example, schools varied in the degree and type of ritualisation of their school assemblies, and in most mixed schools girls showed higher involvement in assembly than boys. However, the degree and type of ritualisation was not related to the mean level of involvement of either sex or the difference in the mean score between the sexes when all the schools were compared.

It must be concluded that generally speaking the organisation does not determine pupil involvement. This does not mean that the organisation does not influence pupil involvement. This conclusion is an important one because it denies the positivistic notion of the structure of an organisation controlling the actions of its members. (For a discussion of this point see Silverman (1970).) Clearly this structure controls their behaviour. If a school has a rule that all pupils must wear the full school uniform it is clearly controlling pupil behaviour in this respect. What is not controlled or determined by the rule is the meaning the pupils place upon that behaviour, which in this case is strongly related to their sex (Chapter 4).

There are a number of possible reasons why in general the organisation of the school does not determine pupil involvement. First, pupils generally experience only one kind of school organisation, that of the school they attend. Even their knowledge of other kinds of organisation is likely to be small, and certainly not framed in the sophisticated ways used in this investigation. Fine differences in the extent and kind of structuring of school activities do not form part of the pupils' definition of the situation. The pupils' definition of the school situation is related to the meanings they bring into the situation related to their age, sex and social class of origin. The school not only defines the pupil, but the pupil also defines the school.

Pupils usually only made comments about the organisation of the school in the questionnaire when it was being changed, as for example when a school was unstreaming or abolishing its prefects, when a relevant comparison could be made. Differences in the organisation between schools are only appreciated by those who investigate them, and probably by teachers drawing upon their experiences of different schools and indirect sources of information. It is possible that the more detailed organisation of schools is part of the teachers' definition of the situation, since they are responsible for its creation and perpetuation. A study of the organisation of the school is therefore likely to explain more about teachers than pupils.

A second explanation concerns the extent to which activities in school are organised. It has several times been pointed out that many of the activities of the school are not organised, they are not structured, but are mediated by individual teachers. Our measurements of pupil involvement were usually of their orientation towards school activities, both organised and non-organised in the technical sense. For example the statement, 'The school expects you to behave in a reasonable way', covers control of behaviour mediated bureaucratically by rules and regulations and also control by individual teachers. It could be that some of the variations in pupil involvement, both within and between schools, may reflect the pupils' dispositions towards forms of teacher behaviour.

This is related to the third explanation. The organisation of the school is maintained by the teachers and in a minor way by the prefects. It could be that the teachers' manner in implementing rules and procedures is just as important, from the pupils' point of view, as the rules and procedures themselves. Girls, in particular, seem to prefer to be asked to do something 'nicely'.

There was one aspect of the organisation of some schools that is a possible exception to the generalisation that organisation and involvement were not directly related. This was the use of streaming, although it should be stressed the relationship did not exist in all schools (Chapter 8). High stream-status was sometimes associated with high mean levels of pupil involvement. Here is a possibility of structural determinism; the organisation controls the actions of its members. This effect may be explained by viewing the school in terms of the identities of its pupils. In previous chapters it was suggested that age- and sex-specialisation within the school mainly confirm the existing age and sex identities of pupils. Ability-specialisation, however, confers a new identity on the pupil, an ability-identity. The most important signal of this identity is the pupil's learning group, and grouping in streams produces the strongest signals. Rejection of the identity of less able, low stream, may be manifest in low school involvement.

However, the meanings that pupils bring into the stream situation may lead to their defining it in different ways. The direct relationship between stream-status and mean involvement was much more common for boys than girls, and most common in grammar schools. For boys, low stream-status not only signals low ability, but because of the link between ability and occupation, low-status occupational destiny. This signal is less important for girls who have a stronger orientation to marriage. Status for women is based on their marital state; being a Miss or Mrs, rather than their occupation.[1] The definition of the streamed situation may be different for boys and girls because the implied consequences have different degrees of importance to them. In a more general sense, school has less long-term importance for girls, which may partly explain their better adaptation to some aspects of it.

A divided system of secondary schooling ascribes gross ability-identities: grammar school, able; modern school, less able. When grammar-school pupils are placed in low streams, their ability-identity of being a grammar-school pupil is denied. This dissonance may be further exacerbated by the school's exhorting all its pupils to the highest aspirations. The situation is likely to be more acute for boys than girls. It is possible that streaming in modern schools operates in the opposite way in creating a high ability-identity for the top-stream pupils to contradict the low-ability one conferred by being sent to such a school.

The relationship between stream-status and mean involvement was not found in all schools. It is possible that its incidence may be related to the orientation of the teachers towards the stream system, and towards the pupils it arranges they should teach. (See Lunn (1970).)

The general relationship between culture, school organisation and pupil involvement are summarised in the paradigm shown in Figure 6.

The paradigm illustrates the point that cultural transmission in schools is not only achieved by the transmission of the educational knowledge and the inculcation of modes of approved behaviour, but also through the pupils' encounter with the organisation of these activities.

The operation of age- and sex-specialisation in this respect has already been mentioned. They transmit conceptions of age and sexuality which largely confirm those already held by the pupils. Ability-specialisation in the form of stratified teaching groups may transmit conceptions of the stratification of the occupational struc-ture. The school assembly and prefectorial system transmit particular conceptions of authority.

---

[1] One question in the pupils' survey was 'At what age do you expect to get married?' Thirty-eight per cent of boys answered 'not sure' compared with 29 per cent of girls. Girls also usually expected to marry earlier than boys. These are crude indices of the stronger orientation of girls towards marriage.

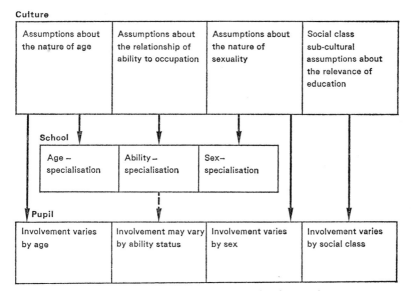

Note The arrows indicate the relationships between the elements in terms of their origins and not their interaction

FIGURE 6

Hilde Himmelweit (1966) has suggested that the use of streaming in schools acts as a signal to the pupil indicating his academic worth. This metaphor can be extended to the rest of the organisation of the school, which can be viewed as a whole set of signals whose messages are all the more powerful for being transmitted so often. Pupils do not, however, automatically react to these signals. The message may be understood, but it is not always accepted.

Some possible educational implications

Michael F. D. Young (1971) has recently made a case for research in the sociology of education to concentrate on sociological rather than educational problems. Although the research forming the basis of this study was financed by the Schools Council it was not carried out to solve specified education problems. At the most general level it was concerned with an old sociological problem, some would say old-fashioned problem, that of social order. One of the outcomes of the research is to suggest that order or social control is also an educational problem from the perspective of headteachers

181

and teachers, although it is not necessarily seen as an acute problem or one that is readily admitted.

Thus there are implications for educational practice that follow from this research because the sociological and educational problems happen to coincide. The implications are, however, only indirect and tentatively suggested because the educational perspective is not the same as the sociological. The former is strongly evaluative, and, as this study shows, also strongly affective. The latter aspires to an objectivity in which values and emotions are given the status of variables in the analysis of the situation.

The study of the organisation of pupil behaviour and learning has described many variations in these aspects of schools. These descriptions may enable more alternatives in organisation to be considered and more informed decisions to be made.

The study of pupil involvement only has direct implications for policy if the educational value-judgment is that high involvement is better than low. If this is the case then it should be recognised that this is a relatively new attitude towards pupils. In the recent past few teachers would have been interested in their pupils' emotional disposition towards, and evaluation of, the processes of the school. The happiness and commitment of pupils as educational aims may still not be accepted by everyone. It could be argued that pupils, even the older ones in secondary schools, do not have the experience or knowledge to know what is best for them, and that some things in education are so intrinsically valuable that they should continue even if they are associated with a negative or even hostile pupil reaction. It could also be argued that the level of a pupil's involvement in the school is much less important than how well he learns, or long-term outcomes in the form of changed attitudes and behaviour.

Assuming that the level of pupil involvement is a matter of importance to teachers, then the results of this research may suggest that attendance at the school assembly should be voluntary, particularly for older pupils. However, its abolition would remove an important focus of involvement for girls. Either abolition or voluntary attendance would reduce its effectiveness as a means of communication and as a consensual rite, although its quality as a religious occasion might be improved.

If wearing of the school uniform were made voluntary then an important source of discontent among boys would be removed. But its abolition would remove an important focus of involvement for most girls, and would probably not be approved by many parents and potential employers.

If more out-of-school activities are provided then the more pupils join them. However, if a school is concerned about social class differences in levels of joining clubs then it could put on such activities during the school day so that working-class pupils may experience them to the same extent as the middle-class. This assumes that voluntary attendance is not an important consideration in the running of such activities.

The provision of games provides an important focus of involvement for most pupils, particularly boys from working-class homes.

The size of a school does not directly relate to the level of involvement shown by its pupils. Larger schools can provide a wider variety of subjects, games and activities than smaller ones.

Older pupils show little approval of the House system, unless it is the focus of pastoral care provision. However, its abolition would remove an important focus of involvement for younger pupils, and if membership excluded older pupils then its importance may be reduced for the younger ones.

The study of the relationship between school organisation and pupil involvement indicates that the use of streaming may be associated with a polarisation of involvement, with the top-stream pupils showing higher involvement than those in bottom streams. This 'effect' is stronger for boys than girls.

Perhaps the most important implication of this part of the research is that, with the possible exception of streaming, there are no particular forms of organisation that are associated with either high or low pupil involvement. It is unlikely that a school could be deliberately organised to produce high involvement at the attitudinal level.

A final point is one that has implications for both educationalists and sociologists. It is the recognition of the evaluative, and perhaps more importantly, the emotional basis of most of the activities in schools.

There is a great deal of spurious rationality in current educational discussions, suggested in phrases such as cost effectiveness, the formulation of objectives and administrative efficiency. When headteachers and teachers give reasons for what they do they are not necessarily being rational. It might be more honest, although more difficult, for them to recognise, or even sometimes admit, that they often do things mainly because they feel them to be right and good.

Sociologists may reflect that the attempt to understand the school becomes a study of the beliefs, values, assumptions and affective dispositions of the wider cultures that the members of the school, and sometimes the sociologist, share.

Appendix A
Some notes on the samples and methodology

1 Pilot samples and validation of methods
2 The schools' survey sample
3 The self-completion questionnaire
4 The analysis of documents
5 Direct observations in schools
6 The interview(s)
7 Item-analysis scales for structural variables
8 The pupils' survey sample
9 Pupils' background information
10 Measurements of involvement
11 The administration of the pupils' questionnaire

1 Pilot samples and validation of methods

All of the methods used in both the surveys were constructed and validated in pilot schools during the first year of the project (1967–8).

As preliminaries to this, the existing research was reviewed and contact made with local schools which included periods of observation, discussions with teachers and informal interviews with head-teachers. In addition, the school experiences of full-time students of the Exeter Institute of Education were drawn upon in a number of loosely structured group discussions.

2 The schools' survey sample

The intention was to survey a sample of maintained secondary schools representative of the national (England and Wales) distribution of schools by size, sex composition and status. This proved to be difficult.

The first difficulty was on obtaining reliable information about the characteristics of schools nationally. The most recent volume of Statistics of Education then available was for 1966. It gave an analysis of schools by size and status, and by status and sex composition, but not by size, status and sex composition. In addition, its information on the proportion of schools by status would clearly be an underestimate of the number of comprehensive schools that would exist when the survey was to be carried out in 1968 and 1969. After inspecting the latest survey by the Comprehensive Schools Committee and the trends in the past editions of Statistics of Education, it was estimated that by 1968–9 the proportion of selective to non-selective schools would change only a little towards more non-selective, that the proportion of comprehensives would rise among the non-selective schools, and that their number would roughly equal that of the selective schools. The assumption was made that the distribution of schools by size would remain reasonably constant for each type of school, as would the proportions of single-sex and mixed schools.

Table 1, Chapter 1, makes a comparison of the final sample with the ideal representation of schools that was calculated when the statistics for 1969 were available. The estimate of the ratio of selective to non-selective proved to be reasonably correct, and the representation of the selective schools is a good one, accepting the rather arbitrary nature of the size classification. The estimate of the proportion of comprehensive schools was too high; ideally thirteen and not seventeen should have been included. It follows that the modern schools are under-represented by about four schools. In addition, the number of large and very large comprehensives was overestimated, so that modern schools of this size are slightly under-represented. The overestimation of the number of comprehensives, particularly the large and very large ones, led to the under-representation of mixed modern schools.

Our resources did not permit the selecting of a national sample of schools. Instead it was selected from the schools of seven local authorities in the south-west of England. Between them they serve a city with half a million population, one of nearly a quarter of a million, two towns of 100,000, many smaller towns and a large rural area.

The Education Committee's *Yearbook* was used as a sampling frame, but due to the rapid changes occurring in secondary education its information was often out of date. Apart from changes of head-teacher, schools were listed which were eventually found to have changed their status, and generally to have become bigger.[1] The

---

[1] An additional problem in a few cases was to decide on what constituted a school. In general the *Yearbook* was taken as the guide but a junior and a senior comprehensive school with separate headteachers were judged to be one school as all the pupils from the junior school transferred to the senior school. The decision was justified as there was found to be a continuity of organisation and exchange of staff between the two schools.

schools were randomly selected so that the sample matched the presumed national distribution by size, status and sex composition. The original intention had been to select the sample from only five local authority areas, but two more were added to deal with replacements for schools who were unwilling or unable to help. Fourteen such replacements were made. Six headteachers declined to help and gave no explicit reasons for doing so. Two others were heavily committed to help with other research and two more did not keep records of pupils' background, which were essential to the analysis. Only one headteacher explicitly objected to the form and purpose of the research, after initially agreeing to help. One declined to help because he was reluctant to provide information about the backgrounds of his pupils. One of the replaced schools had an acting headteacher who was understandably reluctant to help. The final replacement was made after the survey had commenced; the school did not return the questionnaire.

The intention to survey a sample of schools representative of the national distribution of schools by size, status and sex composition was therefore fulfilled as satisfactorily as the conditions permitted, apart from the slight over- and under-representation already referred to. Two other important reservations should be made about the sample. First, it is drawn from one region of the country. Only a national survey could establish the existence of specific regional factors relating to school organisations. Within this regional sample no specific local authority factor was found. The second reservation concerns the replacement of schools in the sample. Sample replacement is a commonplace in this kind of research but it should be recognised that the schools that were replaced may have had particular kinds of organisation. This possibility, unfortunately, cannot be checked.

3 The self-completion questionnaire

The questionnaire was sent through the post to most schools at the end of the summer term of 1968. Others, especially the replacement schools, received them in the autumn term. The questionnaire was not the first contact with the schools. Permission to ask headteachers to help was first obtained from the chief education officers concerned. In the case of two authorities, meetings with the headteachers were arranged in which the purpose and methods of the research were explained and any questions were answered. All the headteachers who attended these meetings agreed to help. All headteachers were sent a letter explaining the research and the help we were asking of them. When assurance of help was given, the self-completion questionnaire was sent off, to be completed by the headteacher, or a teacher of his delegation (often the deputy head), or the school secretary.

The purpose of the questionnaire was to provide information about the characteristics of the pupils and to provide some general idea of the basic organisation of the school. The age and sex compositions were asked for, and information which was used to estimate the schools' social and ability compositions. The social composition was obtained by asking for the fathers' occupations of the second-year pupils. The offer was made for one of the research team to abstract this information from the school records, and this was taken up in a few cases. Where the information was incomplete a supplementary method was used which consisted of giving the second-year pupils a card on which they were asked to write their father's occupation without filling in their own names. The cards were distributed or collected either by teachers, or, in a few cases, by fieldworkers.

The ability composition was obtained by asking for the verbal reasoning quotient, or equivalent, used in secondary selection of the second-year pupils. This information was usually fairly complete. The second year was sampled because it was assumed that there was the maximum chance of the information being complete for this year-group. The information for the first year may not have been collated, and that for older age-groups more likely to have been lost, and to include transfers from other schools without selection-test results.

The rest of the questionnaire consisted of factual questions covering pupil learning groups, curriculum, games, out-of-school activities, examinations, school leavers, uniform, prefectorial, House and pastoral care systems, reports and other minor aspects of school organisation.

4 The analysis of documents

Schools were asked to return the questionnaire together with any documents which would provide insight and information regarding their organisation. Most schools sent something. The documents were commonly school rules, uniform lists, speech-day programmes, school magazines, and, in a few cases, school histories, brochures and staff handbooks.

5 Direct observations in schools

Direct observations were made of the daily routine of each school by a fieldworker. All the girls' schools were observed by Mrs Fry; all the boys' schools (with one exception) by Mr Easthope or myself.

In order to minimise observer bias and render the observations suitable for quantification and analysis, the observations were largely structured using a seventeen-page observation inventory which mainly consisted of single dichotomous observations (seen/not seen), although unstructured observations were also made and noted.

The observer arrived at the school at least ten minutes before pupils were allowed to enter, and observed, often from a car, the pupils arriving and subsequently entering school. 1968 was the first year of the British Standard Time experiment and it caught the observers and the schools unprepared. The dark prevented efficient observation after November, and some schools quickly changed both their entry into school and lateness procedures.

The observer met the headteacher or his delegate as soon as the pupils were in school. Observations of the school assembly usually followed. This required the fieldworker to be in a position to observe the proceedings without (ideally) being observed.

During the morning the observer was conducted around the school by a senior pupil, often a head-prefect, and made observations of the school hall, corridors, notice boards, cloakrooms and play-grounds. Opportunities were taken to ask the guide questions about the organisation of the activities that took place in those areas of the school, and to observe pupil behaviour in those areas.

The morning break was spent in the staffroom or common room, and opportunities were taken to talk to teachers about the school organisation. Two lessons were visited during the course of the morning. Schools were asked to arrange one to be a junior form and the other a senior form, preferably in a non-practical period. The purpose was to observe the extent to which the organisation of activities entered the classrooms in terms of entry and exit procedures and relationship between pupils and staff. For example, did pupils stand when the teacher entered the room.

Lunch was eaten at the school, and in a place that enabled observations to be made of the pupils.

In large schools and in schools on different sites it was sometimes necessary to return to the school for a second morning.

The success of this non-participant observation depended upon the co-operation of the school and upon the observer's presentation of himself. We tried to dress in a manner which would not cause offence or draw attention to ourselves. (This was the one reason for matching the sex of the observer to that of the single-sex school.) In manner we tried to be interested but objective, sympathetic but non-evaluative. Care was taken to thank all who helped either personally or by letter. These things were done not only because they are good methodology, but also for reasons of general politeness.

6 The interview(s)

The interview with the headteacher was carried out in the afternoon following the morning's observation. It varied in length from one and a half to four hours, according to the size and complexity of the school. In some large schools it was found necessary to carry out short supplementary interviews with deputy headteachers, heads of House and departments, sometimes on the following day. The interview schedule was seventy-three pages long and consisted in the main of questions relating to all aspects of the school organisation which were considered to be visible to the pupils. The information from the self-completion questionnaire, the observations and informal inquiries of the morning usually gave a general idea of the organisation so that it was possible to ask detailed questions without going through too many filter questions.

Pugh *et al.* (1968) have suggested that organisational activities may be studied in three ways:

(a) What is officially expected *should* be done.
(b) What is *allowed* to be done.
(c) What is *actually* done.

Most of our data is concerned with (a) and (b), but some elements of (c) were included through the use of observations. It was possible, for example, to make comparisons of the (a) (b) and (c) aspects of the school assembly, lunch, and movement around the school. In general there was a good correspondence between the three aspects of any given activity, but occasionally there was a wide divergence between what the headteacher expected should be done and what was actually observed to be done. In many cases it would have been very difficult to have checked what was actually done. If, for example, it was officially expected that internal examinations were sat twice a year then it was accepted that this actually happened.

Although most of the questions concerned the detailed organisation of the school, the opportunity was taken to ask the headteachers to comment on the value or importance of particular activities, for example the school assembly. These were totally unstructured and where possible noted verbatim.

7 Item-analysis scales for structural variables

The scales were constructed using a specially written computer programme. In outline, the construction began by pruning all items gathered under a given variable heading to exclude those with a frequency greater than 90 per cent and less than 10 per cent, on the grounds of their being non-discriminating within the sample. Next the biserial correlation, or item-analysis value, was calculated for each item. A minimum acceptable value of 0·7 was set, and items with lower values were rejected from the scale. The mean item-analysis value denotes the degree to which the scale approaches unidimensionality or perfection, indicated by a value of 1·00.

An example of such a scale is that for the measurement of age-specialisation of expressive activities. Eleven items were originally classified under this heading. One was eliminated because it occurred in only 4 per cent of the sample. Three others were eliminated because they did not have high enough item-analysis values. The final scale (Table 3, Chapter 1) contains seven items, and a school's score on the scale is obtained by the addition of the number which are present or exist in the school. The range of scores is 0–7.

Fifty-four such item-analysis type scales were produced.[1] They represent a significant advance in the measurement of the organisational structure of schools, but despite delight in their sophistication some important reservations must be made about them. Like Guttman-type scales they tend to be short. This is partly due to the problem of gathering together large numbers of items which are conceptually similar, and also to the pruning procedures which eliminate high- and low-frequency items and those with low item-analysis values. The longest scale has eight items (i.e. has nine points, 0–8), but a few others are two-item, three-point scales. It is possible that the process of constructing the scales may have eliminated analytically important items. Fortunately this possibility could be checked by using each and any item-response as an independent or dependent variable.

Strictly speaking these scales for the measurement of organisational structure only apply to the schools in this investigation, but they could be used with some justification to compare other schools. To some extent there is an analogy with the use of intelligence tests. These are constructed using a representative sample of pupils but are used to measure and compare other pupils.

8 The pupils' survey sample

The purpose of the pupils' survey was to measure the involvement of pupils and to relate their involvement to the organisation of the school they attended. Ideally, all pupils would have been surveyed in all of the seventy-two schools of the schools' survey. The limitations of our resources lead to our taking a sample of pupils from thirty of the original schools.

[1] Not all of the scales are reported.

Within each of the thirty schools, all of the second-year, fourth-year, fifth-year, and where appropriate, seventh-year pupils were surveyed. The choice of these year-groups was reasonably representative of pupils by age, and avoided the possibility of first-year pupils being asked questions about their experience of a school they had only just entered. In addition, the fourth, fifth and seventh years are all possible terminal years in the school. In very large schools pupils were sampled within year-groups. For example, from three of six non-streamed groups, or from first, third, fifth and seventh streams in a seven-stream system.

The original intention was to sample pupils from thirty-two schools which were reasonably representative of the larger sample of seventy two in terms of their organisational structures. A number of factors made this difficult to fulfil. The pupils' survey was planned for the spring term of 1969. This left no interval between it and the schools' survey for a thorough analysis to be made of the organisational variables of the seventy-two schools. Instead the schools were chosen to cover a range of sizes, sex compositions and statuses.

Eleven of the first-choice schools were eventually replaced. Two had commitments to other research, three were too busy, three others were unable to help but gave no explicit reason. Three objected to some of the questions included in the pupils' questionnaire, which had been sent to each headteacher. Three refusals occurred with second-choice schools, one on the basis that it was a 'bad thing to invite criticism'. In one school the headteacher had agreed to help, but when the fieldworker arrived at the school the teachers refused to do so. It was clear that we had innocently intervened in a head and staff conflict situation that was probably nothing to do with our request for help.[1]

We were reluctant to ask schools for help in any but the first few weeks of the summer term, and in the case of the non-selective schools the survey had to be done before Easter to obtain a sample of fourth-year pupils. The outcome was that 7,457 pupils from thirty schools were surveyed. The basic characteristics of the schools are given in Table 4, Chapter 1.

The final sample is not claimed to be (nor was it designed to be) either a representative sample of pupils or a representative sample of schools. It is a representative sample of pupils in schools whose organisational characteristics are known, and may be compared with those of a reasonably representative sample of schools. It was possible to show retrospectively that the schools in the sub-sample of thirty were in fact fairly representative of schools of their kind by status and sex composition, in terms of their structural variables. The

[1] This explains why only two girls' grammar schools appear in the sample instead of the planned number of three.

mean scores on most of the scales measuring structural variables were similar for matched types of school in each of the two samples.

A reservation that was made about the schools' survey sample should be repeated here. It is possible that the schools who were unable or unwilling to help were atypical in some special way or ways. This possibility cannot, of course, be tested.

9 Pupils' background information

Schools were asked to provide from their records information about each pupil's father's occupation and score in verbal reasoning or other tests used in secondary selection. We were able to offer a small honorarium to a head or delegated teacher for this work or overtime payment to a secretary. The information requested was quite factual and there were no fears of distortion due to payment, which was not always taken up. Where information about a pupil's intelligence-test scores were missing, supplementary tests were sent to the schools or taken and administered by the fieldworkers. The Otis Beta Test Form A was used for second and fourth year, and the Differential Aptitude Verbal Reasoning Form A for fifth and seventh years. The results were sent to schools and they were often pleased to have their records made complete.

10 Measurements of involvement

The operationalisation and measurement of involvement may be carried out in a number of different ways. Behaviour, that of pupils in this study, could be studied, directly, or using self-reports of behaviour, or reports of others could be collected. The intensity of involvement could then be inferred by the observer, or rated by a number of observers or judges. Alternatively, involvement could be measured by all the scaling techniques available for the measurement of attitudes.

The pupils' questionnaire included both basic techniques. Pupils were asked to make estimates of the age they would leave school, their expectations of post-school education and occupation. They were also asked to write down the school clubs they attended and the positions of responsibility they held in the school. Our trials in pilot schools had shown that pupils were accurate in their reporting of their club-going and position-holding, when checked with their teachers.

The major part of the questionnaire consisted of fifty-five statements about different aspects of the school, each of which the pupils were asked to tick if they agreed or cross if they disagreed. The decision to use the dichotomous agree/disagree criterion was taken for two reasons. First, our trials with five-point scales of agreement and disagreement showed that the less able pupils were very slow to answer the questions and had difficulty in discriminating their desired response.[1] This forcing of choice was clearly not so acceptable to some older and more intelligent pupils in the survey, a few of whom made reservations to this effect in the final section of the questionnaire which invited any comments or further opinions. This was regrettable, but it was important for all pupils to be presented with the same structuring in order to make acceptable comparisons.

The second reason for the use of the simple tick/cross response was that although the response to each question was available for analysis, each question also formed a part of a scale (or scales) for the measurement of involvement, the scores for which were obtained by the summation of the number of agreements with the questions constituting items of the scales.

Seven scales were constructed and included in the questionnaire, one twenty-six item Thurstone-type scale for general involvement, and six shorter summation scales for involvement in particular aspects of the school.

The items forming the general involvement scale were presented in Table 6, Chapter 2. There were a number of reasons for the choice of a Thurstone-type scale.[2] The construction of such scales entails the use of judges who are presented with a large number of statements which they are asked to rank according to the degree to which agreement with each statement indicates favourability towards that which the scale is intended to measure. The use of judges in constructing the general involvement scale obviated the possibility of our own personal views on what constituted high or low involvement influencing the content of the scale.

The judges used were students or former students following advanced courses at the Bristol and Exeter Institutes of Education. The intention was to obtain a sample of interested, co-operative, practising secondary-school teachers and headteachers. One hundred and thirty-nine were asked to help. There was no reply from forty, and eleven letters were returned marked 'wrong address'. In view of the career mobility associated with the taking of advanced qualifications in education it is likely that many of the forty non-replies had also moved. Twelve replies arrived too late to be included in the scale-construction. Three had stopped teaching in schools. Only two refusals were obtained. Seventy-one judges were eventually used. A retrospective check on the responses of the latecomers' choices

[1] The tick/cross single-column method was also found to be more acceptable than the usual two-column agree/disagree.

[2] See also Chapter 1 for a discussion of the choice.

indicated that they would have made no significant difference to the final scale.

It is not claimed that the teacher–judges were a typical sample of secondary-school teachers. Comparisons of different sets of judges' ranking of items suggest that the nature of the judges may affect the value of the score assigned to each statement but not the interval of the scores between statements, so that when the scale scores are used comparatively, as in this study, the effect of the judges' differences is not important. (See Selltiz (1965).)

It could be argued that the use of teachers as judges produced a scale which represents a teacherly perspective on school involvement, which may differ from that of the pupils. The evidence of the effect of changing judges on scale scores does not support this criticism, but even if the scale does represent a teachers' viewpoint this could be an appropriate one in that the organisation of the school is largely in the hands of the teachers.

The items forming the scales were derived from two principal sources. Exploratory interviews were carried out with small groups of three or four pupils from the pilot schools. The groups varied by age, sex and stream-status. The loosely structured interview ('discussion') covered the main aspects of school life and was tape recorded. To minimise the problem of the socially acceptable response, the pupils, who had been chosen by the school from the top, middle and bottom of each class concerned, were interviewed at the research unit. Some of the scale items were taken from transcripts of pupils' comments made in these interviews.

The second source of items was the use of pupils' written material. Children of different ages and sex in the pilot schools were asked to complete a number of sentences which referred to different aspects of school, e.g. The school assembly is . . .

The teacher–judges were eventually presented with 120 statements for their judgment. The construction of the scale followed the usual procedure, which resulted in the twenty-six item-scale shown in Table 6, Chapter 2. The items represent a variety of aspects of the school and a range of scores. A pupil's score is the mean score for the items agreed with.

The six short scales were constructed to measure involvement in expressive activities, instrumental activities, school assembly, House activities, school uniform and pastoral care.[1]

All the questions forming each scale were ones that received high scores from the teacher–judges. A pupil's score was obtained by the summation of the number of agreements with the items forming the scale. Like Thurstone-type scales, these scales may be regarded as being interval scales, but although they have a fixed zero (no questions

[1] These scales are similar to those used by Sugarman (1967) and King (1969a).

194

agreed with), they may not be regarded as ratio scales. The reliability of these scales is expressed in the high positive correlations between incidence of agreement with each item and the total score.[1]

The advantages of these scales are similar to those of the Thurstone-type scale for general involvement. The use of judges eliminated the possibility of personal bias, and the nature of the scale implies that involvement is not unidimensional, in that a given score may represent a number of different patterns of agreement with the questions.[1] Separate Thurstone-type scales could have been used for these measurements but this would have involved the inclusion of more questions, which because of the greater length of such scales would have considerably lengthened the time taken to complete the questionnaire.

11 The administration of the pupils' questionnaire

The method for the administration of the questionnaire was arrived at through trials in the pilot schools. Using a sample of 120 pupils three different questionnaires were tested; some were completed anonymously, others asked for names, some were administered by teachers, others by fieldworkers. Altogether twelve different situations were created. On the basis of the analysis of the results, our observations, and comments made by teachers, it was concluded that response was not appreciably affected by who administered the questionnaire, or whether it was anonymous or not. To a large extent these factors were rendered unimportant by a simple methodological innovation. At the same time that the pupils were given the questionnaires they were also given a large envelope. The instructions on the front of the questionnaire, which were read aloud by the administrator, whilst the pupils read their own copy, included the sentence, 'when you have finished, place the sheets in the envelope provided and then seal the envelope'.

The procedure followed in the survey was as follows. A fieldworker took the questionnaires to the school on the morning of the survey. The questionnaire was completed in the different teaching groups during the same period of the day to prevent leakage. The questionnaire was administered by the teacher normally taking the class. In some cases it was possible to brief all the teachers who helped beforehand, but in any case printed instructions were given to each one together with a short account of the purpose of the survey and its methodology. In non-selective schools the fieldworker usually offered to help in a second-year low-stream class where pupils might have some difficulties in understanding. The completed questionnaires were collected and taken away by the fieldworker. The whole

[1] Not for a score of 0 or the highest possible score.

operation was designed to cause as little disruption and inconvenience to the school as possible.

The administration of questionnaires to pupils in a school setting has its methodological advantages and disadvantages. The advantages include having a virtually captive sample, and therefore a high response rate. In addition, the completion of a questionnaire is very similar to many school tasks involving reading and selection of responses, and so pupils are well socialised in this respect. The disadvantages are almost corollaries of the advantages. The researcher is utilising the authority system of the school, which may distort the pupils' responses. One fear is that some pupils will tend to give socially acceptable responses, perhaps regarding the questionnaires as a test with right answers. Another, not necessarily contradictory, is that others may give bravado, anti-social responses. Both could occur as a kind of polarisation effect. These possibilities are difficult to test. Our impression is that neither was of any significance, and this we attribute largely to the use of the envelope. There was often a visible reaction on the part of pupils when they saw the envelope, and (we infer) recognition of its implications, which were reinforced by another part of the introduction, 'Your answers are completely confidential and will not be shown to anyone in the school.' This is also confirmed by the wide range of comments, both critical and appreciative, made in the free response section of the questionnaire.

Appendix B
A note on the methods of analysis

The analyses concerned four sets of variables: structural, contextual, pupil involvement and pupil social characteristics.

A number of problems arise in the analysis of so many variables, but these can be reduced by the application of theoretical perspectives drawn from previous studies, and by relating the form of the analysis to the kinds of explanations to be made of the results.

School organisation analysis

The variables concerned were structural and contextual.

Structural variables were generally used as dependent variables in relation to the key contextual variables of school status and sex composition as independent variables. In addition both structural and contextual variables, which were continuous (unlike sex composition and status which are categoric), were correlated.

Pupil involvement analysis

The variables concerned were pupil involvement and pupil social characteristics.

Data were gathered for individual pupils, but all of the analyses were for aggregates of pupils. The principles behind the choice of aggregates or groups of pupils relate to the kinds of explanations posed. This study was concerned with the relationships between school organisation and pupil involvement, and so it was necessary to analyse involvement in the organisation groups in which it was manifest. Hence the basic unit of the analysis of pupil involvement was the individual school.

To have chosen types of school as basic units would have incurred the possibility of committing an aggregative fallacy. (See Robinson (1950); Swift (1970); King and Easthope (1973).) An analysis of the mean scores of all pupils in all grammar schools would not necessarily reveal anything about involvement patterns in any individual grammar school. The school is the membership group of the pupil. An aggregate of all the pupils in all grammar schools is a completely artificial group to which none of the pupils belongs.

The choice of the school as a basic unit for the analysis of involvement also follows from the method of constructing the scales used in its measurement. Many of the questions constituting scale items referred to the pupil's own school, for example, 'The punishments are fair in this school.' In addition, the pupil would be drawing upon his experience of his present school in rating items like 'School work is usually interesting.'

In some analyses mean involvement within individual schools was made a dependent variable in relation to the pupils' age, sex and social class. These within-school aggregates are often rather small, particularly when three independent variables operate, i.e. sex, age and social class, and the numbers are sometimes too small for the differences in mean score to be statistically significant. Nevertheless, such differences may sometimes be socially significant, and conversely a statistically significant difference may have no social significance. For example, middle-class pupils were always a minority in modern schools, and differences in the mean scores for involvement between the social classes keeping age and sex constant were seldom large enough for statistical significance, but if all or nearly all such schools showed the same trend in the direction of the difference in mean scores by social class, then the difference may be of some social significance. To analyse for all modern schools in an effort to achieve statistical significance by increasing the numbers involved would be to commit an aggregative fallacy, since this grouping would not be the membership group of any pupil. In addition it may happen that the false aggregate may not show a statistically significant difference in the mean scores of the groups of pupils in question, because although the pattern of the *difference* in the mean scores may be the same in all individual schools, the *levels* of the scores may vary greatly from one school to another.

School organisation and pupil involvement analysis

All four kinds of variables were used.

Mean involvement scores were used as dependent variables in relation to sex composition and school status as independent

Routledge & Kegan Paul

9 PARK STREET, BOSTON
MASSACHUSETTS   02108
Telephone: 617/742-5863

*The Publishers present their
compliments to the Editor and have
pleasure in sending for review a copy
of the accompanying publication.
They would greatly appreciate
receiving a marked copy of his
journal containing any notice that
may be given to the book.*

*N.B. Reviews should not appear in the
press prior to the date of publication.*

SCHOOL ORGANISATION AND
PUPIL INVOLVEMENT

by

RONALD KING

International Library of Sociology

Published Price $10.95

Date of Publication   6th September 1973

variables. Continuous contextual and structural variables were correlated against mean involvement scores using Kendall's tau (1955). The mean involvement scores for each school were for all pupils and pupils aggregated by sex, age and social class in several permutations.

Appendix C
Additional tables

TABLE A *Social class differences in general involvement*

Girls' Modern

No.	01 WC	01 MC	03 WC	03 MC	06 WC	06 MC	22 WC	22 MC
2nd year mean	5·9	5·7	6·1	6·4	5·4	5·8	5·8	6·0
(n S.D.)	(58 0·56)	(17 0·82)	(53 0·65)	(25 0·33)	(76 0·66)	(28 0·73)	(47 0·58)	(21 0·35)
4th year mean	5·8	5·5	5·9	5·4	5·4	5·3	5·5	5·6
(n S.D.)	(49 0·63)	(10 0·59)	(51 0·61)	(25 0·85)	(53 0·71)	(21 0·76)	(50 0·67)	(17 0·67)
5th year mean	6·1	5·8	5·9	5·9	5·5	5·8	5·5	5·4
(n S.D.)	(13 0·47)	(6 0·72)	(19 0·69)	(23 0·59)	(21 0·62)	(6 0·80)	(19 0·54)	(15 0·62)

Boys' Modern

No.	16 WC	16 MC	21 WC	21 MC	25 WC	25 MC	26 WC	26 MC
2nd year mean	5·5	5·7	5·9	5·9	5·5	5·5	5·7	5·8
(n S.D.)	(40 0·55)	(11 0·58)	(71 0·57)	(38 0·45)	(50 0·54)	(10 0·62)	(47 0·66)	(39 0·47)
4th year mean	5·4	5·5	5·8	5·4	5·5	5·7	5·5	5·6
(n S.D.)	(29 0·70)	(11 0·94)	(75 0·60)	(28 0·63)	(28 0·63)	(10 0·37)	(47 0·73)	(26 0·48)
5th year mean	6·2	6·1	5·9	5·9	5·4	5·9	5·9	5·7
(n S.D.)	(13 0·43)	(9 0·18)	(44 0·44)	(19 0·43)	(23 0·62)	(12 0·53)	(19 0·51)	(17 0·38)

Legend WC = working class; MC = middle class

Mixed Modern No.	04		07		11	
	WC	MC	WC	MC	WC	MC
Boys						
2nd year mean	5·7	5·6	5·7	5·1	5·9	5·7
(n S.D.)	(22 0·73)	(10 0·56)	(21 0·40)	(1 —)	(30 0·43)	(15 0·59)
4th year mean	5·7	5·8	6·0	6·2	5·9	5·8
(n S.D.)	(19 0·80)	(14 0·43)	(19 0·51)	(2 0·03)	(35 0·53)	(21 0·54)
5th year mean	5·9	5·9			6·2	5·9
(n S.D.)	(15 0·52)	(19 0·44)			(12 0·43)	(11 0·47)
Girls						
2nd year mean	6·0	5·8	6·0	6·2	5·7	5·7
(n S.D.)	(27 0·49)	(12 0·80)	(18 0·55)	(3 0·43)	(22 0·54)	(22 0·54)
4th year mean	5·8	5·8	6·2	6·4	5·9	5·9
(n S.D.)	(24 0·65)	(22 0·48)	(15 0·44)	(3 0·25)	(24 0·60)	(19 0·55)
5th year mean	6·1	6·0	6·2	5·8	5·8	6·1
(n S.D.)	(16 0·51)	(18 -048)	(3 0·37)	(1 —)	(5 0·59)	(13 0·44)

TABLE A—*contd*

Mixed Modern No.	15		19		20	
	WC	MC	WC	MC	WC	MC
Boys						
2nd year mean (n S.D.)	5·6 (33 0·67)	5·5 (6 0·72)	5·0 (9 0·90)	6·0 (2 0·23)	5·8 (16 0·46)	5·6 (8 0·56)
4th year mean (n S.D.)	5·6 (40 0·50)	5·7 (21 0·51)	5·4 (7 0·37)	5·5 (7 0·33)	5·7 (20 0·57)	5·3 (13 0·60)
5th year mean (n S.D.)	5·8 (15 0·56)	5·8 (12 0·49)	5·8 (4 0·59)	5·8 (2 0·21)	6·0 (17 0·42)	5·8 (16 0·69)
Girls						
2nd year mean (n S.D.)	6·1 (20 0·47)	5·8 (10 0·63)	5·5 (9 0·65)	5·6 (4 0·30)	6·1 (15 0·45)	6·1 (14 0·53)
4th year mean (n S.D.)	5·8 (33 0·56)	5·8 (19 0·69)	5·4 (12 0·64)	6·0 (6 0·36)	5·9 (16 0·57)	5·9 (5 0·32)
5th year mean (n S.D.)	6·3 (16 0·39)	6·2 (10 0·40)		5·3 (3 0·62)	5·8 (10 0·62)	5·6 (4 0·35)

Girls' _Grammar_ No.	17		18		_Boys'_ _Grammar_ 02		09	
	WC	MC	WC	MC	WC	MC	WC	MC
2nd year mean	5·6	5·6	5·9	5·8	5·9	5·8	5·7	5·7
(n S.D.)	(46 0·70)	(40 0·54)	(49 0·54)	(58 0·63)	(49 0·46)	(36 0·56)	(13 0·65)	(20 0·68)
4th year mean	5·1	5·3	5·8	5·7	5·7	5·8	5·9	5·6
(n S.D.)	(32 0·85)	(46 0·62)	(44 0·49)	(60 0·59)	(47 0·55)	(36 0·51)	(8 0·41)	(14 0·55)
5th year mean	5·6	5·6	5·9	5·8	5·7	5·7	5·4	5·4
(n S.D.)	(26 0·54)	(44 0·68)	(20 0·52)	(44 0·67)	(37 0·74)	(49 0·66)	(12 0·49)	(19 0·61)
7th year mean	6·0	5·9	5·9	5·4	5·5	5·7	5·6	5·5
(n S.D.)	(5 0·27)	(18 0·45)	(7 0·77)	(14 0·46)	(23 0·55)	(42 0·60)	(3 0·11)	(12 0·25)

203

TABLE A—*contd*

Mixed Grammar No.	08		13		27	
	WC	MC	WC	MC	WC	MC
Boys						
2nd year mean	5·7	5·9	5·9	5·7	5·9	5·9
(n S.D.)	(17 0·50)	(27 0·59)	(11 0·76)	(16 0·65)	(5 0·55)	(18 0·44)
4th year mean	5·3	5·4	5·5	5·5	6·1	5·6
(n S.D.)	(14 0·75)	(25 0·70)	(7 0·54)	(19 0·67)	(5 0·62)	(9 0·41)
5th year mean	5·8	5·6	5·9	5·8	5·2	5·6
(n S.D.)	(12 0·57)	(23 0·44)	(11 0·44)	(27 0·60)	(7 1·07)	(15 0·84)
7th year mean	5·7	5·8	6·3	5·6	5·8	5·6
(n S.D.)	(10 0·65)	(19 0·63)	(3 0·17)	(18 0·53)	(4 0·29)	(7 0·37)
Girls						
2nd year mean	6·0	6·0	6·2	6·1	6·0	6·2
(n S.D.)	(24 0·34)	(30 0·52)	(11 0·40)	(24 0·42)	(10 0·50)	(19 0·45)
4th year mean	5·4	5·6	6·1	5·6	5·8	5·8
(n S.D.)	(22 0·53)	(29 0·67)	(10 0·48)	(29 0·93)	(10 0·35)	(20 0·68)
5th year mean	5·7	5·8	5·8	5·8	6·1	5·6
(n S.D.)	(16 0·42)	(34 0·54)	(11 0·37)	(33 0·75)	(8 0·94)	(11 0·65)
7th year mean	6·2	6·0	6·0	5·7	6·0	6·0
(n S.D.)	(12 0·34)	(20 0·46)	(6 0·28)	(15 0·78)	(1 —)	(5 0·55)

Mixed Comprehensive No. 24

	Boys WC	Boys MC	Girls WC	Girls MC
2nd year mean (n S.D.)	—	—	—	—
4th year mean (n S.D.)	5·8 (17 0·44)	6·2 (12 0·40)	5·9 (34 0·61)	5·9 (26 0·73)
5th year mean (n S.D.)	—	—	5·5 (39 0·74)	5·6 (39 0·67)
7th year mean (n S.D.)	—	—	6·0 (18 0·39)	5·8 (15 0·51)

Girls' Comprehensive No. 12

	WC	MC
2nd year mean (n S.D.)	6·0 (46 0·52)	6·0 (22 0·52)
4th year mean (n S.D.)	5·8 (27 0·86)	5·7 (6 0·47)
5th year mean (n S.D.)	6·1 (10 0·86)	6·2 (4 0·34)

TABLE A—*contd*

Mixed Comprehensive	No.	05 WC	05 MC	10 WC	10 MC	14 WC	14 MC
Boys							
2nd year mean		5·8	5·8	5·4	5·2	5·6	5·7
(n S.D.)		(35 0·65)	(8 0·61)	(45 0·57)	(18 0·54)	(55 0·55)	(21 0·47)
4th year mean		5·4	5·4	5·7	5·8	5·4	5·6
(n S.D.)		(39 0·68)	(9 0·49)	(81 0·58)	(40 0·49)	(47 0·65)	(15 0·54)
5th year mean		5·7	5·8	5·7	5·5	5·6	5·5
(n S.D.)		(47 0·53)	(15 0·57)	(46 0·45)	(19 0·60)	(22 0·50)	(16 0·38)
7th year mean		—	—	5·6	5·5	5·8	5·7
(n S.D.)				(3 0·41)	(3 0·32)	(9 0·43)	(7 0·40)
Girls							
2nd year mean		5·7	6·0	5·5	5·5	5·7	5·8
(n S.D.)		(30 0·49)	(4 0·55)	(43 0·72)	(20 0·65)	(67 0·57)	(33 0·57)
4th year mean		5·5	5·8	5·6	5·6	5·3	5·4
(n S.D.)		(33 0·75)	(9 0·44)	(61 0·70)	(30 0·58)	(29 0·73)	(22 0·60)
5th year mean		6·1	6·1	5·9	5·6	5·6	5·5
(n S.D.)		(26 0·44)	(15 0·46)	(28 0·62)	(20 0·58)	(27 0·54)	(17 0·61)
7th year mean		—	—	6·0	6·2	5·9	5·4
(n S.D.)				(5 0·15)	(2 0·13)	(3 0·49)	(3 0·24)

Mixed

Comprehensive No.	23 WC	23 MC	29 WC	29 MC	30 WC	30 MC
Boys						
2nd year mean	5·6	5·9	5·9	6·2	5·5	5·8
(n S.D.)	(42 0·53)	(9 0·35)	(25 0·67)	(16 0·44)	(32 0·58)	(18 0·44)
4th year mean	5·7	6·1	5·9	5·9	5·9	5·4
(n S.D.)	(40 0·55)	(8 0·29)	(25 0·44)	(18 0·45)	(18 0·37)	(11 0·53)
5th year mean	6·1	6·1	5·7	5·7	5·8	5·7
(n S.D.)	(22 0·54)	(8 0·19)	(32 0·59)	(21 0·48)	(18 0·55)	(20 0·53)
7th year mean	5·7	4·9	5·9	4·5	5·9	6·1
(n S.D.)	(4 0·30)	(1 —)	(2 0·25)	(1 —)	(8 0·46)	(10 0·20)
Girls						
2nd year mean	5·8	6·1	5·7	6·1	6·0	6·0
(n S.D.)	(27 0·48)	(10 0·47)	(18 0·47)	(19 0·53)	(26 0·53)	(27 0·56)
4th year mean	5·5	5·6	5·8	5·9	6·1	5·7
(n S.D.)	(32 0·79)	(6 0·66)	(17 0·55)	(14 0·60)	(13 0·56)	(8 0·49)
5th year mean	6·1	5·9	5·9	5·5	6·0	6·0
(n S.D.)	(24 0·40)	(4 0·53)	(26 0·57)	(3 0·63)	(19 0·51)	(29 0·52)
7th year mean	6·0	5·8	5·6	—	6·1	5·8
(n S.D.)	(2 0·25)	(1 —)	(2 0·08)		(1 —)	(4 0·09)

TABLE B *Age and sex differences in general involvement*

Girls' Modern No.	01	03	06	22	Girls' Comprehensive No.	12
2nd year mean	5·8	6·1	5·5	5·8		6·0
(n S.D.)	(88 0·63)	(98 0·64)	(108 0·70)	(77 0·52)		(101 0·51)
4th year mean	5·7	5·7	5·4	5·5		5·8
(n S.D.)	(70 0·64)	(98 0·69)	(79 0·71)	(69 0·66)		(48 0·76)
5th year mean	6·1	5·9	5·6	5·5		6·0
(n S.D.)	(21 0·56)	(54 0·60)	(27 0·68)	(37 0·56)		(20 0·78)

Boys' Modern No.	16	21	25	26
2nd year mean	5·6	5·8	5·5	5·7
(n S.D.)	(63 0·59)	(121 0·57)	(71 0·55)	(97 0·60)
4th year mean	5·4	5·7	5·5	5·5
(n S.D.)	(61 0·71)	(109 0·63)	(45 0·64)	(79 0·66)
5th year mean	6·1	5·9	5·5	5·8
(n S.D.)	(24 0·34)	(66 0·44)	(36 0·62)	(43 0·47)

Girls' Grammar No.	17	18	Boys' Grammar	02	09	28
2nd year mean	5·6	5·8		5·9	5·7	6·1
(n S.D.)	(91 0·62)	(115 0·64)		(94 0·51)	(35 0·63)	(64 0·47)
4th year mean	5·2	5·7		5·7	5·7	6·0
(n S.D.)	(95 0·77)	(107 0·55)		(94 0·58)	(23 0·51)	(62 0·56)
5th year mean	5·5	5·8		5·7	5·4	5·9
(n S.D.)	(79 0·62)	(67 0·63)		(97 0·69)	(34 0·57)	(72 0·53)
7th year mean	5·9	5·7		5·6	5·5	5·7
(n S.D.)	(25 0·41)	(23 0·63)		(77 0·64)	(17 0·23)	(37 0·49)

Mixed Modern No.	04	07	11	15	19	20
Boys						
2nd year mean	5·7	5·6	5·8	5·6	5·3	5·7
(n S.D.)	(44 0·65)	(27 0·51)	(45 0·49)	(43 0·73)	(16 0·85)	(29 0·62)
4th year mean	5·7	5·9	5·9	5·6	5·5	5·6
(n S.D.)	(42 0·66)	(24 0·42)	(63 0·53)	(62 0·51)	(16 0·37)	(51 0·59)
5th year mean	5·9	—	6·0	5·8	5·8	5·7
(n S.D.)	(39 0·51)	(0 —)	(24 0·60)	(27 0·53)	(6 0·50)	(45 0·66)
Girls						
2nd year mean	5·9	6·0	5·8	6·0	5·5	5·9
(n S.D.)	(53 0·59)	(22 0·60)	(51 0·56)	(35 0·54)	(17 0·58)	(40 0·62)
4th year mean	5·9	6·2	5·9	5·8	5·6	5·8
(n S.D.)	(51 0·56)	(26 0·42)	(49 0·56)	(59 0·63)	(19 0·63)	(33 0·61)
5th year mean	6·0	6·1	6·0	6·3	5·3	5·7
(n S.D.)	(37 0·47)	(4 0·30)	(19 0·51)	(30 0·38)	(4 0·54)	(17 0·60)

Mixed Grammar No.	08	13	27	Mixed Comprehensive No.	24
Boys					
2nd year mean	5·8	5·9	6·0		
(n S.D.)	(50 0·56)	(33 0·68)	(24 0·49)		
4th year mean	5·4	5·5	5·7		5·9
(n S.D.)	(43 0·71)	(32 0·63)	(17 0·67)		(32 0·46)
5th year mean	5·6	5·8	5·5		
(n S.D.)	(37 0·49)	(47 0·58)	(27 0·89)		
7th year mean	5·8	5·8	5·7		
(n S.D.)	(33 0·61)	(24 0·54)	(11 0·36)		
Girls					
2nd year mean	6·0	6·2	6·1		
(n S.D.)	(58 0·46)	(42 0·41)	(30 0·48)		
4th year mean	5·5	5·7	5·8		5·9
(n S.D.)	(54 0·61)	(43 0·86)	(31 0·61)		(68 0·66)
5th year mean	5·7	5·8	5·8		5·5
(n S.D.)	(54 0·50)	(53 0·64)	(21 0·82)		(91 0·74)
7th year mean	6·0	5·8	6·0		5·9
(n S.D.)	(36 0·41)	(29 0·70)	(6 0·51)		(37 0·47)

Mixed Comprehensive No.	05	10	14	23	29	30
Boys						
2nd year mean	5·8	5·3	5·6	5·6	6·0	5·6
(n S.D.)	(58 0·66)	(69 0·66)	(81 0·53)	(63 0·58)	(49 0·67)	(51 0·55)
4th year mean	5·5	5·7	5·4	5·8	5·8	5·7
(n S.D.)	(60 0·63)	(142 0·62)	(68 0·68)	(53 0·54)	(48 0·49)	(42 0·50)
5th year mean	5·7	5·6	5·6	6·1	5·7	5·7
(n S.D.)	(69 0·53)	(73 0·57)	(40 0·46)	(33 0·47)	(56 0·56)	(42 0·52)
7th year mean	6·0	5·6	5·8	5·5	5·4	6·0
(n S.D.)	(7 0·49)	(6 0·37)	(16 0·42)	(5 0·42)	(4 0·58)	(18 0·36)
Girls						
2nd year mean	5·7	5·5	5·7	5·8	5·9	6·0
(n S.D.)	(42 0·57)	(66 0·70)	(106 0·57)	(44 0·53)	(42 0·55)	(53 0·54)
4th year mean	5·6	5·5	5·3	5·5	5·8	5·9
(n S.D.)	(46 0·74)	(107 0·67)	(57 0·70)	(41 0·78)	(37 0·59)	(29 0·63)
5th year mean	6·1	5·8	5·6	6·0	5·9	6·0
(n S.D.)	(46 0·46)	(54 0·61)	(47 0·55)	(28 0·43)	(31 0·57)	(48 0·51)
7th year mean	6·0	6·1	5·6	5·9	5·6	5·9
(n S.D.)	(8 0·51)	(7 0·15)	(6 0·47)	(5 0·35)	(2 0·00)	(5 0·13)

Statistically significant mean differences (5 per cent or beyond)
2nd year/4th year boys, school nos 02, 05, 07, 10, 13, 14, 16, 23, 26, 27, 29;
2nd year/4th year girls, school nos 03, 08, 12, 13, 14, 15, 17, 22, 23, 27;
4th year/5th year boys, school nos 04, 05, 08, 13, 14, 16, 21, 23, 26;
4th year/5th year girls, school nos 01, 03, 05, 08, 10, 14, 15, 17, 23;
Girls/boys 2nd year, school nos 07, 13, 15, 20, 30.

TABLE C *Standardisation of expressive activities scale*

Item	Incidence (%)
No eating in playground	11
Pupils leave dining table with whole dining group	11
Scooters prohibited	13
Motor bikes prohibited	13
No school work to be done in formrooms at break	13
No games in formroom at break	13
Pupils line up before entering school	14
Special places in official bus or coach	15
Line up after break	17
Homework forbidden in formrooms	17
Rules about eating on way to school	19
Cars prohibited	19
Special cycle parking places	21
Rules about behaviour on official bus	24
All pupils must buy copy of school magazine	28
Each pupil has special dinner place	28
Adults 'first in queue' rule at bus stops	29
Pupils may not enter classrooms before teachers	31
Special playground entrances	39
Sandwich lunches require permission	40
Pupils queue outside classrooms	40
All pupils must attend swimming gala	44
Restricted access to cloakrooms	47
No records to be played in formrooms	47
No rooms for the exclusive use of pupils	47
Pupils supervised on school bus	49
Each pupil has special dinner table	50
Certain games prohibited in playground	51
Rules about the use of motor transport	53
Individual places allocated in cloakroom	53
Controlled access to stairs and corridors	54
Eating prohibited in formrooms	56
Dinner tables supervised	56
Sandwich lunches forbidden	58
Pupils leave dinner table when instructed	60
Special playground areas	60
Special entry time	64
No drinking tea, etc. in form rooms	65
Rules about hair length or style	65
Journey to hall supervised	65
Permission required to use bicycle	65
Only those with health problems exempt PE	69
Pupils must attend speech day	71
Pupils leave dinner table with other table members	72
Only those with health problems exempt games	78
Pupils may not leave dinner table when they wish	78
Special entry doors	78
Permission required to leave school in dinner hour	79
Queue for dinner	81
Restricted access to formrooms in dinner hour	82
Building cleared of pupils at break	82

Item	Incidence (%)
School diners may not leave school in dinner hour	83
Special cloakroom areas	85
Restricted access to formrooms at break	88
All pupils must attend sports day	90
	(N = 72)

TABLE D *Social class differences in expressive involvement – mean scores on scale*

Girls' modern schools No.		01	03*	06	22*
4th year WC	mean	5·2	5·3	4·7	4·8
	(n S.D.)	(49 0·87)	(51 0·92)	(53 1·18)	(50 1·12)
MC	mean	5·0	4·4	4·6	4·2
	(n S.D.)	(10 0·77)	(25 1·17)	(21 1·05)	(17 0·94)

Mixed grammar schools No.		08	13	27
4th year girls' WC	mean	4·7	5·3	5·0
	(n S.D.)	(22 1·35)	(10 0·64)	(10 0·63)
MC	mean	4·8	4·8	4·7
	(n S.D.)	(29 1·38)	(29 1·30)	(20 0·90)

Mixed Comprehensives No.	05	10	14	23	29	30
5th year girls' WC mean	5·4	5·0	4·7	5·3	5·0	5·4
(n S.D.)	(26 0·74)	(28 1·05)	(27 1·09)	(24 0·84)	(26 1·04)	(10 9·81)
MC mean	5·3	4·8	4·4	4·0	4·7	5·0
(n S.D.)	(15 0·93)	(20 1·25)	(17 1·42)	(4 1·22)	(3 1·25)	(29 1·16)

Boys' Grammar Schools No.		02	09	28
4th year WC	mean	4·7	4·6	5·1
	(n S.D.)	(47 1·42)	(8 1·22)	(15 0·77)
MC	mean	4·7	4·2	4·9
	(n S.D.)	(36 1·10)	(14 1·32)	(43 1·22)

* Significant at the 5 per cent level.

TABLE E *Social class differences in expressive involvement –
percentage occupancy of positions*

Girls' Modern Schools	No.	01	03	06	22		
2nd year WC	%	41	42	38	62		
	(n)	(58)	(53)	(76)	(47)		
MC	%	47	61	39	76		
	(n)	(17)	(23)	(28)	(21)		

Comprehensives	No.	05	10	14	23	29	30
Girls' 5th year WC	%	65	50	56	39	57	50
	(n)	(26)	(28)	(27)	(24)	(26)	(19)
MC	%	73	70	41	75	69	56
	(n)	(15)	(20)	(17)	(4)	(3)	(29)

Boys' Modern	No.	16	21	25	26		
2nd year WC	%	35	37	49	45		
	(n)	(40)	(71)	(50)	(47)		
MC	%	45	41	56	50		
	(n)	(11)	(38)	(10)	(39)		
4th year WC	%	31	51	64	51		
	(n)	(29)	(75)	(28)	(47)		
MC	%	64	54	70	63		
	(n)	(11)	(28)	(10)	(26)		

Boys' Grammar	No.	02	09	28			
2nd year WC	%	47	38	36			
	(n)	(49)	(13)	(11)			
MC	%	60	65	72			
	(n)	(36)	(20)	(46)			

Mixed Grammar	No.	08	13	27			
4th year Boys WC	%	79	88	100			
	(n)	(14)	(7)	(5)			
MC	%	52	63	50			
	(n)	(25)	(19)	(9)			
5th year Boys WC	%	58	81	43			
	(n)	(12)	(11)	(7)			
MC	%	87	85	80			
	(n)	(23)	(27)	(15)			

Statistically significant differences (5 per cent or over by chi-square)
2nd year, school no. 28; 4th year, nos 16, 27; 5th year, nos 23, 08, 27.

TABLE F *Percentage of pupils of different sexes occupying school positions in mixed grammar schools*

School No.		2nd year B	2nd year G	4th year B	4th year G	5th year B	5th year G	7th year B	7th year G
08	%	30	25	44	22	42	17	38	19
	n	50	58	43	54	37	54	33	36
13	%	54	5	88	48	63	37	100	21
	n	33	42	32	43	47	53	24	24
27	%	54	53	76	45	63	71	45	50
	n	24	30	17	31	27	21	11	6

Statistically significant differences (5 per cent or higher by chi-square)
2nd year, school no. 13; 4th year, school nos 08, 13 and 27; 5th year, school
nos 08 and 13; 7th year, school no. 13.

TABLE G *Age differences in expressive involvement – mean scores on scale*

Boys' Grammar	No.	02*	09	28
	2nd year mean	5·0	4·7	5·1
	(n S.D.)	(94 0·99)	(35 1·23)	(64 0·98)
	4th year mean	4·6	4·4	4·4
	(n S.D.)	(94 1·39)	(23 1·28)	(62 1·19)

Mixed Grammar	No.	08*	13	27*
	Girls 2nd year mean	5·3	5·2	5·2
	(n S.D.)	(58 0·93)	(42 0·78)	(30 0·96)
	Girls 4th year mean	4·7	4·9	4·7
	(n S.D.)	(54 1·38)	(43 1·19)	(31 0·09)

* Difference in means of ages 5 per cent significant by t test.

TABLE H *Expressive involvement of girls in grammar schools*

Girls' Grammar No.	17	18	Mixed Grammar No. 08	13	27
2nd year mean	4·5	4·9	5·3	5·2	5·2
(n S.D.)	(91 1·25)	(115 1·14)	(58 0·93)	(42 0·78)	(30 0·96)

TABLE I *Percentage occupancy of positions by school status and sex composition*

Girls' Grammar No.	17	18	Mixed Grammar No.	08	13	27
2nd year % girls (n)	62 (77)	83 (115)		55 (58)	48 (42)	53 (30)

Girls' Modern No.	01	03	06	22
5th year % (n)	100 (21)	72 (54)	85 (27)	71 (38)

Boys' Modern No.	16	21	25	26
5th year % (n)	92 (24)	66 (67)	97 (36)	76 (41)

Mixed Modern No.	04	11	15	19	20
5th year girls % (n)	76 (37)	100 (19)	96 (28)	100 (4)	35 (17)
5th year boys % (n)	62 (39)	92 (24)	68 (28)	100 (6)	44 (45)

Comprehensive No.	05	10	14	23	29	30
5th year girls % (n)	70 (47)	57 (54)	49 (47)	44 (27)	68 (31)	40 (40)
5th year boys % (n)	70 (67)	66 (73)	60 (40)	62 (34)	66 (56)	63 (38)

TABLE J *Age and sex differences in acceptance of school uniform*

Girls' Modern No.	01	03	06	22	Girls' Comprehensive No.	12
2nd year mean (n S.D.)	1·5 (88 0·64)	1·6 (98 0·65)	0·9 (108 0·80)	1·4 (77 0·75)		1·6 (101 0·60)
4th year mean (n S.D.)	1·4 (70 0·68)	1·1 (98 0·77)	0·9 (79 0·70)	1·2 (69 0·76)		1·4 (48 0·73)
5th year mean (n S.D.)	1·6 (21 0·58)	1·3 (54 0·79)	0·7 (27 0·60)	1·1 (37 0·82)		1·8 (20 0·54)

Boys'

Modern No.	16	21	25	26
2nd year				
mean	1·6	1·7	0·8	1·4
(n S.D.)	(63 0·66)	(121 0·57)	(71 0·70)	(97 0·72)
4th year				
mean	1·0	1·2	0·5	0·9
(n S.D.)	(61 0·74)	(109 0·77)	(45 0·54)	(79 0·65)
5th year				
mean	1·4	1·4	0·4	1·1
(n S.D.)	(24 0·70)	(66 0·69)	(36 0·55)	(43 0·68)

Girls' Grammar No.	17	18	*Boys'* Grammar No. 02	09	28
2nd year					
mean	1·3	1·9	1·5	1·1	1·3
(n S.D.)	(91 0·78)	(115 0·74)	(94 0·60)	(35 0·67)	(64 0·74)
4th year					
mean	1·1	0·8	1·2	0·9	0·8
(n S.D.)	(95 0·83)	(107 0·78)	(94 0·81)	(23 0·80)	(62 0·79)
5th year					
mean	1·0	0·6	1·0	0·3	0·5
(n S.D.)	(79 0·80)	(67 0·71)	(97 0·77)	(34 0·46)	(72 0·60)
7th year					
mean	0·9	1·0	1·0	0·8	0·4
(n S.D.)	(25 0·84)	(23 0·71)	(77 0·79)	(17 0·73)	(37 0·48)

Mixed Modern No.	04	07	11	15	19	20
Boys						
2nd year						
mean	1·3	0·7	1·3	1·6	1·2	1·4
(n S.D.)	(44 0·66)	(27 0·61)	(45 0·80)	(43 0·66)	(16 0·81)	(29 0·67)
4th year						
mean	0·9	0·6	1·4	1·0	0·4	1·2
(n S.D.)	(42 0·82)	(24 0·56)	(63 0·79)	(62 0·68)	(16 0·48)	(52 0·78)
5th year						
mean	1·2	—	1·2	0·8	1·2	1·1
(n S.D.)	(39 0·78)	(0 0·00)	(24 0·82)	(28 0·63)	(6 0·90)	(45 0·81)
All mean	1·1	0·6	1·3	1·1	0·8	1·2
(n S.D.)	(125 0·78)	(51 0·59)	(132 0·80)	(133 0·73)	(38 0·81)	(126 0·79)
Girls						
2nd year						
mean	1·6	0·9	1·4	1·6	1·1	1·7
(n S.D.)	(53 0·60)	(22 0·69)	(51 0·69)	(35 0·54)	(17 0·76)	(40 0·55)

TABLE J—*contd*

Mixed Modern No.	04	07	11	15	19	20
Girls contd						
4th year mean	1·5	0·7	1·7	1·5	1·1	1·8
(n S.D.)	(51 0·64)	(26 0·73)	(49 0·59)	(59 0·65)	(19 0·76)	(33 0·41)
5th year mean	1·6	0·5	1·6	1·8	1·0	1·2
(n S.D.)	(37 0·59)	(4 0·50)	(19 0·67)	(30 0·56)	(4 0·71)	(17 0·71)
All mean	1·6	0·7	1·5	1·6	1·1	1·6
(n S.D.)	(141 0·61)	(52 0·71)	(119 0·66)	(124 0·61)	(40 0·75)	(90 0·58)

Mixed Grammar No.	08	13	27	*Mixed Comprehensive* No.	24
Boys					
2nd year mean	1·3	1·4	1·4		
(n S.D.)	(50 0·80)	(33 0·78)	(24 0·64)		
4th year mean	0·9	1·1	1·0		1·3
(n S.D.)	(43 0·80)	(32 0·74)	(17 0·69)		(32 0·77)
5th year mean	1·1	0·8	0·7		
(n S.D.)	(37 0·66)	(47 0·75)	(27 0·70)		
7th year mean	1·0	0·8	0·6		
(n S.D.)	(33 0·69)	(24 0·69)	(11 0·77)		
All mean	1·1	1·0	1·0		
(n S.D.)	(163 0·76)	(136 0·79)	(79 0·75)		
Girls					
2nd year mean	1·5	1·5	1·4		
(n S.D.)	(58 0·72)	(42 0·73)	(30 0·80)		
4th year mean	1·2	0·9	0·9		1·2
(n S.D.)	(54 0·73)	(43 0·74)	(31 0·76)		(68 0·78)
5th year mean	1·4	1·1	0·9		1·0
(n S.D.)	(54 0·74)	(53 0·80)	(21 0·68)		(91 0·79)
7th year mean	1·1	0·9	1·5		1·2
(n S.D.)	(36 0·81)	(24 0·81)	(6 0·76)		(37 0·74)
All mean	1·3	1·1	1·1		
(n S.D.)	(202 0·76)	(162 0·80)	(88 0·79)		

Mixed Compre-hensive No.	05	10	14	23	29	30
Boys						
2nd year						
mean	1·0	1·0	1·2	1·3	1·5	1·4
(n S.D.)	(50 0·80)	(69 0·75)	(81 0·73)	(63 0·75)	(49 0·70)	(51 0·77)
4th year						
mean	1·0	1·0	0·8	1·4	1·2	1·4
(n S.D.)	(60 0·77)	(142 0·75)	(68 0·74)	(53 0·75)	(48 0·75)	(42 0·61)
5th year						
mean	1·0	0·9	0·7	0·9	1·2	1·2
(n S.D.)	(69 0·81)	(73 0·71)	(40 0·71)	(33 0·85)	(56 0·75)	(42 0·80)
7th year						
mean	1·0	0·7	0·8	1·2	0·8	0·7
(n S.D.)	(7 0·76)	(6 0·75)	(16 0·83)	(5 0·75)	(4 0·43)	(18 0·73)
All mean	1·0	1·0	1·0	1·2	1·3	1·3
(n S.D.)	(186 0·79)	(290 0·74)	(205 0·77)	(154 0·79)	(157 0·75)	(153 0·77)
Girls						
2nd year						
mean	1·3	0·9	1·4	1·5	1·7	1·5
(n S.D.)	(42 0·80)	(66 0·83)	(106 0·67)	(44 0·66)	(42 0·56)	(53 0·72)
4th year						
mean	1·2	0·7	0·9	1·1	1·5	1·1
(n S.D.)	(46 0·71)	(107 0·77)	(57 0·75)	(41 0·68)	(37 0·60)	(29 0·73)
5th year						
mean	1·4	0·9	1·1	1·4	1·6	1·1
(n S.D.)	(46 0·71)	(54 0·75)	(47 0·79)	(28 0·72)	(31 0·60)	(48 0·86)
7th year						
mean	1·0	1·1	0·8	1·4	1·5	1·0
(n S.D.)	(8 0·71)	(7 0·35)	(6 0·69)	(5 0·49)	(2 0·50)	(6 0·63)
All mean	1·3	0·8	1·2	1·3	1·6	1·3
(n S.D.)	(142 0·74)	(234 0·79)	(216 0·76)	(118 0·69)	(112 0·59)	(136 0·79)

Statistically significant differences of mean scores (5 per cent or higher)
All boys/all girls, school nos 04, 05, 11, 13, 14, 16, 20, 29;
2nd year/4th year boys, school nos 02, 04, 08, 14, 15, 16, 21, 25, 26, 28;
2nd year/4th year girls, school nos 03, 12, 13, 18, 23, 27, 30.

TABLE K *Age and sex differences in involvement in school assembly*

Girls' Modern No.	01	03	06	22	*Girls' Compre-hensive* No	12
2nd year						
mean	1·5	1·5	1·0	0·9		1·4
(n S.D.)	(88 0·75)	(98 0·81)	(108 0·90)	(77 0·88)		(101 0·77)

TABLE K—*contd*

Girls' Modern No.	01	03	06	22	Girls' Compre-hensive No.	12
4th year mean	1·3	0·8	0·6	0·5		1·0
(n S.D.)	(70 0·86)	(98 0·88)	(79 0·82)	(69 0·73)		(48 0·85)
5th year mean	0·9	1·1	0·5	0·5		1·7
(n S.D.)	(21 0·87)	(54 0·92)	(27 0·74)	(37 0·79)		(20 0·64)

Boys' Modern No.	16	21	25	26
2nd year mean	0·8	0·8	0·9	1·0
(n S.D.)	(63 0·89)	(121 0·88)	(71 0·89)	(97 0·86)
4th year mean	0·4	0·7	0·5	0·5
(n S.D.)	(61 0·73)	(109 0·86)	(45 0·78)	(79 0·79)
5th year mean	0·6	0·5	0·2	0·4
(n S.D.)	(24 0·81)	(66 0·82)	(36 0·53)	(43 0·78)

Girls' Grammar No.	17	18	Boys' Grammar No.	02	09	28
2nd year mean	0·8	0·9		0·7	0·7	1·0
(n S.D.)	(91 0·93)	(115 0·86)		(94 0·89)	(35 0·87)	(64 0·91)
4th year mean	0·5	0·6		0·5	0·3	0·8
(n S.D.)	(95 0·81)	(107 0·77)		(94 0·82)	(23 0·70)	(62 0·86)
5th year mean	0·7	0·6		0·6	0·4	0·5
(n S.D.)	(79 0·84)	(67 0·79)		(97 0·84)	(34 0·59)	(72 0·76)
7th year mean	1·1	0·4		0·3	0·2	0·3
(n S.D.)	(25 0·82)	(23 0·77)		(77 0·67)	(17 0·64)	(37 0·62)

Mixed Modern No.	04	07	11	15	19	20
Boys 2nd year mean	0·8	0·9	0·9	1·0	0·9	0·8
(n S.D.)	(44 0·86)	(27 0·92)	(45 0·94)	(43 0·93)	(16 0·86)	(29 0·91)
4th year mean	0·5	1·0	0·6	0·7	0·5	0·6
(n S.D.)	(42 0·79)	(24 0·93)	(63 0·81)	(62 0·91)	(16 0·79)	(52 0·82)
5th year mean	0·5	—	0·8	0·2	0·3	0·6
(n S.D.)	(39 0·75)	—	(24 0·92)	(28 0·50)	(6 0·47)	(45 0·82)

218

All mean	0·6	0·9	0·7	0·7	0·6	0·6
(n S.D.)	(125 0·82)	(51 0·93)	(132 0·88)	(133 0·89)	(38 0·81)	(126 0·85)

Girls
2nd year

mean	1·1	1·0	1·3	1·3	1·2	1·7
(n S.D.)	(53 0·85)	(22 0·90)	(51 0·86)	(35 0·85)	(17 0·88)	(40 0·64)

4th year

mean	0·9	1·3	0·7	1·0	0·9	1·0
(n S.D.)	(51 0·84)	(26 0·87)	(49 0·85)	(59 0·88)	(19 0·94)	(33 0·92)

5th year

mean	0·5	0·8	0·8	1·4	0·5	0·9
(n S.D.)	(37 0·76)	(4 0·43)	(19 0·89)	(30 0·91)	(4 0·50)	(17 0·94)

All mean	0·9	1·2	1·0	1·2	1·0	1·3
(n S.D.)	(141 0·85)	(52 0·89)	(119 0·90)	(124 0·90)	(40 0·91)	(90 0·89)

Mixed Grammar No. 08 13 27   *Mixed Comprehensive* No. 24

Boys
2nd year

mean	1·0	0·7	0·9	
(n S.D.)	(50 0·91)	(33 0·90)	(24 0·88)	

4th year

mean	0·3	0·2	0·1	0·8
(n S.D.)	(43 0·68)	(32 0·51)	(17 0·24)	(32 0·83)

5th year

mean	0·3	0·2	0·4	
(n S.D.)	(37 0·65)	(47 0·59)	(27 0·62)	

7th year

mean	0·6	0·5	0·3	
(n S.D.)	(33 0·81)	(24 0·71)	(11 0·62)	

All mean	0·6	0·4	0·5	
(n S.D.)	(163 0·83)	(136 0·72)	(79 0·73)	

Girls
2nd year

mean	1·3	1·0	1·1	
(n S.D.)	(58 0·87)	(42 0·87)	(30 0·92)	

4th year

mean	0·7	0·4	0·7	1·2
(n S.D.)	(54 0·86)	(43 0·69)	(31 0·89)	(68 0·87)

5th year

mean	0·8	0·8	0·8	0·8
(n S.D.)	(54 0·91)	(53 0·94)	(21 0·91)	(91 0·91)

7th year

mean	1·0	0·9	0·7	1·2
(n S.D.)	(36 0·93)	(24 0·95)	(6 0·75)	(37 0·90)

TABLE K—*contd*

Mixed Grammar No.	08	13	27	*Mixed Comprehensive* No. 24
Girls contd				
All mean	1·0	0·8	0·90	
(n S.D.)	(202 0·92)	(162 0·90)	(88 0·91)	

Mixed Comprehensive No.	05	10	14	23	29	30
Boys						
2nd year						
mean	0·9	0·5	0·4	1·1	1·1	0·7
(n S.D.)	(50 0·92)	(69 0·67)	(81 0·75)	(63 0·89)	(49 0·90)	(51 0.88)
4th year						
mean	0·6	0·4	0·3	0·8	0·5	0·5
(n S.D.)	(60 0·84)	(142 0·71)	(68 0·65)	(53 0·90)	(48 0·76)	(42 0·76)
5th year						
mean	0·4	0·3	0·1	1·0	0·5	0·5
(n S.D.)	(69 0·75)	(73 058)	(40 0·26)	(33 0·92)	(56 0·78)	(42 0·79)
7th year						
mean	0·3	0·0	0·4	0·4	0·3	0·8
(n S.D.)	(7 0·70)	(6 0·00)	(16 0·70)	(5 0·80)	(4 0·43)	(18 0·90)
All mean	0·6	0·4	0·3	1·0	0·7	0·6
(n S.D.)	(186 0·84)	(290 0·67)	(205 0·66)	(154 0·92)	(157 0·86)	(153 0·83)
Girls						
2nd year						
mean	1·1	0·6	1·0	1·3	1·1	1·1
(n S.D.)	(42 0·89)	(66 0·83)	(106 0·87)	(44 0·89)	(42 0·86)	(53 0·92)
4th year						
mean	0·7	1·1	0·5	0·7	0·8	1·4
(n S.D.)	(46 0·88)	(107 0·92)	(57 0·77)	(41 0·86)	(37 0·92)	(29 0·81)
5th year						
mean	0·9	0·9	0·4	1·0	1·1	0·8
(n S.D.)	(46 0·92)	(54 0·89)	(47 0·70)	(28 0·87)	(31 0·89)	(48 0·93)
7th year						
mean	0·9	0·1	0·3	1·0	2·0	0·3
(n S.D.)	(8 0·78)	(7 0·35)	(6 0·75)	(5 0·63)	(2 0·22)	(5 0·98)
All mean	0·9	0·9	0·7	1·0	1·0	1·1
(n S.D.)	(142 0·91)	(234 0·91)	(216 0·86)	(118 0·90)	(112 0·90)	(135 0·93)

Statistically significant differences of mean score (5 per cent or higher)
All boys/all girls, school nos 04, 05, 10, 11, 13, 14, 15, 19, 20, 27, 30;
2nd year/4th year boys, school nos 04, 08, 13, 16, 25, 26, 27, 29;
2nd year/4th year girls, school nos 03, 05, 06, 08, 11, 12, 13, 14, 17, 18, 20, 22, 23.

TABLE L Age and social class differences in House involvement – Grammar school boys

School No.	02 WC	02 MC	02 All	09 WC	09 MC	09 All	28 WC	28 MC	28 All
2nd year mean (n S.D.)	1·7 (49 0·63)	1·6 (36 0·58)	1·6 (94 0·64)	1·5 (13 0·63)	1·4 (20 0·74)	1·5 (35 0·69)	1·6 (11 0·50)	1·4 (46 0·70)	1·5 (64 0·77)
4th year mean (n S.D.)	1·6 (47 0·74)	1·4 (36 0·83)	1·5 (94 0·78)	1·4 (8 0·86)	1·1 (14 0·70)	1·1 (23 0·80)	1·3 (15 0·77)	1·1 (43 0·81)	1·2 (62 0·79)
5th year mean (n S.D.)	1·4 (37 0·72)	1·2 (49 0·85)	1·3 (97 0·82)	1·3 (12 0·85)	0·5 (19 0·75)	0·8 (34 0·90)	0·8 (11 0·83)	0·8 (52 0·81)	0·8 (72 0·83)
7th year mean (n S.D.)	0·6 (23 0·83)	1·1 (42 0·89)	0·9 (77 0·90)	1·0 (3 0·82)	1·1 (12 0·86)	0·9 (17 0·87)	0·3 (8 0·66)	0·5 (27 0·72)	0·5 (37 0·76)

School No.	08 WC	08 MC	08 All	13 WC	13 MC	13 All	27 WC	27 MC	27 All
2nd year mean (n S.D.)	1·6 (17 0·59)	1·3 (27 0·84)	1·3 (50 0·84)	1·6 (11 0·64)	1·6 (16 0·50)	1·6 (33 0·60)	1·8 (5 0·40)	1·5 (18 0·76)	1·5 (24 0·71)
4th year mean (n S.D.)	1·1 (14 0·74)	0·9 (25 0·91)	1·0 (43 0·88)	1·9 (7 0·35)	1·5 (19 0·75)	1·4 (32 0·82)	1·6 (5 0·49)	1·4 (9 0·68)	1·4 (17 0·69)
5th year mean (n S.D.)	1·3 (12 0·92)	0·8 (23 0·92)	0·9 (37 0·94)	1·5 (11 0·98)	1·4 (27 0·73)	1·3 (47 0·83)	0·7 (7 0·45)	1·3 (15 0·77)	1·0 (27 0·77)
7th year mean (n S.D.)	0·6 (11 0·77)	0·8 (19 0·89)	0·8 (33 0·88)	1·7 (3 0·47)	1·2 (18 0·71)	1·2 (24 0·87)	0·3 (4 0·43)	1·0 (7 0·93)	0·7 (11 0·86)

Statistically significant differences of mean scores (5 per cent or higher)
All 2nd year/all 7th year, school nos 02, 08, 09, 13, 27, 28;
WC/MC 7th year, school nos 02; 5th year school no. 08.

TABLE M *Age and social class differences in satisfaction with pastoral care in grammar schools*

Boys

School No.	02	09	28	08	13	27
2nd year						
mean	1·3	1·1	1·4	1·2	1·6	1·3
(n S.D.)	(94 0·74)	(35 0·84)	(66 0·70)	(50 0·77)	(33 0·60)	(24 0·73)
4th year						
mean	1·1	1·4	1·4	1·0	1·1	0·9
(n S.D.)	(94 0·78)	(23 0·65)	(62 0·68)	(43 0·73)	(32 0·82)	(17 0·83)
5th year						
mean	1·2	0·7	1·3	1·1	1·1	0·6
(n S.D.)	(97 0·79)	(34 0·74)	(72 0·68)	(37 0·75)	(47 0·70)	(27 0·74)
7th year						
mean	0·9	0·8	1·1	1·0	1·3	1·0
(n S.D.)	(77 0·79)	(17 0·62)	(37 0·66)	(34 0·77)	(24 0·66)	(11 0·60)

Girls

School No.	17	18	08	13	27
2nd year					
mean	1·0	1·2	1·6	1·6	1·4
(n S.D.)	(91 0·71)	(115 0·78)	(58 0·53)	(42 0·58)	(30 0·66)
4th year					
mean	0·5	1·0	0·9	1·1	0·7
(n S.D.)	(95 0·68)	(107 0·80)	(54 0·81)	(43 0·80)	(31 0·62)
5th year					
mean	0·9	1·0	1·2	1·2	1·1
(n S.D.)	(79 0·78)	(67 0·72)	(54 0·72)	(53 0·83)	(21 0·75)
7th year					
mean	0·8	1·0	1·3	1·3	1·0
(n S.D.)	(25 0·78)	(23 0·86)	(36 0·60)	(24 0·79)	(6 0·58)
All WC					
mean	1·0	1·3	1·3	1·5	1·2
(n S.D.)	(109 0·79)	(120 0·75)	(74 0·76)	(38 0·60)	(29 0·75)
All MC					
mean	0·8	1·0	1·3	1·2	1·0
(n S.D.)	(143 0·83)	(179 0·78)	(113 0·71)	(101 0·82)	(55 0·66)

Statistically significant differences in mean scores (5 per cent or higher)
2nd year/7th year boys, school nos. 02, 28,; girls, no. 08;
WC/MC, school nos. 13, 17, 18.

TABLE N *Sex and social class differences in percentage membership of school teams*

Girls' Modern	No.	01	03	06	22	Girls' Comprehensive	No.	12
WC %		20	15	13	28			16
n		(120)	(123)	(150)	(116)			(83)
MC %		36	24	7	34			22
n		(33)	(71)	(55)	(53)			(32)

Boys' Modern	No.	16	21	25	26
WC %		23	25	33	29
n		(82)	(190)	(101)	(113)
MC %		36	31	41	56
n		(31)	(85)	(32)	(82)

Mixed Modern	No.	04	07	11	15	19	20
Boys WC %		32	33	31	35	45	32
n		(56)	(40)	(77)	(89)	(20)	(53)
MC %		42	33	51	68	36	21
n		(43)	(3)	(47)	(39)	(11)	(39)
Girls WC %		22	17	31	36	38	14
n		(67)	(36)	(51)	(69)	(21)	(43)
MC %		25	14	34	31	31	25
n		(52)	(7)	(56)	(39)	(13)	(24)

Girls' Grammar	No.	17	18	Boys' Grammar	No.	02	09	28
WC %		34	12			49	51	41
n		(109)	(120)			(156)	(36)	(46)
MC %		37	20			40	54	46
n		(148)	(179)			(163)	(65)	(172)

Mixed Grammar	No.	08	13	27
Boys WC %		31	75	67
n		(54)	(32)	(21)
MC %		43	58	51
n		(94)	(80)	(49)

TABLE N—*contd*

Mixed Grammar No.		08	13	27			
Girls							
WC	%	19	26	55			
	n	(74)	(38)	(29)			
MC	%	20	31	55			
	n	(113)	(101)	(55)			

Mixed Comprehensive No.		05	10	14	23	24	30
Boys							
WC	%	39	27	26	43	31	36
	n	(124)	(175)	(133)	(108)	(84)	(76)
MC	%	42	32	20	39	32	25
	n	(36)	(80)	(59)	(26)	(56)	(59)
Girls							
WC	%	34	15	14	25	22	29
	n	(92)	(137)	(126)	(85)	(63)	(59)
MC	%	28	8	17	19	25	31
	n	(32)	(72)	(75)	(21)	(36)	(68)

Statistically significant differences (5 per cent or higher by chi-square)
Boys WC/MC, school nos 11, 15 and 26;
Girls WC/MC, school no. 18.

TABLE O *Sex differences in percentage agreement with 'I like doing games'*

Mixed Grammar No.	08	13	27			
Boys %	77	82	76			
n	(164)	(136)	(79)			
Girls %	69	79	83			
n	(202)	(162)	(88)			

Mixed Modern No.	04	07	11	15	19	20
Boys %	66	90	83	84	66	76
n	(125)	(51)	(132)	(133)	(38)	(127)
Girls %	67	75	73	72	82	66
n	(141)	(52)	(119)	(124)	(40)	(94)

Mixed Compre-hensive No.	05	10	14	23	29	30
Boys %	86	80	82	88	85	78
n	(186)	(290)	(205)	(44)	(42)	(153)
Girls %	79	65	67	81	87	77
n	(142)	(234)	(216)	(118)	(112)	(136)

Statistically significant differences (5 per cent or higher by chi-square)
School nos 07, 11, 15, 19, 10 and 14.

TABLE P *Social class differences in the frequency of joining school clubs*

Girls' Modern No.	01	03	06	22	*Girls' Compre-hensive* No.	12
WC mean	0·4	1·0	0·5	0·4		0·6
(n S.D.)	(120 0·89)	(123 1·21)	(150 1·15)	(116 1·15)		(83 1·16)
MC mean	0·4	1·4	0·5	0·3		1·3
(n S.D.)	(33 0·64)	(71 1·32)	(55 1·26)	(53 0·44)		(32 2·05)

Boys' Modern No.	16	21	25	26
WC mean	1·0	0·4	0·4	0·7
(n S.D.)	(82 1·06)	(190 0·93)	(101 0·79)	(113 1·17)
MC mean	0·8	0·7	0·7	0·8
(n S.D.)	(31 1·19)	(85 1·00)	(32 1·13)	(82 0·97)

Mixed Modern No.	04	07	11	15	19	20
Boys WC mean	0·4	0·4	0·4	0·5	0·1	0·7
(n S.D.)	(56 0·68)	(40 0·89)	(77 0·75)	(89 1·17)	(20 0·30)	(53 0·93)
MC mean	0·8	0·0	0·4	0·7	0·5	1·3
(n S.D.)	(43 1·27)	(3 0·00)	(47 0·53)	(39 1·43)	(11 0·66)	(39 1·42)

Girls' Grammar No.	17	18	*Boys' Grammar* No. 02	09	28
WC mean	1·0	0·6	1·7	1·4	1·8
(n S.D.)	(109 1·38)	(120 1·07)	(156 1·41)	(36 1·23)	(46 2·20)
MC mean	1·5	0·7	2·0	1·2	1·9
(n S.D.)	(148 1·51)	(179 1·11)	(163 1·50)	(65 1·69)	(172 1·66)

TABLE P—*contd*

Mixed Grammar No.	08		13		27	

Boys

WC mean	0·8		0·9		0·5	
(n S.D.)	(54	1·20)	(32	1·22)	(21	0·73)
MC mean	0·9		1·7		0·5	
(n S.D.)	(94	1·13)	(80	1·69)	(49	0·86)

Girls

WC mean	0·5		1·1		0·5	
(n S.D.)	(74	0·78)	(38	1·17)	(29	0·86)
MC mean	0·7		1·6		0·3	
(n S.D.)	(113	0·94)	(101	1·64)	(55	0·55)

Mixed *Compre-* *hensive* No.	05		10		14		23		29		30	

Boys

WC mean	1·1		0·5		0·6		0·3		0·6		0·7	
(n S.D.)	(124	1·42)	(175	1·06)	(133	0·87)	(108	0·72)	(84	1·24)	(76	1·20)
MC mean	1·1		0·7		1·0		0·4		0·5		1·6	
(n S.D.)	(36	1·36)	(80	1·19)	(59	1·17)	(26	0·74)	(56	1·12)	(59	1·95)

Girls

WC mean	1·1		0·4		0·5		1·0		0·3		0·9	
(n S.D.)	(92	1·62)	(137	0·77)	(126	0·75)	(85	0·95)	(63	0·50)	(59	1·28)
MC mean	0·9		0·5		1·2		1·0		0·3		1·2	
(n S.D.)	(32	1·47)	(72	0·99)	(75	1·35)	(21	0·98)	(36	0·75)	(68	1·66)

Statistically significant differences of mean scores (5 per cent or higher)
WC/MC boys, school nos. 13, 14, 19, 21, 30; girls, school nos. 03, 13, 14, 17.

TABLE Q   *Age and sex differences in the frequency of joining school clubs in grammar schools*

Girls' Grammar No.	17		18		*Boys'* Grammar No. 02		09		28	
2nd year										
mean	1·7		0·9		1·6		2·6		2·2	
(n S.D.)	(91	1·56)	(115	1·18)	(94	1·33)	(35	1·73)	(64	1·62)
4th year										
mean	1·0		0·2		1·8		1·0		1·3	
(n S.D.)	(95	1·33)	(107	0·64)	(94	1·24)	(23	1·22)	(62	1·29)
5th year										
mean	0·7		0·6		1·6		0·8		1·8	
(n S.D.)	(79	0·94)	(67	1·02)	(97	1·64)	(34	1·97)	(72	1·98)
7th year										
mean	2·8		1·3		2·6		0·1		2·2	
(n S.D.)	(25	1·26)	(23	1·57)	(77	1·43)	(17	0·24)	(37	1·57)

Mixed						
Grammar No.	08		13		27	
	Boys	*Girls*	*Boys*	*Girls*	*Boys*	*Girls*

	Boys	*Girls*	*Boys*	*Girls*	*Boys*	*Girls*
2nd year						
mean	0·9	0·6	1·4	1·9	0·2	0·1
(n S.D.)	(50 1·10)	(58 1·01)	(33 1·45)	(42 1·18)	(24 0·58)	(30 0·54)
4th year						
mean	0·7	0·4	1·1	1·4	0·8	0·5
(n S.D.)	(43 0·92)	(54 0·65)	(32 1·34)	(43 1·47)	(17 1·04)	(31 0·56)
5th year						
mean	0·6	0·6	1·1	1·1	0·5	0·6
(n S.D.)	(37 1·14)	(54 0·73)	(47 1·30)	(53 1·24)	(27 0·74)	(21 0·79)
7th year						
mean	1·1	0·9	3·1	2·0	1·1	0·8
(n S.D.)	(33 1·29)	(36 1·06)	(24 1·63)	(24 2·27)	(11 0·67)	(6 0·69)

Statistically significant differences of mean scores (5 per cent or higher)
2nd year/7th year boys, school nos. 02, 13, 27;
2nd year/7th year girls, school nos. 17, 27.

TABLE R *Sex, age and social class differences in percentage
expectation of post-school education*

Girls'									*Girls' Compre-*		
Modern No.	01		03		06		22		*hensive* No.	12	
	WC	MC	WC	MC	WC	MC	WC	MC		WC	MC
2nd year											
%	38	53	62	87	42	75	36	67		39	41
n	(58)	(17)	(53)	(23)	(76)	(28)	(47)	(21)		(46)	(22)
4th year											
%	27	40	61	80	43	33	56	76		37	67
n	(49)	(10)	(51)	(25)	(53)	(21)	(50)	(17)		(27)	(6)
5th year											
%	31	17	68	96	67	83	100	93		80	75
n	(13)	(6)	(19)	(23)	(21)	(6)	(19)	(15)		(10)	(4)

Boys'								
Modern No.	16		21		25		26	
	WC	MC	WC	MC	WC	MC	WC	MC
2nd year								
%	45	55	49	58	28	20	49	56
n	(40)	(11)	(71)	(38)	(50)	(10)	(47)	(39)

TABLE R—*contd*

Boys' Modern No.	16		21		25		26	
	WC	MC	WC	MC	WC	MC	WC	MC
4th year								
%	59	64	67	75	64	80	55	65
n	(29)	(11)	(75)	(28)	(38)	(10)	(47)	(26)
5th year								
%	77	100	86	79	87	75	68	88
n	(13)	(9)	(44)	(19)	(23)	(12)	(19)	(17)

Girls' Grammar No.	17		18		Boys' Grammar No.	02		09		28	
	WC	MC	WC	MC		WC	MC	WC	MC	WC	MC
2nd year											
%	80	77	86	91		78	86	77	85	100	85
n	(46)	(40)	(49)	(58)		(49)	(36)	(13)	(20)	(11)	(46)
4th year											
%	63	89	80	85		77	86	75	79	80	84
n	(32)	(46)	(44)	(60)		(47)	(36)	(8)	(14)	(15)	(43)
5th year											
%	65	75	83	83		81	82	75	84	82	96
n	(26)	(44)	(20)	(47)		(37)	(49)	(12)	(19)	(11)	(52)
7th year											
%	100	94	86	93		91	100	67	92	100	96
n	(5)	(18)	(7)	(14)		(23)	(42)	(3)	(12)	(8)	(27)

Mixed Modern No.	04		07		11		15		19		20	
	WC	MC	WC	MC	WC	MC	WC	MC	WC	MC	WC	MC
Boys												
2nd year												
%	41	60	29	100	47	27	55	67	33	50	63	38
n	(22)	(10)	(21)	(1)	(30)	(15)	(33)	(6)	(9)	(2)	(16)	(8)
4th year												
%	47	71	37	50	40	49	61	62	29	57	75	46
n	(19)	(14)	(19)	(2)	(35)	(21)	(41)	(21)	(7)	(7)	(20)	(13)
5th year												
%	93	100	—	—	75	64	53	75	75	100	71	88
n	(15)	(19)	(0)	(0)	(12)	(11)	(15)	(12)	(4)	(2)	(17)	(16)
Girls												
2nd year												
%	52	83	33	67	59	63	40	50	11	75	47	43
n	(27)	(12)	(18)	(3)	(22)	(24)	(20)	(10)	(9)	(4)	(15)	(14)
4th year												
%	50	55	27	0	21	42	46	58	58	57	31	60
n	(24)	(22)	(15)	(3)	(24)	(19)	(33)	(19)	(12)	(6)	(16)	(5)
5th year												
%	75	89	0	0	80	69	94	90	—	100	60	50
n	(16)	(18)	(3)	(1)	(5)	(13)	(16)	(10)	(0)	(3)	(10)	(4)

Mixed Grammar No.	08		13		27		Mixed Comprehensive No.	24	
	WC	MC	WC	MC	WC	MC		WC	MC
Boys									
2nd year									
%	65	85	36	69	80	78			
n	(17)	(27)	(11)	(16)	(5)	(18)			
4th year									
%	57	88	77	63	60	84		41	42
n	(14)	(25)	(7)	(19)	(5)	(9)		(71)	(12)
5th year									
%	67	78	100	85	100	67			
n	(12)	(23)	(11)	(27)	(7)	(15)			
7th year									
%	73	89	67	89	100	86			
n	(11)	(19)	(3)	(18)	(4)	(7)			
Girls									
2nd year									
%	83	87	91	88	60	58			
n	(24)	(30)	(11)	(24)	(10)	(19)			
4th year									
%	95	83	80	69	90	85		41	69
n	(22)	(29)	(10)	(29)	(10)	(20)		(34)	(26)
5th year									
%	81	91	73	91	88	100		62	77
n	(16)	(34)	(11)	(33)	(8)	(11)		(39)	(39)
7th year									
%	100	95	83	93	100	40		100	93
n	(12)	(20)	(6)	(15)	(1)	(5)		(18)	(15)

Mixed Comprehensive No.	05		10		14		23		29		30	
	WC	MC	WC	MC	WC	MC	WC	MC	WC	MC	WC	MC
Boys												
2nd year												
%	57	38	33	39	42	48	24	67	52	50	38	61
n	(35)	(8)	(45)	(18)	(55)	(21)	(42)	(9)	(25)	(16)	(32)	(18)
4th year												
%	44	89	52	77	45	60	35	38	64	83	58	64
n	(39)	(9)	(81)	(40)	(47)	(15)	(40)	(8)	(25)	(18)	(18)	(11)
5th year												
%	79	60	80	79	59	69	82	88	97	67	83	85
n	(47)	(15)	(46)	(19)	(22)	(16)	(22)	(8)	(32)	(21)	(18)	(20)
7th year												
%	100	100	67	100	89	71	75	0	100	100	100	100
n	(3)	(4)	(3)	(3)	(9)	(7)	(4)	(1)	(2)	(1)	(8)	(10)

TABLE R—*contd*

Mixed Compre-hensive No.	05		10		14		23		29		30	
	WC	MC	WC	MC	WC	MC	WC	MC	WC	MC	WC	MC
Girls												
2nd year												
%	30	50	26	50	34	42	26	60	44	63	62	74
n	(30)	(4)	(43)	(20)	(67)	(33)	(27)	(10)	(18)	(19)	(26)	(27)
4th year												
%	30	33	41	30	17	55	28	50	35	36	23	50
n	(33)	(9)	(61)	(30)	(29)	(22)	(32)	(6)	(17)	(14)	(13)	(8)
5th year												
%	62	53	32	50	33	53	63	75	46	67	79	76
n	(26)	(15)	(28)	(20)	(27)	(17)	(24)	(4)	(26)	(3)	(19)	(29)
7th year												
%	67	75	60	100	100	67	100	100	100	—	100	75
n	(3)	(4)	(5)	(2)	(3)	(3)	(2)	(1)	(2)	(0)	(1)	(4)

Statistically significant differences (5 per cent or higher by chi-square)
2nd year WC/MC, school nos. 03, 06 and 22;
4th year WC/MC girls, school nos. 17, 24 and 14; boys, school nos. 08, 10;
5th year WC/MC girls, school no. 03; boys, school no. 29.

TABLE S *Age and sex differences in instrumental involvement*

Girls' Modern No.	01	03	06	22
2nd year				
mean	5·3	5·3	4·9	5·2
(n S.D.)	(88 1·08)	(98 1·02)	(108 1·31)	(77 1·16)
4th year				
mean	5·0	4·8	4·8	4·6
(n S.D.)	(70 1·20)	(98 1·34)	(79 1·27)	(69 1·47)
5th year				
mean	5·3	5·4	5·1	5·2
(n S.D.)	(21 0·76)	(54 0·87)	(27 1·12)	(37 1·08)

Boys' Modern No.	16	21	25	26
2nd year				
mean	5·0	5·4	4·9	5·2
(n S.D.)	(63 1·15)	(121 0·99)	(71 1·33)	(97 1·08)
4th year				
mean	4·4	5·1	5·4	4·6
(n S.D.)	(61 1·27)	(109 1·24)	(45 0·88)	(79 1·58)
5th year				
mean	5·7	5·3	5·5	5·4
(n S.D.)	(24 0·69)	(66 1·04)	(36 0·80)	(43 0·79)

Mixed Comprehensive No.	05	10	14	23	29	30
Boys						
2nd year						
mean	4·9	4·9	4·9	5·1	5·2	5·1
(n S.D.)	(50 1·28)	(69 1·44)	(81 1·23)	(63 1·17)	(49 1·33)	(51 1·22)
4th year						
mean	4·6	5·5	4·6	5·2	5·3	4·8
(n S.D.)	(60 1·46)	(142 0·85)	(68 1·15)	(53 1·15)	(48 0·94)	(42 1·21)
5th year						
mean	5·1	5·3	5·0	5·4	4·9	5·2
(n S.D.)	(69 1·11)	(73 1·03)	(40 1·05)	(33 0·95)	(56 1·29)	(42 1·20)
Girls						
2nd year						
mean	4·9	4·9	5·3	5·3	5·1	5·2
(n S.D.)	(42 1·18)	(66 1·20)	(106 1·06)	(44 0·97)	(42 1·07)	(53 1·18)
4th year						
mean	4·4	4·6	4·4	5·0	4·9	4·8
(n S.D.)	(46 1·58)	(107 1·33)	(57 1·48)	(41 1·06)	(37 1·17)	(24 1·16)
5th year						
mean	5·6	5·3	5·0	5·3	5·5	5·2
(n S.D.)	(46 0·65)	(54 0·83)	(47 0·99)	(28 1·10)	(31 0·84)	(37 1·21)

Mixed Modern No.	04	07	11	15	19	20
Boys						
2nd year						
mean	5·1	4·9	5·0	5·1	4·3	5·4
(n S.D.)	(44 1·15)	(27 1·24)	(45 1·04)	(43 1·37)	(16 1·49)	(29 0·85)
Girls						
2nd year						
mean	5·1	5·5	5·3	5·5	4·4	5·5
(n S.D.)	(53 1·36)	(22 0·58)	(51 1·19)	(35 0·87)	(17 1·29)	(40 0·95)

Mixed Grammar No.	08	13	27
Boys			
2nd year			
mean	4·9	4·9	5·3
(n S.D.)	(50 1·07)	(33 1·29)	(24 0·89)
Girls			
2nd year			
mean	5·1	5·1	5·5
(n S.D.)	(58 0·98)	(42 1·19)	(30 0·62)

Statistically significant differences of mean scores (5 per cent or higher)
2nd year/4th year girls, school no 03, 22, 14; boys 16, 21, 26;
4th year/5th year girls, school no 03, 05, 10, 14, 22, 29; boys 16, 26;
2nd year girls/2nd year boys, school no 07, 11, 14.

231

APPENDIX C

TABLE T *General involvement and streaming – second year*

Girls' Modern				*Girls' Grammar*		*Girls' Comprehensive*
No.	01	03	32	26	17	12
Top stream mean (n S.D.)	5·9 (30 0·75)	6·4 (33 0·30)	6·0 (28 0·38)	5·9 (33 0·50)	5·7 (28 0·54)	5·8 (26 0·53)
2nd top stream mean (n S.D.)	—	6·1 (35 0·63)	—	—	—	—
2nd stream mean (n S.D.)	5·8 (32 0·55)	5·8 (30 0·76)	5·9 (21 0·52)	5·7 (37 0·55)	5·6 (30 0·65)	6·2 (25 0·47)
3rd stream mean (n S.D.)	5·8 (26 0·57)	—	5·8 (12 0·64)	5·4 (27 0·66)	5·7 (33 0·52)	6·2 (22 0·36)
4th stream mean (n S.D.)	—	—	5·6 (16 0·49)	—	—	5·7 (18 0·48)
5th stream mean (n S.D.)	—	—	—	—	—	6·3 (8 0·43)

Boys' Modern				*Boys' Grammar*
No.	16	21	25	28
Top stream mean (n S.D.)	5·6 (21 0·52)	6·0 (30 0·44)	5·3 (21 0·41)	6·2 (24 0·42)
2nd top stream mean (n S.D.)	5·4 (27 0·61)	6·0 (33 0·49)	—	6·1 (28 0·47)
2nd stream mean (n S.D.)	5·7 (15 0·58)	5·6 (31 0·67)	5·7 (30 0·62)	5·8 (12 0·50)
2nd, 2nd stream mean (n S.D.)	—	5·7 (27 0·54)	—	—
3rd stream mean (n S.D.)	—	—	5·4 (20 0·44)	—

Mixed Modern No.	07			11			15		
	Boys	Girls	All	Boys	Girls	All	Boys	Girls	All
Top stream mean	5·7	6·0	5·8	5·9	5·6	5·7	5·7	6·2	6·0
(n S.D.)	(16 0·43)	(9 0·37)	(25 0·44)	(16 0·33)	(16 0·38)	(32 0·38)	(14 0·51)	(15 0·51)	(29 0·56)
2nd stream mean	5·5	6·0	5·8	5·8	6·0	5·9			
(n S.D.)	(11 0·30)	(13 0·62)	(24 0·56)	(11 0·33)	(18 0·38)	(29 0·37)			—
3rd stream mean				6·0	5·9	5·9	5·7	5·8	5·7
(n S.D.)			—	(9 0·68)	(15 0·79)	(24 0·75)	(20 0·82)	(15 0·51)	(35 0·70)
4th stream mean				5·5	6·3	5·7			
(n S.D.)			—	(9 0·58)	(2 0·24)	(11 0·62)			—
5th stream mean							5·1	5·6	5·3
(n S.D.)			—			—	(9 0·56)	(5 0·23)	(14 0·53)

Mixed Modern No.	19			20			Mixed Grammar 27		
	Boys	Girls	All	Boys	Girls	All	Boys	Girls	All
Top stream mean	5·6	5·4	5·5	5·7	6·0	5·9	5·9	6·0	5·9
(n S.D.)	(7 0·57)	(11 0·53)	(18 0·56)	(14 0·47)	(19 0·69)	(33 0·63)	(14 0·38)	(12 0·48)	(26 0·44)
2nd top stream mean				5·8	6·1	6·0			
(n S.D.)				(11 0·57)	(14 0·51)	(25 0·56)			
2nd stream mean	5·0	5·7	5·3	5·6	5·8	5·7	6·1	6·2	6·1
(n S.D.)	(9 0·92)	(6 0·63)	(15 0·89)	(4 0·70)	(7 0·46)	(11 0·61)	(10 0·57)	(18 0·47)	(28 0·51)

TABLE T—*contd*

Mixed Comprehensive No.	05			23			29		
	Boys	*Girls*	*All*	*Boys*	*Girls*	*All*	*Boys*	*Girls*	*All*
Top stream mean (n S.D.)	6·0 (19 0·62)	6·0 (17 0·35)	6·0 (36 0·52)	5·4 (18 0·39)	5·7 (12 0·48)	5·5 (30 0·48)	6·3 (12 0·33)	6·1 (19 0·33)	6·1 (31 0·51)
2nd top stream mean (n S.D.)	—	—	—	6·0 (17 0·49)	6·0 (14 0·51)	6·0 (31 0·47)	—	—	—
2nd stream mean (n S.D.)	5·6 (20 0·56)	5·5 (15 0·57)	5·6 (35 0·65)	5·7 (16 0·57)	5·8 (11 0·53)	5·7 (27 0·56)	—	—	—
3rd stream mean (n S.D.)	5·8 (11 0·46)	5·7 (10 0·71)	5·7 (21 0·60)	5·4 (12 0·74)	5·7 (7 0·48)	5·5 (19 0·67)	6·1 (18 0·51)	6·1 (14 0·50)	6·1 (32 0·51)
5th stream mean (n S.D.)	—	—	—	—	—	—	5·7 (19 0·83)	5·6 (9 0·30)	5·7 (28 0·71)

Mixed Comprehensive No.	Boys	30 Girls	All	10 Boys
Top stream mean	5·8	6·1	6·0	5·7
(n S.D.)	(11 0·43)	(18 0·27)	(29 0·37)	(21 0·40)
2nd stream mean	5·8	5·9	5·8	—
(n S.D.)	(11 0·48)	(16 0·93)	(27 0·67)	
3rd stream mean	—	—	—	5·3
(n S.D.)				(29 0·52)
4th stream mean	5·6	6·2	5·8	—
(n S.D.)	(15 0·57)	(10 0·52)	(25 0·61)	
5th stream mean	5·3	6·1	5·6	4·9
(n S.D.)	(14 0·55)	(9 0·39)	(23 0·60)	(19 0·80)

Note. In school no. 10 boys were taught separately from girls, who were in non-streamed groups.

TABLE U   *General involvement and streaming – fourth year*

Girls' Modern	No.	01	03	22	Girls' Comprehensive No.	12
Top stream mean (n S.D.)		5·6 (21 0·61)	5·6 (31 0·88)	5·5 (24 0·61)		6·1 (20 0·56)
2nd top stream mean (n S.D.)		—	5·5 (32 0·70)	5·6 (31 0·60)		—
2nd stream mean (n S.D.)		5·9 (18 0·56)	5·9 (16 0·77)	5·1 (14 0·74)		5·5 (15 0·93)
2nd, 2nd stream mean (n S.D.)		5·7 (30 0·68)	—	—		5·7 (13 0·65)
3rd stream mean (n S.D.)		—	5·8 (19 0·55)	—		—

Boys' Modern	No.	01	03	22		26
		16	21	25		
Top stream mean (n S.D.)		5·7 (26 0·50)	5·8 (34 0·50)	5·3 (22 0·69)		5·7 (33 0·56)
2nd stream mean (n S.D.)		5·3 (23 0·84)	5·7 (33 0·63)	5·8 (17 0·46)		5·4 (25 0·74)
3rd stream mean (n S.D.)		5·0 (12 0·61)	5·8 (21 0·63)	5·7 (6 0·52)		5·4 (21 0·65)

Girls' Grammar / Boys' Grammar

	Girls' Grammar		Boys' Grammar	
No.	17	18	02	28
Top stream mean (n S.D.)	5·1 (34 0·90)	5·8 (26 0·52)	5·9 (33 0·49)	6·1 (24 0·40)
2nd top stream mean (n S.D.)	—	5·7 (29 0·58)	—	—
2nd stream mean (n S.D.)	5·4 (29 0·52)	5·6 (25 0·64)	5·6 (35 0·61)	5·9 (18 0·69)
2nd, 2nd stream mean (n S.D.)	—	5·8 (27 0·44)	—	—
3rd stream mean (n S.D.)	5·1 (32 0·78)	—	5·4 (26 0·51)	—

Mixed Comprehensive

	23			24			29		
No.	Boys	Girls	All	Boys	Girls	All	Boys	Girls	All
Top stream mean (n S.D.)	5·8 (14 0·62)	6·1 (9 0·46)	5·9 (23 0·58)	6·0 (18 0·47)	6·3 (11 0·31)	6·1 (29 0·43)	5·9 (26 0·49)	5·5 (6 5·5)	5·8 (32 0·51)
2nd top stream mean (n S.D.)	—	—	—	—	5·8 (28 0·76)	5·8 (28 0·76)	—	—	—
2nd stream mean (n S.D.)	5·6 (10 0·48)	5·1 (13 0·70)	5·3 (23 0·66)	5·8 (14 0·42)	6·3 (12 0·26)	6·0 (26 0·43)	—	—	—
2nd, 2nd stream mean (n S.D.)	—	—	—	—	5·6 (17 0·60)	5·6 (17 0·60)	—	—	—

237

TABLE U—contd

Mixed Comprehensive No.	23			24			29		
	Boys	Girls	All	Boys	Girls	All	Boys	Girls	All
3rd stream mean (n S.D.)	5·8 (29 0·50)	—	5·8 (29 0·50)	—	—	—	5·8 (11 0·55)	5·9 (17 0·00)	5·8 (28 0·55)
2nd, 3rd stream mean (n S.D.)	—	5·4 (19 0·77)	5·4 (19 0·77)	—	—	—	—	—	—
5th stream mean (n S.D.)	—	—	—	—	—	—	5·7 (11 0·41)	5·8 (11 0·62)	5·8 (22 0·54)

Mixed Comprehensive No.	30			10
	Boys	Girls	All	Boys
Top stream mean (n S.D.)	5·6 (16 0·53)	6·0 (14 0·36)	5·8 (30 0·49)	5·8 (31 0·39)
2nd stream mean (n S.D.)	—	—	—	6·0 (31 0·51)
3rd stream mean (n S.D.)	—	—	—	5·6 (30 0·46)
4th stream mean (n S.D.)	5·8 (17 0·50)	5·7 (10 0·80)	5·7 (27 0·63)	5·8 (28 0·70)
5th stream mean (n S.D.)	—	—	—	5·0 (22 0·64)
6th stream mean (n S.D.)	5·6 (9 0·44)	6·0 (9 0·59)	5·8 (18 0·57)	—

Mixed Modern No.	07			15			19		
	Boys	Girls	All	Boys	Girls	All	Boys	Girls	All
Top stream mean (n S.D.)	6·1 (15 0·38)	6·2 (14 0·35)	6·2 (29 0·37)	5·7 (29 0·44)	—	5·7 (29 0·44)	5·5 (7 0·48)	5·7 (11 0·52)	5·6 (18 0·52)
2nd top stream mean (n S.D.)	—	—	—	—	6·0 (27 0·52)	6·0 (27 0·52)	—	—	—
2nd stream mean (n S.D.)	5·6 (9 0·48)	6·1 (12 0·42)	5·9 (21 0·52)	5·6 (13 0·55)	5·8 (8 0·44)	5·7 (21 0·52)	5·5 (9 0·25)	5·4 (8 0·72)	5·5 (17 0·53)
3rd stream mean (n S.D.)	—	—	—	5·6 (20 0·55)	—	5·6 (20 0·55)	—	—	—
2nd, 3rd stream mean (n S.D.)	—	—	—	—	5·6 (24 0·73)	5·6 (24 0·73)	—	—	—

Mixed Grammar No.	08			27 Mixed Modern No.			11		
	Boys	Girls	All	Boys	Girls	All	Boys	Girls	All
Top stream mean (n S.D.)	5·8 (8 0·64)	5·6 (16 0·54)	5·7 (24 0·58)	5·5 (9 0·69)	5·7 (16 0·70)	5·6 (25 0·70)	6·0 (19 0·52)	6·1 (13 0·54)	6·0 (32 0·53)
2nd stream mean (n S.D.)	4·9 (9 0·90)	5·7 (12 0·33)	5·4 (21 0·77)	5·8 (8 0·59)	5·9 (16 0·48)	5·9 (24 0·52)	5·7 (13 0·51)	5·6 (20 0·63)	5·7 (33 0·59)
3rd stream mean (n S.D.)	5·4 (14 0·53)	5·1 (14 0·77)	5·2 (28 0·67)	—	—	—	6·0 (20 0·49)	6·0 (12 0·32)	6·0 (32 0·43)
4th stream mean (n S.D.)	5·5 (12 0·50)	5·7 (12 0·43)	5·6 (24 0·48)	—	—	—	5·6 (11 0·51)	5·8 (4 0·41)	5·7 (15 0·49)

TABLE V · General involvement and streaming – fifth year

Boys' Modern No.	25	Boys' Grammar No.	02	28
Top stream mean	5·7		6·0	5·8
(n S.D.)	(12 0·26)		(31 0·58)	(28 0·51)
2nd top stream mean	—		5·7	6·0
(n S.D.)	—		(31 0·62)	(26 0·53)
2nd stream mean	5·2		5·6	6·0
(n S.D.)	(17 0·59)		(25 0·59)	(18 0·54)
3rd stream mean	—		5·0	—
(n S.D.)	—		(10 0·83)	—

Girls' Grammar No.	17	18	Girls' Comprehensive No. 12
Top stream mean	5·8	5·8	6·3
(n S.D.)	(28 0·59)	(21 0·68)	(12 0·39)
2nd top stream mean	—	5·9	—
(n S.D.)	—	(25 0·42)	
2nd stream mean	5·6	6·3	5·5
(n S.D.)	(25 0·56)	(0 0·25)	(6 0·98)
2nd, 2nd stream mean	—	5·5	—
(n S.D.)	—	(12 0·80)	
3rd stream mean	5·2	—	—
(n S.D.)	(26 0·56)	—	

TABLE V—contd

Mixed Modern	No.	11			15		
		Boys	Girls	All	Boys	Girls	All
Top stream mean (n S.D.)		6·0 (15 0·46)	6·3 (8 0·41)	6·1 (23 0·46)	—	6·2 (22 0·40)	6·2 (22 0·40)
2nd top stream mean (n S.D.)		—	—	—	5.8 (23 0.56)	—	5.8 (23 0.56)
2nd stream mean (n S.D.)		5·9 (9 0·50)	5·9 (11 0·50)	5·9 (20 0·50)	5·8 (4 0·25)	6·4 (8 0·33)	6·2 (12 0·40)

Mixed Grammar	No.	08			27			Mixed Comprehensive No. 10
		Boys	Girls	All	Boys	Girls	All	Boys
Top stream mean (n S.D.)		5·6 (5 0·20)	5·9 (17 0·53)	5·8 (22 0·49)	6·1 (11 0·35)	5·6 (13 0·79)	5·8 (24 0·68)	5·7 (29 0·44)
2nd stream mean (n S.D.)		5·5 (15 0·46)	5·5 (13 0·50)	5·5 (28 0·48)	5·1 (16 0·94)	6·1 (8 0·76)	5·5 (24 0·99)	5·5 (13 0·72)
3rd stream mean (n S.D.)		5·3 (8 0·40)	5·8 (12 0·28)	5·6 (20 0·41)	—	—	—	5·5 (19 0·51)
4th stream mean (n S.D.)		6·1 (9 0·25)	6·0 (12 0·46)	6·0 (21 0·40)	—	—	—	5·7 (12 0·66)

TABLE V—*contd*

Mixed Comprehensive No.	24 Girls	29			30		
		Boys	Girls	All	Boys	Girls	All
Top stream mean (n S.D.)	5·9 (22 0·54)	5·9 (18 0·54)	6·0 (12 0·44)	6·0 (30 0·51)	5·7 (13 0·61)	6·0 (17 0·46)	5·9 (30 0·55)
2nd stream mean (n S.D.)	5·7 (23 0·65)	5·5 (19 0·47)	5·7 (11 0·36)	5·5 (30 0·43)	5·7 (10 0·67)	6·0 (14 0·44)	5·9 (24 0·57)
3rd stream mean (n S.D.)	5·1 (24 0·69)	5·7 (12 0·54)	6·8 (2 0·10)	5·8 (14 0·62)	5·8 (12 0·54)	5·7 (10 0·64)	5·7 (22 0·59)
4th stream mean (n S.D.)	5·7 (20 0·57)	6·2 (7 0·39)	5·7 (11 0·66)	5·8 (18 0·64)	—	—	—
6th stream mean (n S.D.)	—	—	—	—	5·8 (7 0·40)	6·2 (7 0·42)	6·0 (14 0·46)

Note. There were no boys in the fifth year of school no. 24.

TABLE W *Percentage expectation of post-school education and streaming – second year*

Girls' Modern No.	01	03	22	Girls' Grammar No. 17	Girls' Comprehensive No. 12
Top stream %	60	94	54	82	67
(n)	(30)	(33)	(28)	(28)	(26)
2nd top stream %		69			
(n)		(35)			
2nd stream %	31	37	71	77	23
(n)	(32)	(30)	(21)	(30)	(25)
3rd stream %	23		42	82	55
(n)	(26)		(12)	(33)	(22)
4th stream %		6			50
(n)		(16)			(18)
5th stream %					0
(n)					(8)

Boys' Modern No.	16	21	25	26	Boys' Grammar No. 28
Top stream %	76	73	43	63	96
(n)	(21)	(30)	(21)	(33)	(24)
2nd top stream %	41	55			93
(n)	(27)	(33)			(28)
2nd stream %	19	42	23	57	67
(n)	(15)	(31)	(30)	(37)	(12)
2nd, 2nd stream %		48			
(n)		(27)			
3rd stream %			10	33	
(n)			(20)	(27)	

Mixed Modern No.	07		11		15	
	Boys	Girls	Boys	Girls	Boys	Girls
Top stream %	19	78	38	50	92	60
(n)	(16)	(9)	(16)	(16)	(14)	(15)
2nd stream %	10	0	36	53		
(n)	(11)	(13)	(11)	(18)		
3rd stream %			67	75	55	40
(n)			(9)	(15)	(20)	(15)
4th stream %			25	0		
(n)			(9)	(2)		
5th stream %					0	0
(n)					(9)	(5)

243

TABLE W—*contd*

Mixed Modern No.	19 Boys	19 Girls	20 Boys	20 Girls	Mixed Grammar	27 Boys	27 Girls
Top stream %	57	40	53	50		86	67
(n)	(7)	(11)	(14)	(19)		(14)	(12)
2nd top stream %			64	38			
(n)			(11)	(14)			
2nd stream %	10	0	0	57		70	56
(n)	(9)	(6)	(4)	(7)		(10)	(18)

Mixed Comprehensive No.	05 Boys	05 Girls	23 Boys	23 Girls		29 Boys	29 Girls
Top stream %	74	53	21	58		75	58
(n)	(19)	(17)	(18)	(12)		(12)	(19)
2nd top stream %			65	57			
(n)			(17)	(14)			
2nd stream %	29	20	20	0			
(n)	(20)	(15)	(16)	(11)			
3rd stream %	27	0	17	0		44	43
(n)	(11)	(10)	(12)	(7)		(18)	(14)
4th stream %						40	56
(n)						(19)	(9)

Mixed Comprehensive No.	30 Boys	30 Girls	10 Boys
Top stream %	91	89	57
(n)	(11)	(18)	(21)
2nd stream %	64	75	
(n)	(11)	(16)	
3rd stream %			28
(n)			(29)
4th stream %	33	33	
(n)	(15)	(10)	
5th stream %	14	44	18
(n)	(14)	(9)	(19)

TABLE X *General involvement and non-streaming in the second year of mixed schools*

School No.	04		08		13		14	
	Boys	*Girls*	*Boys*	*Girls*	*Boys*	*Girls*	*Boys*	*Girls*
1st group mean (n S.D.)	5·8 (13 0·68)	5·9 (14 0·43)	5·9 (14 0·55)	6·2 (15 0·36)	5·9 (14 0·66)	6·1 (10 0·34)	5·4 (15 0·39)	5·7 (21 0·51)
2nd group mean (n S.D.)	5·9 (11 0·54)	6·1 (13 0·79)	5·7 (15 0·62)	6·0 (11 0·47)	5·7 (11 0·69)	6·1 (12 0·42)	5·4 (15 0·50)	5·3 (22 0·72)
3rd group mean (n S.D.)	5·1 (9 0·47)	6·1 (14 0·59)	6·0 (13 0·42)	6·0 (11 0·43)	6·1 (8 0·61)	6·3 (19 0·43)	5·7 (16 0·44)	5·9 (23 0·46)
4th group mean (n S.D.)			5·4 (7 0·46)	5·9 (17 0·51)			5·9 (18 0·52)	5·8 (20 0·37)
5th group mean (n S.D.)							5·5 (17 0·59)	5·8 (20 0·58)

TABLE Yi *Uniform definition scale for boys*

Item	f
Shirt	46
Jumper	38
Shoes	30
Top coat	30
Scarf	25
Socks	24

Mean item analysis value 0·843; mean score = 3·33 (N = 58; S.D. = 2·00).

TABLE Yii *Uniform definition scale for girls*

Item	f
Blazer	51
Shoes	44
Socks/stockings	44
Top coat	44
Scarf	33

Mean item analysis value 0·807; mean score = 3·72 (N = 58; S.D. = 1·39).

TABLE Zi *Prescription of uniform scale for boys*

Item	f
Tie	50
Trousers	46
Blazer	45
Shirt	40
Shoes	28
Socks	20
Jumper	15
Top coat	14

Mean item analysis value 0·902; mean score = 4·45 (N = 58; S.D. = 2·39).

TABLE Zii *Prescription of uniform scale for girls*

Item	f
Tie	45
Shoes	40
Socks/stockings	39
Top coat	25
Hat/beret	14
Blazer	12

Mean item analysis value 0·811; mean score = 3·02 (N = 58; S.D. = 1·70).

Bibliography

ABRAMS, P. (1971) 'A sociological portrait: age and generation', *New Society*, 18.

ALBROW, M. (1970) *Bureaucracy*, Pall Mall Press.

ANDERSON, C. A. (1961) 'A skeptical note on education and mobility', *American Journal of Sociology*, 6.

ANDERSON, J. G. (1968) *Bureaucracy in Education*, Johns Hopkins Press.

ARCHER, M. S. and VAUGHAN, M. (1972) *Social Conflict and Educational Change, 1780–1850*, Cambridge University Press.

BANKS, O. (1955) *Parity and Prestige in English Secondary Education*, Routledge & Kegan Paul.

BARON, G. (1955) 'The English notion of the school', unpublished paper, University of London Institute of Education.

BENN, C. and SIMON, B. (1970) *Half-Way There*, McGraw-Hill.

BERGER, P. L. (1966) *Invitation to Sociology*, Penguin.

BERNSTEIN, B. B. (1966a) 'Sources of Consensus and Disaffection in Education', *Journal of the Association of Assistant Mistresses*, 17.

BERNSTEIN, B. B. (1971) 'On the classification and framing of educational knowledge', in YOUNG, M. F. D., ed. (1971).

BERNSTEIN, B. B. and DAVIES, B. (1969) 'Some sociological comments on Plowden', in *Perspectives on Plowden*, ed. R. S. Peters, Routledge & Kegan Paul.

BERNSTEIN, B. B., ELVIN, H. L. and PETERS, R. S. (1966b) 'Ritual in education', *Philosophical Transactions of the Royal Society of London*, series B, no. 779, vol. 251.

BIDWELL, C. E. (1965) 'The school as a formal organisation', in *Handbook of Organisations*, ed. J. G. March, Rand McNally.

BLAKE, J. and DAVIS, K. (1964) 'Norms, values and sanctions', in *Handbook of Modern Sociology*, ed. R. E. Faris, Rand McNally.

BLAU, P. M. and SCOTT, W. R. (1963) *Formal Organisations*, Chandler.

BOCOCK, R. J. (1970) 'Ritual: civic and religious', *British Journal o, Sociology*, 21.

BROWN, A. F. and HOUSE, J. H. (1967) 'The organisational component in education', *Review of Educational Research*, 37.

247

CAMPBELL, F. (1968) 'Latin and the élite tradition in education', *British Journal of Sociology*, 19.

CAMPBELL, W. J. (1965) 'School size: its influence on pupils', *Journal of Educational Administration*, 3.

CAPLOW, T. (1964) *Principles of Organisation*, Harcourt, Brace.

CENTRAL ADVISORY COUNCIL FOR EDUCATION (1959) 15 *to* 18 (Crowther Report) HMSO.

CHAPMAN, J. (1971) 'School Councils: in theory and practice', *Journal of Moral Education*, 1.

COHEN, A. K. (1955) *Delinquent Boys: The Culture of the Gang*, Free Press.

CORWIN, R. G. (1965) *A Sociology of Education*, Appleton–Century Crofts.

DALE, R. R. (1969) *Mixed or Single-Sex School*, Routledge & Kegan Paul.

DAVIS, K. and MOORE, W. E. (1945) 'Some principles of stratification', *American Sociological Review*, 10.

DOUGLAS, J. B. W. (1964) *The Home and the School*, MacGibbon & Kee.

DOUGLAS, M. (1966) *Purity and Danger*, Routledge & Kegan Paul.

DURKHEIM, E. (1956) *Education and Sociology*, Free Press.

DURKHEIM, E. (1961) *Moral Education*, Free Press.

EGGLESTON, S. J. (1967) *The Social Context of the School*, Routledge & Kegan Paul.

EISENSTADT, S. N. (1956) *From Generation to Generation*, Free Press.

ETZIONI, A. (1961) *A Comparative Analysis of Complex Organisations* Free Press.

ETZIONI, A. (1964) *Modern Organisation*, Prentice–Hall.

FORD, J. (1970) *Social Class and the Comprehensive School*, Routledge & Kegan Paul.

GOFFMAN, I. (1961) *Asylums*, Doubleday.

GOODY, J. (1961) 'Religion and ritual: the definitional problem', *British Journal of Sociology*, 12.

GOSLIN, D. A. (1965) *The School in Contemporary Society*, Scott Foresman.

GOULDNER, A. W. (1959) 'Organisational analysis', in *Sociology Today*, eds R. K. Merton, L. Broom and L. S. Cottrell, Basic Books.

HALL, R. H. (1963) 'The concept of bureaucracy', *American Journal of Sociology*, 69.

HARGREAVES, D. H. (1967) *Social Relations in a Secondary School*, Routledge & Kegan Paul.

HARRIS, C. C. (1969) 'Reform in a normative organisation', *Sociological Review*, 17.

HIMMELWEIT, H. T. (1954) 'Social status and secondary education since the 1944 Act: some data from London', in *Social Mobility in Britain*, ed. D. V. Glass, Routledge & Kegan Paul.

HIMMELWEIT, H. T. (1963) 'Socio-economic background and personality', in *Current Perspectives in Social Psychology*, eds E. P. Hollander and R. G. Hunt, Oxford University Press.

HIMMELWEIT, H. T. (1966) 'Social background, intelligence and school structure', in *Genetic and Environmental Factors in Human Ability*, eds J. E. Meade and A. S. Parkes, Oliver & Boyd.

HIMMELWEIT, H. T., HALSEY, A. H. and OPPENHEIM, A. N. (1954) 'The views of adolescents on some aspects of the social class structure', *British Journal of Sociology*, 3.

HININGS, C. R., PUGH, D. S., HICKSON, D. J. and TURNER, C. (1967) 'An approach to the study of bureaucracy', *Sociology*, 1.

HOLLY, D. N. (1965) 'Profiting from a comprehensive school', *British Journal of Sociology*, 16.

HOMANS, G. C. (1964) 'Bringing men back in', *American Sociological Review*, 29.

HOROBIN, G., *et al.* (1967) 'The social differentiation of ability', *Sociology*, 1.

JACKSON, B. (1964) *Streaming: An Education System in Miniature*, Routledge & Kegan Paul.

KATZ, D. and KAHN, R. L. (1966) *The Social Psychology of Organisations*, Wiley.

KELLMER-PRINGLE, M. L., BUTLER, N. R. and DAVIE, R. V. (1966) *11,000 Seven-Year-Olds*, Longman.

KENDALL, M. G. (1955) *Rank Correlation Methods*, Griffin.

KING, R. A. (1968) 'The headteacher and his authority', in *Headship in the 1970's*, ed. B. R. Allen, Blackwell.

KING, R. A. (1969a) *Values and Involvement in a Grammar School*, Routledge & Kegan Paul.

KING, R. A. (1969b) *Education* (Social structure of modern Britain series), Longman.

KING, R. A. (1971) 'Unequal access in education: sex and social class', *Social and Economic Administration*, 5.

KING, R. A. (1972) 'Parents and schools', *Secondary Education*, 2.

KING, R. A. and EASTHOPE, G. (1971) 'The structure of careers' guidance in secondary schools', *Vocational Aspect of Education*, 23.

KING, R. A. and EASTHOPE, G. (1973) 'Social class and friendship choice in school', *Research in Education*, vol. II.

KING, R. A. and FRY, J. (1972) 'School magazines', *English in Education*, 6.

KLUCKHOHN, C. (1964) *Mirror for Man*, Premier.

KLUCKHOLN, F. R. and STRODTBECK, F. L. (1961) *Variations in Value Orientations*, Row Peterson.

LACEY, C. (1970) *Hightown Grammar*, Manchester University Press.

LAMBERT, R. (1966) Introduction to *The Public Schools, a Factual Survey*, by G. Kalton, Longman.

LAMBERT, R., HIPKIN, J. and STAGG, S. (1968) *New Wine in Old Bottles?*, Bell.

LEACH, E. (1964) *Political Systems of Highland Burma*, Athlone.

LEAT, D. (1972) 'Misunderstanding Verstehen', *Sociological Review*, 20.

LEVY, P. and PUGH, D. (1969) 'Scaling and multivariate analyses in the study of organisational variables', *Sociology*, 3.

LUNN, J. B. (1970) *Streaming in the Primary School*, NFER.

MCINTYRE, D., MORRISON, A. and SUTHERLAND, J. (1966) 'Social and educational variables relating to teachers' assessments of primary school children', *British Journal of Educational Psychology*, 36.

MACK, E C. (1938) *Public Schools and British Opinion 1780–1860*, Methuen.

MANNHEIM, K. (1936) *Ideology and Utopia*, Kegan Paul.

MARSDEN, D. (1969) 'Which comprehensive principle?', *Comprehensive Education*, 13.

MAYS, J. B., QUINE, W. and PICKETT, K. (1968) *School of Tomorrow*, Longman.

MEAD, M. (1949) *Male and Female*, Morrow.

MERTON, R. K. (1959) Introduction to *Sociology Today*, eds R. K. Merton, L. Broom and L. S. Cottrell, Basic Books.

MITCHELL, G. D. (1964) 'Education, ideology and social change in England', in *Explorations in Social Change*, ed. G. K. Zollschan and W. Hirsch, Routledge & Kegan Paul.

MITCHELL, S., and SHEPHERD, M. (1967) 'The child who dislikes going to school', *British Journal of Educational Psychology*, 37.

MONKS, T. G. (1968) *Comprehensive Education in England and Wales*, NFER.

MUSGROVE, F. (1971) *Patterns of Power and Authority in English Education*, Methuen.

PARSONS, T. (1951) *The Social System*, Free Press.

PARSONS, T. (1954) *Essays in Sociological Theory*, Free Press.

PARSONS, T. (1959a) 'General theory in sociology', in *Sociology Today*, eds R. K. Merton, L. Broom and L. S. Cottrell, Basic Books.

PARSONS, T. (1959b) 'The school class as a social system', *Harvard Educational Review*, 29.

PARSONS, T. and BALES, R. F. (1956) *Family, Socialisation and Interaction Process*, Routledge & Kegan Paul.

PEABODY, R. L. (1962) 'Perceptions of organisational authority', *Administrative Science Quarterly*, 7.

PRIME MINISTER'S COMMITTEE (1963) *Higher Education* (Robbins Report), HMSO.

PUGH, D. S., HICKSON, D. J., HININGS, C. R., TURNER, C. and LUPTON, T. (1963) 'A conceptual scheme for organisational analysis', *Administrative Science Quarterly*, 8.

PUGH, D. S., HICKSON, D. J., HININGS, C. R. and TURNER, C. (1968) 'Dimensions of organisational structure', *Administrative Science Quarterly*, 13.

ROBERTSON, R. (1972) 'A sociological portrait: religion', *New Society*, 19.

ROBINSON, W. S. (1950) 'Ecological correlations and the behaviour of individuals', *American Sociological Review*, 15.

ROSE, A. M. (ed.) (1962) *Human Behaviour and Social Processes*, Routledge & Kegan Paul.

SARASON, S. B. and GLADWIN, T. (1958) 'Psychological and cultural problems', in *Mental Subnormality*, eds R. L. Masland, S. B. Sarason and T. Gladwin, Basic Books.

SCHOOLS COUNCIL (1968) *Young School Leavers*, Enquiry No. 1, HMSO.

SELLTIZ, C., JAHODA, M., DEUTSCH, M. and COOK, S. T. (1965) *Research Methods in Social Relations*, Methuen.

SILVERMAN, D. (1970) *The Theory of Organisations*, Heinemann.

SIMON, B. (1965) *Education and the Labour Movement 1870–1920*, Lawrence & Wishart.

SUGARMAN, B. N. (1967) 'Involvement in youth culture, academic achievement and conformity in school', *British Journal of Sociology*, 18.

SWIFT, D. F. (1970) 'Recent research in the sociology of education', *Report of the Joint DES/ATCDE Conference on the Sociology of Education in Colleges of Education*, DES.

SYLVESTER, D. W. (1970) *Educational Documents 800–1816*, Methuen.

TURNER, R. H. (1964) *The Social Context of Ambition*, Chandler.

TURNER, V. W. (1964) 'Symbols in Ndembu ritual', in *Closed Systems and Open Minds*, ed. M. Gluckman, Oliver & Boyd.

WALLER, W. (1932) *The Sociology of Teaching*, Wiley.

WEBER, M. (1948) *From Max Weber: Essays in Sociology*, eds H. Gerth and C. W. Mills, Routledge & Kegan Paul.

WEINBERG, I. (1967) *The English Public Schools*, Atherton.

WHITE, J. (1968) 'Instruction in obedience?', *New Society*, 292.

WILKINSON, J. (1966) *The Prefects*, Oxford University Press.

WILSON, A. B. (1959) 'Residential segregation of social classes and aspirations of high school boys', *American Sociological Review*, 24.

WITKIN, R. W. (1971) 'Social class influence on the amount and type of positive evaluation of school lessons', *Sociology*, 5.

WOBER, M. (1971) *English Girls' Public Schools*, Allen Lane.

WOOD, S. M. (1966) 'Uniform, its significance as a factor in role-relationships', *Sociological Review*, 14.

WRIGHT, D. (1971) 'A sociological portrait: sex differences', *New Society*, 18.

YOUNG, M. F. D. (ed.) (1971) Introduction to *Knowledge and Control*, Collier-Macmillan.

Index

International Library of Sociology

Edited by
John Rex
University of Warwick

Founded by
Karl Mannheim

as The International Library of Sociology
and Social Reconstruction

*This Catalogue also contains other Social Science
series published by Routledge*

Routledge & Kegan Paul   London and Boston

68-74 Carter Lane   London EC4V 5EL
9 Park Street   Boston   Mass 02108

Contents

● *Books so marked are available in paperback*
All books are in Metric Demy 8vo format (216 × 138mm approx.)

GENERAL SOCIOLOGY

Belshaw, Cyril. The Conditions of Social Performance. *An Exploratory Theory. 144 pp.*

Brown, Robert. Explanation in Social Science. *208 pp.*

● Rules and Laws in Sociology.

Cain, Maureen E. Society and the Policeman's Role. *About 300 pp.*

Gibson, Quentin. The Logic of Social Enquiry. *240 pp.*

Gurvitch, Georges. Sociology of Law. *Preface by Roscoe Pound. 264 pp.*

Homans, George C. Sentiments and Activities: *Essays in Social Science. 336 pp.*

Johnson, Harry M. Sociology: *a Systematic Introduction. Foreword by Robert K. Merton. 710 pp.*

Mannheim, Karl. Essays on Sociology and Social Psychology. *Edited by Paul Keckskemeti. With Editorial Note by Adolph Lowe. 344 pp.*

Systematic Sociology: *An Introduction to the Study of Society. Edited by J. S. Erös and Professor W. A. C. Stewart. 220 pp.*

Martindale, Don. The Nature and Types of Sociological Theory. *292 pp.*

● **Maus, Heinz.** A Short History of Sociology. *234 pp.*

Mey, Harald. Field-Theory. *A Study of its Application in the Social Sciences. 352 pp.*

Myrdal, Gunnar. Value in Social Theory: *A Collection of Essays on Methodology. Edited by Paul Streeten. 332 pp.*

Ogburn, William F., and **Nimkoff, Meyer F.** A Handbook of Sociology. *Preface by Karl Mannheim. 656 pp. 46 figures. 35 tables.*

Parsons, Talcott, and **Smelser, Neil J.** Economy and Society: *A Study in the Integration of Economic and Social Theory. 362 pp.*

● **Rex, John.** Key Problems of Sociological Theory. *220 pp.*

Urry, John. Reference Groups and the Theory of Revolution.

FOREIGN CLASSICS OF SOCIOLOGY

● **Durkheim, Emile.** Suicide. *A Study in Sociology. Edited and with an Introduction by George Simpson. 404 pp.*

Professional Ethics and Civic Morals. *Translated by Cornelia Brookfield. 288 pp.*

● **Gerth, H. H.,** and **Mills, C. Wright.** From Max Weber: *Essays in Sociology. 502 pp.*

Tönnies, Ferdinand. Community and Association. *(Gemeinschaft und Gesellschaft.) Translated and Supplemented by Charles P. Loomis. Foreword by Pitirim A. Sorokin. 334 pp.*

SOCIAL STRUCTURE

Andreski, Stanislav. Military Organization and Society. *Foreword by Professor A. R. Radcliffe-Brown. 226 pp. 1 folder.*

Coontz, Sydney H. Population Theories and the Economic Interpretation. *202 pp.*

Coser, Lewis. The Functions of Social Conflict. *204 pp.*

Dickie-Clark, H. F. Marginal Situation: *A Sociological Study of a Coloured Group.* *240 pp. 11 tables.*

Glass, D. V. (Ed.). Social Mobility in Britain. *Contributions by J. Berent, T. Bottomore, R. C. Chambers, J. Floud, D. V. Glass, J. R. Hall, H. T. Himmelweit, R. K. Kelsall, F. M. Martin, C. A. Moser, R. Mukherjee, and W. Ziegel. 420 pp.*

Glaser, Barney, and **Strauss, Anselm L.** Status Passage. *A Formal Theory. 208 pp.*

Jones, Garth N. Planned Organizational Change: *An Exploratory Study Using an Empirical Approach. 268 pp.*

Kelsall, R. K. Higher Civil Servants in Britain: *From 1870 to the Present Day. 268 pp. 31 tables.*

König, René. The Community. *232 pp. Illustrated.*

● **Lawton, Denis.** Social Class, Language and Education. *192 pp.*

McLeish, John. The Theory of Social Change: *Four Views Considered. 128 pp.*

Marsh, David C. The Changing Social Structure of England and Wales, 1871-1961. *288 pp.*

Mouzelis, Nicos. Organization and Bureaucracy. *An Analysis of Modern Theories. 240 pp.*

Mulkay, M. J. Functionalism, Exchange and Theoretical Strategy. *272 pp.*

Ossowski, Stanislaw. Class Structure in the Social Consciousness. *210 pp.*

SOCIOLOGY AND POLITICS

Hertz, Frederick. Nationality in History and Politics: *A Psychology and Sociology of National Sentiment and Nationalism. 432 pp.*

Kornhauser, William. The Politics of Mass Society. *272 pp. 20 tables.*

Laidler, Harry W. History of Socialism. *Social-Economic Movements: An Historical and Comparative Survey of Socialism, Communism, Co-operation, Utopianism; and other Systems of Reform and Reconstruction. 992 pp.*

Mannheim, Karl. Freedom, Power and Democratic Planning. *Edited by Hans Gerth and Ernest K. Bramstedt. 424 pp.*

Mansur, Fatma. Process of Independence. *Foreword by A. H. Hanson. 208 pp.*

Martin, David A. Pacifism: *an Historical and Sociological Study. 262 pp.*

Myrdal, Gunnar. The Political Element in the Development of Economic Theory. *Translated from the German by Paul Streeten. 282 pp.*

Wootton, Graham. Workers, Unions and the State. *188 pp.*

FOREIGN AFFAIRS: THEIR SOCIAL, POLITICAL AND ECONOMIC FOUNDATIONS

Mayer, J. P. Political Thought in France from the Revolution to the Fifth Republic. *164 pp.*

CRIMINOLOGY

Ancel, Marc. Social Defence: *A Modern Approach to Criminal Problems.* *Foreword by Leon Radzinowicz. 240 pp.*

Cloward, Richard A., and **Ohlin, Lloyd E.** Delinquency and Opportunity: *A Theory of Delinquent Gangs. 248 pp.*

Downes, David M. The Delinquent Solution. *A Study in Subcultural Theory. 296 pp.*

Dunlop, A. B., and **McCabe, S.** Young Men in Detention Centres. *192 pp.*

Friedlander, Kate. The Psycho-Analytical Approach to Juvenile Delinquency: *Theory, Case Studies, Treatment. 320 pp.*

Glueck, Sheldon, and **Eleanor.** Family Environment and Delinquency. *With the statistical assistance of Rose W. Kneznek. 340 pp.*

Lopez-Rey, Manuel. Crime. *An Analytical Appraisal. 288 pp.*

Mannheim, Hermann. Comparative Criminology: *a Text Book. Two volumes. 442 pp. and 380 pp.*

Morris, Terence. The Criminal Area: *A Study in Social Ecology. Foreword by Hermann Mannheim. 232 pp. 25 tables. 4 maps.*

● **Taylor, Ian, Walton, Paul,** and **Young, Jock.** The New Criminology. *For a Social Theory of Deviance.*

SOCIAL PSYCHOLOGY

Bagley, Christopher. The Social Psychology of the Epileptic Child. *320 pp.*

Barbu, Zevedei. Problems of Historical Psychology. *248 pp.*

Blackburn, Julian. Psychology and the Social Pattern. *184 pp.*

● **Brittan, Arthur.** Meanings and Situations. *224 pp.*

● **Fleming, C. M.** Adolescence: Its Social Psychology. *With an Introduction to recent findings from the fields of Anthropology, Physiology, Medicine, Psychometrics and Sociometry. 288 pp.*

● The Social Psychology of Education: *An Introduction and Guide to Its Study. 136 pp.*

Homans, George C. The Human Group. *Foreword by Bernard DeVoto. Introduction by Robert K. Merton. 526 pp.*

Social Behaviour: *its Elementary Forms. 416 pp.*

Klein, Josephine. The Study of Groups. *226 pp. 31 figures. 5 tables.*

Linton, Ralph. The Cultural Background of Personality. *132 pp.*

Mayo, Elton. The Social Problems of an Industrial Civilization. *With an appendix on the Political Problem. 180 pp.*

Ottaway, A. K. C. Learning Through Group Experience. *176 pp.*

Ridder, J. C. de. The Personality of the Urban African in South Africa. *A Thematic Apperception Test Study. 196 pp. 12 plates.*

● **Rose, Arnold M.** (Ed.). Human Behaviour and Social Processes: *an Inter-actionist Approach. Contributions by Arnold M. Rose, Ralph H. Turner, Anselm Strauss, Everett C. Hughes, E. Franklin Frazier, Howard S. Becker, et al. 696 pp.*

Smelser, Neil J. Theory of Collective Behaviour. *448 pp.*
Stephenson, Geoffrey M. The Development of Conscience. *128 pp.*
Young, Kimball. Handbook of Social Psychology. *658 pp. 16 figures. 10 tables.*

SOCIOLOGY OF THE FAMILY

Banks, J. A. Prosperity and Parenthood: *A Study of Family Planning among The Victorian Middle Classes. 262 pp.*
Bell, Colin R. Middle Class Families: *Social and Geographical Mobility. 224 pp.*
Burton, Lindy. Vulnerable Children. *272 pp.*
Gavron, Hannah. The Captive Wife: *Conflicts of Household Mothers. 190 pp.*
George, Victor, and Wilding, Paul. Motherless Families. *220 pp.*
Klein, Josephine. Samples from English Cultures.
  1. Three Preliminary Studies and Aspects of Adult Life in England. *447 pp.*
  2. Child-Rearing Practices and Index. *247 pp.*
Klein, Viola. Britain's Married Women Workers. *180 pp.*
  The Feminine Character. *History of an Ideology. 244 pp.*
McWhinnie, Alexina M. Adopted Children. *How They Grow Up. 304 pp.*
Myrdal, Alva, and Klein, Viola. Women's Two Roles: *Home and Work. 238 pp. 27 tables.*
Parsons, Talcott, and Bales, Robert F. Family: Socialization and Interaction Process. *In collaboration with James Olds, Morris Zelditch and Philip E. Slater. 456 pp. 50 figures and tables.*

SOCIAL SERVICES

Bastide, Roger. The Sociology of Mental Disorder. *Translated from the French by Jean McNeil. 260 pp.*
Carlebach, Julius. Caring For Children in Trouble. *266 pp.*
Forder, R. A. (Ed.). Penelope Hall's Social Services of England and Wales. *352 pp.*
George, Victor. Foster Care. *Theory and Practice. 234 pp.*
  Social Security: *Beveridge and After. 258 pp.*
● Goetschius, George W. Working with Community Groups. *256 pp.*
Goetschius, George W., and Tash, Joan. Working with Unattached Youth. *416 pp.*
Hall, M. P., and Howes, I. V. The Church in Social Work. *A Study of Moral Welfare Work undertaken by the Church of England. 320 pp.*
Heywood, Jean S. Children in Care: *the Development of the Service for the Deprived Child. 264 pp.*
Hoenig, J., and Hamilton, Marian W. The De-Segration of the Mentally Ill. *284 pp.*
Jones, Kathleen. Mental Health and Social Policy, 1845-1959. *264 pp.*

King, Roy D., Raynes, Norma V., and **Tizard, Jack.** Patterns of Residential Care. *356 pp.*

Leigh, John. Young People and Leisure. *256 pp.*

Morris, Mary. Voluntary Work and the Welfare State. *300 pp.*

Morris, Pauline. Put Away: *A Sociological Study of Institutions for the Mentally Retarded. 364 pp.*

Nokes, P. L. The Professional Task in Welfare Practice. *152 pp.*

Timms, Noel. Psychiatric Social Work in Great Britain (1939-1962). *280 pp.*

● Social Casework: *Principles and Practice. 256 pp.*

Young, A. F., and **Ashton, E. T.** British Social Work in the Nineteenth Century. *288 pp.*

Young, A. F. Social Services in British Industry. *272 pp.*

SOCIOLOGY OF EDUCATION

Banks, Olive. Parity and Prestige in English Secondary Education: a Study in Educational Sociology. *272 pp.*

Bentwich, Joseph. Education in Israel. *224 pp. 8 pp. plates.*

● **Blyth, W. A. L.** English Primary Education. *A Sociological Description.*
1. Schools. *232 pp.*
2. Background. *168 pp.*

Collier, K. G. The Social Purposes of Education: *Personal and Social Values in Education. 268 pp.*

Dale, R. R., and **Griffith, S.** Down Stream: *Failure in the Grammar School. 108 pp.*

Dore, R. P. Education in Tokugawa Japan. *356 pp. 9 pp. plates*

Evans, K. M. Sociometry and Education. *158 pp.*

Foster, P. J. Education and Social Change in Ghana. *336 pp. 3 maps.*

Fraser, W. R. Education and Society in Modern France. *150 pp.*

Grace, Gerald R. Role Conflict and the Teacher. *About 200 pp.*

Hans, Nicholas. New Trends in Education in the Eighteenth Century. *278 pp. 19 tables.*

● Comparative Education: *A Study of Educational Factors and Traditions. 360 pp.*

Hargreaves, David. Interpersonal Relations and Education. *432 pp.*

● Social Relations in a Secondary School. *240 pp.*

Holmes, Brian. Problems in Education. *A Comparative Approach. 336 pp.*

King, Ronald. Values and Involvement in a Grammar School. *164 pp.*

School Organization and Pupil Involvement. *A Study of Secondary Schools.*

● **Mannheim, Karl,** and **Stewart, W. A. C.** An Introduction to the Sociology of Education. *206 pp.*

Morris, Raymond N. The Sixth Form and College Entrance. *231 pp.*

● **Musgrove, F.** Youth and the Social Order. *176 pp.*

● **Ottaway, A. K. C.** Education and Society: An Introduction to the Sociology of Education. *With an Introduction by W. O. Lester Smith. 212 pp.*

Peers, Robert. Adult Education: *A Comparative Study. 398 pp.*

Pritchard, D. G. Education and the Handicapped: *1760 to 1960. 258 pp.*
Richardson, Helen. Adolescent Girls in Approved Schools. *308 pp.*
Stratta, Erica. The Education of Borstal Boys. *A Study of their Educational Experiences prior to, and during Borstal Training. 256 pp.*

SOCIOLOGY OF CULTURE

Eppel, E. M., and **M.** Adolescents and Morality: *A Study of some Moral Values and Dilemmas of Working Adolescents in the Context of a changing Climate of Opinion. Foreword by W. J. H. Sprott. 268 pp. 39 tables.*
● **Fromm, Erich.** The Fear of Freedom. *286 pp.*
   The Sane Society. *400 pp.*
Mannheim, Karl. Essays on the Sociology of Culture. *Edited by Ernst Mannheim in co-operation with Paul Kecskemeti. Editorial Note by Adolph Lowe. 280 pp.*
Weber, Alfred. Farewell to European History: *or The Conquest of Nihilism Translated from the German by R. F. C. Hull. 224 pp.*

SOCIOLOGY OF RELIGION

Argyle, Michael. Religious Behaviour. *224 pp. 8 figures. 41 tables.*
Nelson, G. K. Spiritualism and Society. *313 pp.*
Stark, Werner. The Sociology of Religion. *A Study of Christendom.*
   Volume I. *Established Religion. 248 pp.*
   Volume II. *Sectarian Religion. 368 pp.*
   Volume III. *The Universal Church. 464 pp.*
   Volume IV. *Types of Religious Man. 352 pp.*
   Volume V. *Types of Religious Culture. 464 pp.*
Watt, W. Montgomery. Islam and the Integration of Society. *320 pp.*

SOCIOLOGY OF ART AND LITERATURE

Jarvie, Ian C. Towards a Sociology of the Cinema. *A Comparative Essay on the Structure and Functioning of a Major Entertainment Industry. 405 pp.* •
Rust, Frances S. Dance in Society. *An Analysis of the Relationships between the Social Dance and Society in England from the Middle Ages to the Present Day. 256 pp. 8 pp. of plates.*
Schücking, L. L. The Sociology of Literary Taste. *112 pp.*

SOCIOLOGY OF KNOWLEDGE

Mannheim, Karl. Essays on the Sociology of Knowledge. *Edited by Paul Kecskemeti. Editorial Note by Adolph Lowe. 353 pp.*
Remmling, Gunter W. (Ed.). Towards the Sociology of Knowledge. *Origins and Development of a Sociological Thought Style.*
Stark, Werner. The Sociology of Knowledge: *An Essay in Aid of a Deeper Understanding of the History of Ideas. 384 pp.*

URBAN SOCIOLOGY

Ashworth, William. The Genesis of Modern British Town Planning: *A Study in Economic and Social History of the Nineteenth and Twentieth Centuries. 288 pp.*
Cullingworth, J. B. Housing Needs and Planning Policy: *A Restatement of the Problems of Housing Need and 'Overspill' in England and Wales. 232 pp. 44 tables. 8 maps.*
Dickinson, Robert E. City and Region: *A Geographical Interpretation. 608 pp. 125 figures.*
   The West European City: *A Geographical Interpretation. 600 pp. 129 maps. 29 plates.*
● The City Region in Western Europe. *320 pp. Maps.*
Humphreys, Alexander J. New Dubliners: *Urbanization and the Irish Family. Foreword by George C. Homans. 304 pp.*
Jackson, Brian. Working Class Community: *Some General Notions raised by a Series of Studies in Northern England. 192 pp.*
Jennings, Hilda. Societies in the Making: *a Study of Development and Redevelopment within a County Borough. Foreword by D. A. Clark. 286 pp.*
● **Mann, P. H.** An Approach to Urban Sociology. *240 pp.*
Morris, R. N., and **Mogey, J.** The Sociology of Housing. *Studies at Berinsfield. 232 pp. 4 pp. plates.*
Rosser, C., and **Harris, C.** The Family and Social Change. *A Study of Family and Kinship in a South Wales Town. 352 pp. 8 maps.*

RURAL SOCIOLOGY

Chambers, R. J. H. Settlement Schemes in Tropical Africa: *A Selective Study. 268 pp.*
Haswell, M. R. The Economics of Development in Village India. *120 pp.*
Littlejohn, James. Westrigg: *the Sociology of a Cheviot Parish. 172 pp. 5 figures.*
Mayer, Adrian C. Peasants in the Pacific. *A Study of Fiji Indian Rural Society. 248 pp. 20 plates.*
Williams, W. M. The Sociology of an English Village: *Gosforth. 272 pp. 12 figures. 13 tables.*

SOCIOLOGY OF INDUSTRY AND DISTRIBUTION

Anderson, Nels. Work and Leisure. *280 pp.*
● **Blau, Peter M.,** and **Scott, W. Richard.** Formal Organizations: *a Comparative approach. Introduction and Additional Bibliography by J. H. Smith. 326 pp.*
Eldridge, J. E. T. Industrial Disputes. *Essays in the Sociology of Industrial Relations. 288 pp.*
Hetzler, Stanley. Applied Measures for Promoting Technological Growth. *352 pp.*
Technological Growth and Social Change. *Achieving Modernization. 269 pp.*
Hollowell, Peter G. The Lorry Driver. *272 pp.*
Jefferys, Margot, *with the assistance of Winifred Moss.* Mobility in the Labour Market: *Employment Changes in Battersea and Dagenham. Preface by Barbara Wootton. 186 pp. 51 tables.*
Millerson, Geoffrey. The Qualifying Associations: *a Study in Professionalization. 320 pp.*
Smelser, Neil J. Social Change in the Industrial Revolution: *An Application of Theory to the Lancashire Cotton Industry, 1770-1840. 468 pp. 12 figures. 14 tables.*
Williams, Gertrude. Recruitment to Skilled Trades. *240 pp.*
Young, A. F. Industrial Injuries Insurance: *an Examination of British Policy. 192 pp.*

DOCUMENTARY

Schlesinger, Rudolf (Ed.). Changing Attitudes in Soviet Russia.
2. The Nationalities Problem and Soviet Administration. *Selected Readings on the Development of Soviet Nationalities Policies. Introduced by the editor. Translated by W. W. Gottlieb. 324 pp.*

ANTHROPOLOGY

Ammar, Hamed. Growing up in an Egyptian Village: *Silwa, Province of Aswan. 336 pp.*
Brandel-Syrier, Mia. Reeftown Elite. *A Study of Social Mobility in a Modern African Community on the Reef. 376 pp.*
Crook, David, and **Isabel.** Revolution in a Chinese Village: *Ten Mile Inn. 230 pp. 8 plates. 1 map.*
Dickie-Clark, H. F. The Marginal Situation. *A Sociological Study of a Coloured Group. 236 pp.*
Dube, S. C. Indian Village. *Foreword by Morris Edward Opler. 276 pp. 4 plates.*
India's Changing Villages: *Human Factors in Community Development. 260 pp. 8 plates. 1 map.*

Firth, Raymond. Malay Fishermen. *Their Peasant Economy. 420 pp. 17 pp. plates.*

Gulliver, P. H. Social Control in an African Society: a Study of the Arusha, Agricultural Masai of Northern Tanganyika. *320 pp. 8 plates. 10 figures.*

Ishwaran, K. Shivapur. *A South Indian Village. 216 pp.*

Tradition and Economy in Village India: *An Interactionist Approach. Foreword by Conrad Arensburg. 176 pp.*

Jarvie, Ian C. The Revolution in Anthropology. *268 pp.*

Jarvie, Ian C., and **Agassi, Joseph.** Hong Kong. *A Society in Transition. 396 pp. Illustrated with plates and maps.*

Little, Kenneth L. Mende of Sierra Leone. *308 pp. and folder.*

Negroes in Britain. *With a New Introduction and Contemporary Study by Leonard Bloom. 320 pp.*

Lowie, Robert H. Social Organization. *494 pp.*

Mayer, Adrian C. Caste and Kinship in Central India: *A Village and its Region. 328 pp. 16 plates. 15 figures. 16 tables.*

Smith, Raymond T. The Negro Family in British Guiana: *Family Structure and Social Status in the Villages. With a Foreword by Meyer Fortes. 314 pp. 8 plates. 1 figure. 4 maps.*

SOCIOLOGY AND PHILOSOPHY

Barnsley, John H. The Social Reality of Ethics. *A Comparative Analysis of Moral Codes. 448 pp.*

Diesing, Paul. Patterns of Discovery in the Social Sciences. *362 pp.*

Douglas, Jack D. (Ed.). Understanding Everyday Life. *Toward the Reconstruction of Sociological Knowledge. Contributions by Alan F. Blum. Aaron W. Cicourel, Norman K. Denzin, Jack D. Douglas, John Heeren, Peter McHugh, Peter K. Manning, Melvin Power, Matthew Speier, Roy Turner, D. Lawrence Wieder, Thomas P. Wilson and Don H. Zimmerman. 370 pp.*

Jarvie, Ian C. Concepts and Society. *216 pp.*

Roche, Maurice. Phenomenology, Language and the Social Sciences. *About 400 pp.*

Sahay, Arun. Sociological Analysis.

Sklair, Leslie. The Sociology of Progress. *320 pp.*

International Library of Anthropology

General Editor Adam Kuper

Brown, Paula. The Chimbu. *A Study of Change in the New Guinea Highlands.*

Van Den Berghe, Pierre L. Power and Privilege at an African University.

International Library
of Social Policy
General Editor Kathleen Jones

Holman, Robert. Trading in Children. *A Study of Private Fostering.*
Jones, Kathleen. History of the Mental Health Services. *428 pp.*
Thomas, J. E. The English Prison Officer since 1850: *A Study in Conflict.*
258 pp.

Primary Socialization, Language
and Education
General Editor Basil Bernstein

Bernstein, Basil. Class, Codes and Control. *2 volumes.*
   1. *Theoretical Studies Towards a Sociology of Language. 254 pp.*
   2. *Applied Studies Towards a Sociology of Language. About 400 pp.*
Brandis, Walter, and **Henderson, Dorothy.** Social Class, Language and
   Communication. *288 pp.*
Cook-Gumperz, Jenny. Social Control and Socialization. *A Study of Class
   Differences in the Language of Maternal Control.*
Gahagan, D. M., and **G. A.** Talk Reform. *Exploration in Language for Infant
   School Children. 160 pp.*
Robinson, W. P., and **Rackstraw, Susan, D. A.** A Question of Answers.
   2 volumes. 192 pp. and 180 pp.
Turner, Geoffrey, J., and **Mohan, Bernard, A.** A Linguistic Description and
   Computer Programme for Children's Speech. *208 pp.*

Reports of the Institute of Community Studies

Cartwright, Ann. Human Relations and Hospital Care. *272 pp.*
   Parents and Family Planning Services. *306 pp.*
   Patients and their Doctors. *A Study of General Practice. 304 pp.*
● **Jackson, Brian.** Streaming: *an Education System in Miniature. 168 pp.*
Jackson, Brian, and **Marsden, Dennis.** Education and the Working Class:
   *Some General Themes raised by a Study of 88 Working-class Children
   in a Northern Industrial City. 268 pp. 2 folders.*
Marris, Peter. The Experience of Higher Education. *232 pp. 27 tables.*
Marris, Peter, and **Rein, Martin.** Dilemmas of Social Reform. *Poverty and
   Community Action in the United States. 256 pp.*
Marris, Peter, and **Somerset, Anthony.** African Businessmen. *A Study of
   Entrepreneurship and Development in Kenya. 256 pp.*
Mills, Richard. Young Outsiders: *a Study in Alternative Communities.*

Runciman, W. G. Relative Deprivation and Social Justice. *A Study of Attitudes to Social Inequality in Twentieth Century England. 352 pp.*
Townsend, Peter. The Family Life of Old People: *An Inquiry in East London. Foreword by J. H. Sheldon. 300 pp. 3 figures. 63 tables.*
Willmott, Peter. Adolescent Boys in East London. *230 pp.*
The Evolution of a Community: *a study of Dagenham after forty years. 168 pp. 2 maps.*
Willmott, Peter, and **Young, Michael.** Family and Class in a London Suburb. *202 pp. 47 tables.*
Young, Michael. Innovation and Research in Education. *192 pp.*
● **Young, Michael,** and **McGeeney, Patrick.** Learning Begins at Home. *A Study of a Junior School and its Parents. 128 pp.*
Young, Michael, and **Willmott, Peter.** Family and Kinship in East London. *Foreword by Richard M. Titmuss. 252 pp. 39 tables.*
The Symmetrical Family.

Reports of the Institute for Social Studies in Medical Care

Cartwright, Ann, Hockey, Lisbeth, and **Anderson, John L.** Life Before Death.
Dunnell, Karen, and **Cartwright, Ann.** Medicine Takers, Prescribers and Hoarders. *190 pp.*

Medicine, Illness and Society
General Editor   W. M. Williams

Robinson, David. The Process of Becoming Ill.
Stacey, Margaret. *et al.* Hospitals, Children and Their Families. *The Report of a Pilot Study. 202 pp.*

Monographs in Social Theory
General Editor   Arthur Brittan

Bauman, Zygmunt. Culture as Praxis.
Dixon, Keith. Sociological Theory. *Pretence and Possibility.*
Smith, Anthony D. The Concept of Social Change. *A Critique of the Functionalist Theory of Social Change.*

Routledge Social Science Journals

The British Journal of Sociology. *Edited by Terence P. Morris. Vol. 1, No. 1, March 1950 and Quarterly. Roy. 8vo. Back numbers available. An international journal with articles on all aspects of sociology.*

Economy and Society. *Vol. 1, No. 1. February 1972 and Quarterly. Metric Roy. 8vo. A journal for all social scientists covering sociology, philosophy, anthropology, economics and history. Back numbers available.*

Year Book of Social Policy in Britain, The. *Edited by Kathleen Jones. 1971. Published Annually.*

Printed in Great Britain by Lewis Reprints Limited
Brown Knight & Truscott Group, London and Tonbridge